Digitalization of Higher Education using Cloud Computing

Chapman & Hall/CRC Cloud Computing for Society 5.0

Series Editors: ***Vishal Bhatnagar and Vikram Bali***

Digitalization of Higher Education using Cloud Computing
Edited by: S.L. Gupta, Nawal Kishor, Niraj Mishra, Sonali Mathur, Utkarsh Gupta

Cloud Computing Technologies for Smart Agriculture and Healthcare
Edited by: Urmila Shrawankar, Latesh Malik, Sandhya Arora

For more information about this series please visit: www.routledge.com/Chapman--HallCRC-Cloud-Computing-for-Society-50/book-series/CRCCCS

Digitalization of Higher Education using Cloud Computing

Implications, Risk, and Challenges

Edited by
S. L. Gupta
Nawal Kishor
Niraj Mishra
Sonali Mathur
Utkarsh Gupta

A CHAPMAN & HALL BOOK

First edition published 2022
by CRC Press
6000 Broken Sound Parkway NW, Suite 300, Boca Raton, FL 33487-2742

and by CRC Press
2 Park Square, Milton Park, Abingdon, Oxon OX14 4RN

CRC Press is an imprint of Taylor & Francis Group, LLC

Library of Congress Cataloging-in-Publication Data
Names: Gupta, S. L., editor.
Title: Digitalization of higher education using cloud computing: implications, risk, & challenges/edited by S.L. Gupta, Nawal Kishor, Niraj Mishra, Sonali Mathur, Utkarsh Gupta.
Description: First edition. | Boca Raton, FL: C&Hall/CRC Press, 2022. |
Series: Cloud computing for society 5.0 | Includes bibliographical references and index. |
Summary: "Digitalization of Higher Education sector using Cloud Computing: Implications, Risk ,and Challenges focuses on multi-faceted strategies to be adopted by HEIs to deal with the emerging issues related to teaching-learning processes using cloud computing, technological interventions, curriculum overhaul, experiential learning, multi-disciplinary approach and continuous innovations and digitalization. Also, strategic pragmatism is expected to resolve issues pertaining Information Classification: General to skill-gaps and skill upgradation which have become imperative due to technological transformations. In the current evolving phase of Education Technology (EdTech) both the faculty and the students need be adept in adjusting to the ever-changing requirements of the teaching learning process. It is apparent that skills such as critical thinking, innovative and novel perspectives, emotional intelligence, transformational leadership, systems thinking and design thinking will soon become crucial for survival in HEIs. In order to prepare and train leaders for future workplaces, HEIs must align their teaching in alignment with cloud computing, pedagogy and curriculum accordingly. Skill advancement of educators must go on parallelly to the skill evolutions and requirements of new-age workplaces. Discusses digitalization of education Discusses transforming higher education Talks about usage of digital technologies to enhance education Connects academia across the globe Provides Tools for online classes, virtual classrooms and virtual laboratories This book is primarily aimed at policy makers of higher education, teachers, students and regulators of universities"– Provided by publisher.
Identifiers: LCCN 2021032668 (print) | LCCN 2021032669 (ebook) | ISBN 9781032066134 (hardback) |
ISBN 9781032066158 (paperback) | ISBN 9781003203070 (ebook)
Subjects: LCSH: Education, Higher–Effect of technological innovations on. |
Internet in higher education. | Cloud computing.
Classification: LCC LB2395.7 .D55 2022 (print) | LCC LB2395.7 (ebook) | DDC 378.1/7344678–dc23
LC record available at https://lccn.loc.gov/2021032668
LC ebook record available at https://lccn.loc.gov/2021032669

ISBN: 978-1-032-06613-4 (hbk)
ISBN: 978-1-032-06615-8 (pbk)
ISBN: 978-1-003-20307-0 (ebk)

DOI: 10.1201/9781003203070

Typeset in Palatino
by Newgen Publishing UK

Contents

Preface

The opportunities and challenges faced by Higher Education Institutions (HEIs) in recent times due to technological disruptions have forced both academia and industry to realign their strategies for survival and growth. With the acceleration of cloud computing in higher education, it has now become imperative for educators to constantly upskill and reskill in order to meet the requirements of the future of work, particularly in the digital age. Technological advancement is an unstoppable wave and the lack of relevant skills to handle the disruptions in higher education will become a huge challenge if not addressed promptly. This is the new phase of Education 4.0 where HEIs are aligning themselves using cloud computing applications and thus preparing both faculties and students to embrace the changes happening in the teaching and learning processes. Today, the biggest challenge is skills shortage and the biggest question is how to bridge this skills gap. Upskilling is the way forward and most HEIs need to become equipped to handle technological disruptions by creating a skill-focused environment using cloud computing.

This book focuses on multi-faceted strategies to be adopted by HEIs to deal with the emerging issues related to teaching-learning processes using cloud computing, technological interventions, curriculum overhaul, experiential learning, multi-disciplinary approach and continuous innovations and digitalization. Also, strategic pragmatism is expected to resolve issues pertaining to skills gaps and skill upgradation which have become imperative due to technological transformations. In the current evolving phase of Education Technology (EdTech) both faculties and students need to be adept in adjusting to the ever-changing requirements of the teaching-learning process. It is apparent that skills such as critical thinking, innovative and novel perspectives, emotional intelligence, transformational leadership, systems thinking and design thinking will soon become crucial for survival in HEIs. In order to prepare and train leaders for future workplaces, HEIs must align their teaching with cloud computing, pedagogy and curriculum accordingly. Skills advancement of educators must occur in parallel with the skills evolutions and requirements of new-age workplaces.

Evolution of technology and the consequent changes in institutional and social settings are omnipresent and are having a profound impact on our functioning. The evolutionary path guided by these technological disruptions is here to stay, is irreversible, and is touching our lives at each moment in diverse ways, sometimes through choice but often without our consent. With the persistent support and encouragement of our perspective, we have compiled a book that should serve as an important resource for both scholarly and practical needs. It gathers together the challenges associated with digitalization using cloud computing techniques, the trends in education technology and how higher education institutions should prepare to achieve the goals of Education 4.0 using cloud computing.

S. L. Gupta
Ranchi, India
Nawal Kishor
New Delhi, India
Niraj Mishra
Ranchi, India
Sonali Mathur
New Delhi, India
Utkarsh Gupta
Connecticut, United States of America

Editors' Biographies

S. L. Gupta is currently working as Director, Birla Institute of Technology, Noida. Previously he worked as Dean of Waljat College of Applied Sciences, Muscat, Oman. He brings with him a rich experience of 27 years in academia. His professional qualifications include an Executive Programme in Retail Management from IIM-Kolkata and a PGDBM (Marketing) from CMD Modinagar, India and M.Com from University of Rajasthan, Jaipur, India. His fields of specialization are Sales and Distribution Management, Marketing Research, Marketing of Service, Retail Management and Research Methodology. He has to his credit many publications in national and international journals. He has published eight books, as well as research papers on his area of specialization, which are internationally recognized and recommended in many universities and colleges.

Nawal Kishor, Ph.D., PGDIM, M.Com, is Professor and former Director, School of Management Studies, Indira Gandhi National Open University, New Delhi, India. He is the Managing Editor of the leading journal, *The Indian Journal of Commerce* and the Editor of *Indian Journal of Open Learning*. He has been engaged in teaching, training, research and other academic and administrative activities for the last 30 years. He has been involved in the development of B.Com, M.Com, PGDIBO, BBA (Retail), M.Phil and Ph.D. programmes along with the conduct of orientation programmes, workshops, refresher courses, faculty development programmes, etc. He has published more than 60 research papers in international and national reputed journals. He has presented more than 15 research papers at international and national conferences. He has been actively involved as key note speaker, technical session chairman, guest of honour and resource person at various international and national Conferences. His areas of interest are: International Business Management, International Marketing, Marketing Management, Consumer Behaviour, General Management, Organizational Behaviour, Human Resource Management, Foreign Trade, Export Import Procedures and Documentation, Retail Management and Distance Education. He has visited the USA, Canada, Australia, France, Germany, UK, the Netherland, Italy, Switzerland, Ethiopia, Singapore, Hongkong, UAE and Namibia for academic purposes. He received Best Researcher Silver Medal for the 'Second Best Research Paper Award' 2014.

Niraj Mishra is currently working in the Department of Management, Birla Institute of Technology, Mesra, Ranchi, India. Prior to this he was the Head of Department of Management, Waljat College of Applied Sciences, Muscat, Oman. Dr. Mishra completed his M.B.A degree from Birla Institute of Technology, Mesra, India and Ph.D. in Management from BR Ambedkar Bihar University, India. He has published several research papers in areas of service marketing, e-services and quality management. Dr. Mishra has participated in many national and international conferences and presented research papers. He has also received the Best Paper Award for one of his papers presented at an international conference. He is guiding Ph.D. scholars in various universities in India in the area of e-services. Dr. Mishra has served as Deputy Head of Department of Management, Quality Coordinator (Academic) at Waljat College of Applied Sciences and is the Chairman of Risk Management Committee of the college. He has played an active role in preparation of strategic plans and operational plans, risk register and various HR policies of the college.

Sonali Mathur is associated with JSS Academy of Technical Education, Noida and has worked since 2010 as Assistant Professor in the Computer Science & Engineering Department. She received her B.E. in Computer Science and Engineering from M.J.P. Rohilkhand University, Bareilly, M.Tech in Information Technology from Guru Gobind Singh Indraprastha University, and has completed her Ph.D. in Data Warehouse Testing and Security from Birla Institute of Technology, Mesra, Ranchi. Confirmed more than 16 years of teaching and research experience and published research papers in various journals and conferences, her areas of interest include Data warehouse, data mining, security and testing.

Utkarsh Gupta is currently pursuing an M.B.A in Marketing and Business Analytics from the University of Connecticut, US. He is also serving as the President at UConn Graduate Consulting, where he manages a team of 50 consultants. He has extensive work experience in developing marketing and sales strategy for startups. He has worked as decision scientist in Mu Sigma delivering data-based strategy solutions to fortune 500 companies. He had a brief stint with the Coca-Cola company's global headquarters in Atlanta developing marketing strategies.

List of Contributors

Amjed Sid Ahmed
Department of Computing and IT, Global College of Engineering and Technology, Muscat, Oman

Renu Bala
Chaudhary Devi Lal University, Sirsa, Haryana, India

Kulvinder Kaur Batth
Department of Commerce, K. C. College, Mumbai, India

Pawan Kumar Chand
Chitkara Business School, Chitkara University, Punjab, India

Marshal Fith
Waljat College of Applied Sciences, Muscat, Sultanate of Oman

Srinivasa K. G.
Department of CSE, National Institute of Technical Teachers Training and Research, Chandigarh, India

Isha Gupta
Amity University, Noida, Uttar Pradesh, India

Rajan Gupta
Centre for Information Technologies & Applied Mathematics, University of Nova Gorica, Nova Gorica, Slovenia

S. L. Gupta
Birla Institute of Technology, Mesra, Ranchi, India

Sandeep Gupta
Department of Computer Science and Engineering, JIMS Engineering Management Technical Campus, Greater Noida, India

Ahmad Hosseini
Department of Foundation Studies, Global College of Engineering and Technology, Muscat, Oman

Manjula Jain
College of Management, Teerthankar Mahaveer University, Moradabad, India

Deepika Jhamb
Chitkara Business School, Chitkara University, Punjab, India

Muralidhar Kurni
Department of Computer Science, School of Science, GITAM (Deemed to be University), Hyderabad, India

Mazhar Hussain Malik
Department of Computing and IT, Global College of Engineering and Technology, Muscat, Oman

Nandita Mishra
Linköping University, LINKÖPING, Sweden

Niraj Mishra
Department of Management, Birla Institute of Technology, Mesra, Ranchi, India

Subhendu Kumar Mishra
Centurion University of Technology and Management, R. Sitapur, Odisha 761211, India

Balamurugan Muthuraman
Department of Administrative and Financial Sciences, Oman College of Management & Technology, Halban, Sultanate of Oman

Saibal Kumar Pal
Defense Research & Development Organization, New Delhi, India

Deepak Tandon
International Management Institute, New Delhi, India

Jency Treesa
Department of Commerce, St Teresa's College (Autonomous), Ernakulam, Kerala, India

Nitin Tyagi
Department of Electronics and Communication Engineering, JIMS Engineering Management Technical Campus, Greater Noida, India

Krishan Kumar Saraswat
Department of Computer Science and Engineering, JIMS Engineering Management Technical Campus, Greater Noida, India

Aarti Singh
FORE School of Management, New Delhi, India

Shekhar Singh
Department of Computer Science and Engineering, JIMS Engineering Management Technical, Campus, Greater Noida, India

Abhaya Ranjan Srivastava
Department of Management, Birla Institute of Technology, Mesra (Lalpur Extension Centre), Ranchi, Jharkhand, India

N. Viswanadham
Department of Accounting and Finance, Faculty of Business Administration, St. Augustine University of Tanzania, Mwanza, Tanzania

Pooja Yadav
Birla Institute of Technology, Mesra (Lalpur Extension Centre), Ranchi, Jharkhand, India

Mohammad Yawar
Waljat College of Applied Sciences, Muscat, Sultanate of Oman

Section A

Cloud Enabled Digitalization of Higher Education

1

Education Tools and Technologies in the Digital Age for Society 5.0

Balamurugan Muthuraman

Assistant Professor, Administrative & Financial Sciences, Oman College of Management & Technology, Muscat, Sultanate of Oman

1.1 Introduction

In the modern world, technology has a great impact on human life, society, and business development. Technology changes education as well. It creates a demand for knowledge and, through expansion of teaching and learning, enhances skills and knowledge. Education is increasingly using digital technologies. It is more crucial than ever for our college students to be technologically literate. We are making them ready for jobs that don't even yet exist, so it's critical to keep pace with the sector and to integrate new technology into the schoolroom to ensure our students are engaged in their learning.

Having a supportive environment is critical in teaching. Technology that matches most requirements is imperative, and digital sources must be easy for students to apply as well as for the teacher to implement within the curriculum. College students are accustomed to using different technologies for their study, which can help them to gain knowledge in unique ways, and result-oriented outcomes can be gained from the study (Bates 2015).

DOI: 10.1201/9781003203070-2

There are three main goals for buying virtual tools in faculties. The first is to make schools extra green and achieve higher productivity in teaching and learning. The capability to teach more in a shorter time, and to accomplish that more cheaply has been a regular aim for training and education structures and this will remain so for many years. The second driver is pupils' self-directed learning, demanding that teaching must be transformed by lecturers, educators, and basis officers so that pupils can become more actively engaged with their studying and so that it relates to their actual lifestyles. The third driving force is the concern to prepare scholars to compete in the job market and to meet the changing needs of the work environment. Related to this, the goal conveys the perception that people with good technological capabilities will strengthen the countrywide financial system (Cuban and Jandrić 2015).

1.2 Literature Review

The research paper by Amiel and Reeves (2008) found that technology in the education sector plays an important role in transforming teaching methods in the classroom. Williamson (2016) found that the modern education system requires digital educational control. Knox (2019) suggested that the post-digital education system provides deep and long-term relationships between human technology. Hawlitschek and Joeckel (2017) suggested that a fun learning environment, based on play, produces more effective improvement and support to the learning.

1.3 Education Tools

Smart phones, laptops, personal digital assistants may be used within education. Such digital devices assist the learner to investigate in line with their own tempo and environment. Due to the improvement in internet connection speeds, connection can be applied in any handheld tool for gaining knowledge. Mobile-assisted language gaining knowhow is a new idea. Now many universities are supplying online publications to reach out to more students. These handheld gadgets are used because of the primary device in online certification and online courses. Mobile gadgets exchange pupil and teacher roles in studying. Students can broaden, deliver, talk, engage, and compare with the assistance of cell devices. Audio-based and video-based study contents, plus internet-based contents, Word files, flash documents, and PDFs can all be downloaded on a mobile tool.

For university students of any age, it is beneficial to use technology in many aspects of their lives. Therefore, virtual equipment inside the schoolroom is becoming increasingly vital. Traditional techniques for education are already going through a change to conform to the dreams of twenty-first-century college students and to enhance the professional practice of instructors. The virtual destiny is going on now. Using technology for schooling provokes a student's interest, will increase their engagement, and results in better knowledge and comprehension. These elements are a challenge for every effective instructor, and these days they may be implemented by employing the use of digital gadgets within the classroom.

1.3.1 Corporate E-Learning

There is currently a huge transformation happening in educational areas. The statistics show that significant growth is expected in electronic learning (e-learning) from 2020 to 2024. The overall e-learning sector earns nearly $38 billion. There are some e-learning companies, like EdTech and Coursera, valued at over $1 billion, and these major companies will be the driving force for the transformation of traditional learning into online education. There is a prediction that global e-learning companies will reach $50 billion in income by 2026. At the same time, the growth rate is expected to increase by 15% by 2026 and it shows e-learning companies are major shareholders in the market share of the e-learning industry. To compare, in 1995 e-learning usage was only 4% in the area of education, whereas 90% of education sectors are now used the e-learning system (Sander 2021).

Corporate companies are adopting e-learning systems for staff development purposes and to improve employee performance. It provides effective information to increase employee performance levels with a lower cost compared to traditional (face-to-face) learning. For example, IBM managers are trained five times more with one-third of the total training cost and the company saved $200 million, which is nearly 30% of IBM's previous year's training budget. Dow Chemical company moved from face-to-face training to e-learning model tools and the company saved $34 million. The company training cost reduces per learner from $95 to $11. E-learning systems not only reduce the cost but also save the employee training time by nearly 40% to 60% compared to traditional learning systems (Statista Research Department 2015).

During the e-learning process, employee involvement is increased by 18% compared to the traditional learning system. Due to increased employee involvement, company productivity also increased nearly 30%. Employees are spending more time in e-learning courses during the training period. Shell is a major market shareholder in the oil industry globally; the company has given training at regular intervals and the oil industry must improve productivity. During the past few decades the company has adopted e-learning for employee training. This has produced good results and the company has saved over $200 million with the delivery of more than 12,000 virtual lessons. The largest airliner manufacturer of Airbus has more than 100,000 staff members spread over 35 countries. Airbus created an e-learning library and provided training to their staff members around the world, with more than 6,900 content, and with a large cost reduction in training due to the e-learning system (Sander 2021).

1.3.2 Global E-Learning Industry

In the twenty-first century, the global e-learning industry is increasing every year by nearly 19% and the growth is estimated to reach $243 billion. The e-learning industry captures the major market share globally, firstly in the United States, followed by Europe, and Latin America and Asia play an important role in the usage of the e-learning process in the industry. The prediction in 2015 was that the e-learning industry globally would earn more than $243 billion a year, and investors are ready to invest in this industry, as with augmented reality and virtual reality technologies. Because of the predicted investment by 2026, the global e-learning industry will earn nearly $336.98 billion based on increased demand (KPMG 2015).

Mobile learning (m-learning) is a part of the e-learning system due to the increasing usage of mobile gadgets. The m-learning system growth rate is 23% per year and it is one of the most important and fast-growing e-learning industry markets. In the education industry, digital learning growth has increased 900% since 2000. The global learning management system market growth is expected to increase 19.1% by 2026 with earnings of $29 billion (Statista Research Department 2015). The student retention rates in the e-learning system expect to reach a maximum of 60%. In major global educational institutions, of the total number of students in these institutions, nearly 20% of students are registered on online courses. 57% of school students are using m-learning system in major countries (KPMG 2015).

1.4 Major E-Learning Tools in the Twenty-First Century

- **Prezi**
  Prezi is a virtual software program for developing interactive presentations. According to their studies, Prezi facilitates you in making presentations that are more effective, more persuasive, more powerful, and more enticing in comparison to those made with PowerPoint. If you haven't tried the software, we strongly suggest that you test it out and gift it to your students.
- **Haiku Deck**
  A virtual device with whose help you can easily make presentations on your iPad, iPhone, and on the net. The device works online and offers a big database of stock images with which you may create photograph-based slides. Haiku Deck is effective for creating presentations on the go and delivering them from your pocket. Haiku Deck can be additionally integrated into Google Classroom, which is very well known these days.
- **Animoto**
  Video is one of the most attractive mediums of the modern world, which is why you have to incorporate it into your study room. Animoto is one of the virtual tools for classrooms that can be used by each instructor and student for educational purposes. Animoto facilitates you to create animated motion pictures effortlessly. You can create picture slideshows, link various films together, and add textual content and extra images to provide an enticing video.
- **Explain Everything**
  Explain Everything is all about interplay in virtual surroundings. This digital tool allows students and teachers to collaborate on an interactive whiteboard, thus encouraging group activities. The software also can be incorporated with Schoolwork, Dropbox, Evernote, GDrive, OneDrive, and other beneficial apps. With the drag-and-drop alternatives, Explain Everything is exquisitely easy, and intuitive to painting applications.
- **Educreations**
  As an interactive whiteboard and screencasting tool, Educreations is an alternative to Explain Everything. Educreations will let you provide an explanation for any form of the idea in interactive digital surroundings, which means that you can train and study from anywhere. The app allows you to develop a technique for each student via replaying their paintings and permitting them to examine at their own pace.
- **Socrative**
  Socrative is virtual equipment for the schoolroom support to examine the students' learning based on their knowledge. The entertainment aspect of Socrative is the best learning tool for college students. They can laugh while taking a look at it! You can incorporate various checks and comply with the results in actual time.

1.5 Digital Age Technologies in Education

Technology can be a useful resource in instructional success via two strategies: the elimination of physical barriers to studying and the evaluation of differentiation. Every learning technologies strategy must be tested within the framework of digital learning created for students, and the trainer is in a great position to rate their success and impact in academic settings.

The function of education, in a traditional instructional setting, is to facilitate, through improved performance and effectiveness, the training of knowledge and abilities. To examine this thesis, we want to first outline some definitions. Efficiency may be defined as the speed at which we obtain know-how. At the same time as the duration, effectiveness is related to the amount of imparted information that is operationally mastered. When technology is placed in an educational setting, consisting of a university, both students and teachers can be regarded as freshmen. Thus, we will go beyond the belief that any growth in teacher expertise and utilization has an impact on progressed studying college students. Ultimately, the technology must serve to develop pupil achievement in college.

1.5.1 Use of Digital Tools in Education

The various technologies enhance learning in a geography lesson, where two classes in different colleges may link up via the internet to discuss concerns over a selected global issue. The groups should work collectively to appreciate the use of e-learning tools. In conditions with limited network, this will be executed at all the classes through video or mail or Short Message Service (SMS).

The college students are fully engaged in the digital education system and it involves the empowered contributors in a conversation from which studying materializes. For instance, rookies operating on a calculation orient modeling software can start to have conversations about what they see on a laptop display and it does not require any terminology. The instructor can then add precise language into the communication as the venture develops.

Digital generation can frequently also be interesting for rookies and creates a more engaging opportunity. At the same time, it is vital to ensure that those students not secure in learning with virtual tools are given equal opportunity to engage in e-learning. The digital era provides instant and quick feedback for both the student and the instructor.

1.5.2 The Challenges of Digital Technologies Within the Classroom

- The technology took a lot of time and resources to invest in software and provide security to the learners. It needs to be verified as powerful and efficient in comparison to more conventional school room methods. Classroom digital technology is a continuous learning process for the teachers and schools in evaluating their competence and usefulness.
- There is a 'digital divide' between the ones who have access to the virtual era and the net and those that don't.
- Keeping technology up-to-date is expensive, as systems can quickly become obsolete.
- There can be issues with the prevailing planned structure, for instance, inconsistent speed of internet connections.

- Major challenges include how to prevent cyber-bullying, personal information hacking, right of entry to the unlawful or restricted website, and distractions of social networking.
- Some aspects of the digital era can be negative. For instance, bad posture and eye stress are commonplace problems, as are running computing tool computer systems use for long periods. Also, Repetitive Strain Injury (RSI) can occur after continuous usage of electronic gadgets like mobile, laptop, and so on.

1.5.3 The Use of Virtual Technologies in the Schoolroom with Teacher Support

- Teachers may want to increase the use of digital technologies in the classroom, developing their awareness of several virtual technologies and considering cautiously both how and why they may be used to help college students. The huge choice of software and devices is a plus point of the story. The consideration of what reading may be executed and the manner the technology can also additionally assist is essential to its powerful deployment.
- The SAMR (Substitution, Augmentation, Modification, Redefinition) model is a useful reference whilst studying the realization of digital generation in the classroom.

Since computers are generally not widely used in many schools, teaching is ruled by traditional methods. It is dominated by front-facing tuition, where the trainer has little interaction with students. Failure of college students to thrive at their own pace becomes one of the drawbacks of this type of teaching. In essence, we have students who are not uniform in knowledge. This variation is regularly hampered by the way of trainer evaluation work and how to transfer information to a collection of youngsters with divers understanding. The instructor chooses to deliver average-to-good coaching, wherein students with inadequate information might now not get important knowledge. Conversely, for the most advanced kids, teaching could be uninteresting

1.6 Conclusion

Using digital resources can help college students visualize many things in technology, instead of counting on verbal descriptions. It can also help to quantify concepts that might be more difficult and time-consuming otherwise. Technology is a companion of training and there is no reason to resist its advance. By incorporating virtual technology within the classroom, you grow to be an effective educator who fosters innovation.

Technology has already served as a crucial feature in schooling in a couple of areas. Specifically, the digital era has been of terrific use in enhancing the effectiveness and performance of the educational reviews of every student and trainer. Continued use and improvement can serve to further benefit education, and suggestions based on the improvement of existing trends in schooling should be pursued for advances in academic success.

1.7 What Next?

On the one hand, people of the schooling community may be exchange pioneers rather than digitalizing global followers. On the other hand, trade takes time and may encounter resistance from the schooling community. Now is the time to step back and reflect on the challenges ahead and the possibilities provided via digital education to equip current society and prepare for the future, no longer just to reply to the needs of the hard work marketplace but also to shape it.

References

Ackermann, Edith. 1996. *Constructionism in practice: Designing, thinking, and learning in a digital world.* London: Routledge.

Amiel, Tel, and Thomas C. Reeves. 2008. "Design-based research and educational technology: Rethinking technology and the research agenda." *Journal of Educational Technology & Society* 11, no. 4, 29–40.

Bates, Tony. 2015 *Teaching in a digital age: Guidelines for design teaching and learning*. Ontario: BC campus.

Beetham, Helen, and Rhona Sharpe, 2007. *Rethinking pedagogy for a digital age: Designing and delivering e-learning*. London: Routledge.

Cuban, Larry, and Petar Jandrić. 2015. "The dubious promise of educational technologies: Historical patterns and future challenges." *E-Learning and Digital Media* 12, no. 3–4, 425–439.

Green, Lucy Santos. 2014. "Through the looking glass." *Knowledge Quest* 43, no. 1, 36.

Hawlitschek, Anja, and Sven Joeckel. 2017. "Increasing the effectiveness of digital educational games: The effects of a learning instruction on students' learning, motivation and cognitive load." *Computers in Human Behavior* 72, 79–86.

Knox, Jeremy. 2019. "What does the 'postdigital' mean for education? Three critical perspectives on the digital, with implications for educational research and practice." *Postdigital Science and Education* 1, no. 2, 357–370.

KPMG. 2015. "Corporate Education Corporate Digital Learning" 1–38. KPMG/IMD.

Kumar, B., Senthil, D., Nivedhitha, M. R., Chitra Mai, and A. Perumal. 2016. "Digital tools for effective learning." *International Research Journal of Engineering and Technology* 3, 381–384.

Luckin, Rosemary, Brett Bligh, Andrew Manches, Shaaron Ainsworth, Charles Crook, and Richard Noss. 2012. "Decoding learning: The proof, promise and potential of digital education." Nesta. https://media.nesta.org.uk/documents/decoding_learning_report.pdf.

Mutch, Carol. 2013. *Doing educational research.* Wellington, New Zealand: Nzcer Press.

Sander, Tamm. 2021. "100 Essential E-Learning Statistics for 2021". https://e-student.org/e-learning-statistics/.

Statista Research Department. 2015. "E-learning market size 2104 and 2022".

Williamson, Ben. 2016. "Digital education governance: An introduction." *European Educational Research Journal* 15, no. 1, 3–13.

2

Digitalization in Higher Education: Students' Issues and Challenges

Pooja Yadav

Research Scholar, Birla Institute of Technology, Mesra (Lalpur Extension Centre), Ranchi, Jharkhand, India

Abhaya Ranjan Srivastava

Assistant Professor, Department of Management, Birla Institute of Technology, Mesra (Lalpur Extension Centre), Ranchi, Jharkhand, India

DOI: 10.1201/9781003203070-3

2.1 Introduction

In the last 15 years the mode of teaching in higher educational institutions has changed considerably. It is very hard to find professors these days who do not use modern technology in their classroom delivery. At present various platforms such as YouTube, Facebook, Wikipedia, Google etc. are being used to deliver lectures, and abundant information is present in these platforms. Online education has created a wide variety of new courses and added new options for teaching; it has also increased enrolment in many academic institutions.

Online education has no boundaries and therefore the internationalization of education has become a common phenomenon. There is a wide variety of means of online education which has increased the accessibility to major world colleges, universities and institutions in various countries which are now evaluating the productivity of their investment in technology.

Higher education systems have experienced notable changes driven by digital technology which results in a dependence on the technology. Ownership of digital skills is considered to be an essential requirement for innovation, creativity and efficiency. Therefore the universities are trying to prepare their curriculum on the basis of these skills.

Jones Kavalier and Flannigan (2006) defined digital literacy as "skills for reading and interpreting the media in order to reproduce verbal and visual information and implementation and evaluation of new information received from the digital environment".

In this ever growing and ever changing digital age a number of students are slowly but steadily moving towards digital courses in almost every field, whether it is business, art, technology, programming language, etc. Digital learning is also known as e-learning and digital classrooms are coming up quickly all around the world. Not only is digitalization providing technologically advanced media but it is also providing more flexibility for learners, as it allows them to study at any time and at any place. The students also find it is easy to choose what they want to learn and what they don't. So these advantages have made online learning very popular with students. These various basic principles have improved the engagement level of students as well as their interest.

With the advent of digitalization in education, the emergence of ICT (information and communication technology) has proved the way to introduce some breakthrough in different areas such as banking, education, health, business, trade and commerce, etc.

Globally, education is one of the sectors which has witnessed dramatic changes in recent times. On the one hand, it is helping countries to develop, but on the other it suffers from ailments of access and affordability. Digital education has three components:

(a) Content
(b) Technological platform
(c) Delivery infrastructure

When talking about India, the Indian IT sector has enough capacity and character to provide excellent online material on various online platforms.

Digital education evolved during the 1990s in the developed economies such as the United States. Subsequently other developed nations of the world have started to realize the cost benefit of digital education and seen the future. According to research conducted by Harvard University, professors are now selling their notes and lectures to various online platforms.

2.2 Methodology

The present research is based on primary and secondary data. The primary data has been collected from a self-administered questionnaire and the secondary data has been collected from articles, journals, websites, etc.

2.3 Research Questions

The present study focuses on the following questions:

(a) What is digitalization in higher education?
(b) What are the various advantages and disadvantages of digitalization in higher education?
(c) What is the impact of digitalization on students' learning process?
(d) What are the key issues and challenges faced by students as a result of the digitalization of higher education?
(e) What measures are there to minimize the issues and challenges faced by the students due to the digitalization of higher education?

2.4 Literature Review

Parker, Lenhart, and Moore (2011) have described in their study how the universities have experienced various changes in making technological platforms a part of education, including distance and online education. Higher education systems have already experienced noteworthy changes which are driven by digital technology and have resulted in a significant dependence on technology. For example, research scholars use digital libraries to access knowledge resources, usage of virtual laboratories etc. (Duderstadt 2003).

Jones-Kavalier and Flannigan (2006) have stated in their study that "digital literacy" includes various skills for reading and interpreting the media so as to reproduce verbal and visual information. The Educational Testing Service of America (2002) has proposed the concept of "digital competence" which means the ability to use the full range of digital technologies.

Tyner (2014) has stated in her study that the higher education institutions have responded to the dramatic move to advanced technology and are trying to evolve digital plans and strategies.

Margaryan et al. (2011) have suggested that extensive understanding of technologies is required for high-quality education and how these technologies can improve the learning process and learner's performance outcomes. According to Kirkwood and Price (2013a, 2013b) the higher education sector has been transformed over the last decade. Various emerging technologies are changing business operation models in all sectors. The emerging technologies include mobile devices (phones, tablets, laptops), advanced analytics, cloud-based IT, etc. With the help of these technologies, universities have improved the experience of teaching and learning processes.

Although digitalization has made the learning process easy it is not without complications and hindrances. Some of the factors underlying the weaknesses of digitalization are a lack of trust in tools and technology, an inability to accept modern technologies and development, an inability to change the existing work environment and add new techniques and capabilities (Hill et al. 2015; Teo et al. 2008).

According to Lea (2013), the IT departments in higher education institutions are not well equipped with the latest technological advancements. Henderson, Selwyn and Aston (2015) have stated in their study that various digital technologies are considered an important component of student education and they are related to considerable changes in the ways students learn and experience the online teaching process. The traditional approaches of teaching are less prevalent in the current digital age (Dabbagh and Kitsantas 2012).

Various empirical studies have shown students' use of technology in recent years. Kennedy et al. (2008) have elaborated in their study that there is a lack of uniformity in the pattern of technology adoption, especially when technological advancements are introduced into the learning process of students. Jones and Cross (2009) have examined how students use hardware and the internet for learning and leisure activities. In their study the respondents ascribed importance to activities such as assessment of the content and expressed a preference for using the internet to communicate instead of sharing content in person. Bose (2009) has described in his study how advanced technologies and analytics have widened and transformed the potential of higher education institutions. With the help of technology, universities are collecting data from internal and external sources to gain a considerable advantage by analyzing the data logically to make the most of its potential. The results of this analysis can be used to improve the academic performance of the students, retaining the students, etc.

Another concept – that is, cloud-based IT – is delivering various ingenious changes to organizations. According to Vaquero et al. (2009), the technology is defined as follows: "clouds are a large pool of easily usable and accessible virtualized resources (such as hardware, development platforms and/or services)". Cloud-based IT has the potential to accelerate business activities in respect of higher education institutions and to change their traditional organizational structure as it provides greater accessibility for less financial outlay and more securely than the traditional system.

Another dramatic change in the education system has come about due to the coronavirus pandemic, or COVID-19. The pandemic has created various changes in the teaching–learning process in the higher education system and has also impacted the way faculties and students interact with each other. So, due to this pandemic, universities and colleges were constrained to conduct the class exclusively online (Shoaibh et al. 2020). In this pandemic situation, many governments in various countries have taken numerous steps in order to avoid the spread of the deadly coronavirus and also to ensure the flow of the educational institutions (Ali 2020)

2.5 Some Facts and Findings of Global Online Learning

Online education has brought about a significant shift in the process of teaching and learning. Some important facts and statistics are mentioned below to assess the worldwide adoption of online learning:

(1) In the current situation of the pandemic (COVID-19), online learning is considered as safe and secure for students as well as for teachers and as the only viable option for providing continuity of education.

COVID-19 has reduced mobility and necessitated physical distancing among people as face-to-face interaction is not safe.

(2) According to Syngene Research, 2019, the Compound Annual Growth Rate (CAGR) of online learning would be 9.1 percent from 2018 to 2026. The growth is likely to be even higher because of the coronavirus pandemic.

(3) According to Palvia et al. 2018, around 99 percent of the students enrolled in undergraduate degree programs online are physically located in the country where their educational institution is located.

(4) A survey has revealed that around 52 percent of the graduate students in USA have suggested that online college level education provides a better learning experience (Duffin 2019).

(5) According to Dos Santos, 2019, The USA, China, India, South Korea and UK are likely to invest more in e-learning.

(6) Technavio 2018 has stated that approximately 59 percent of online learning material comes from US e-learning platform worldwide. According to an estimate, more than 30 percent of American students enroll in at least one online course.

(7) A report presented by the European University Association has stated that the main objective of higher education in Europe in using online teaching and learning is to improve the quality of higher education (Gaebel 2015).

(8) Duffin (2019) has stated in her study that there are more female students who enroll for online education than males. As per the report, in the US 65 percent of undergraduate and 54 percent of graduate online students are female.

(9) Another finding of a report has shown that 86 percent of 1,500 students believe that the learning value obtained by them from online courses equaled their payment.

2.6 Digitalization of Education in India

In India, in the past few years there has been a rise in digital and online classrooms at various levels of learning because of the advent of various technologies like cloud data centers, virtualization, etc. and there has been a huge opportunity for technology to be synchronized with the education industry in India.

With the introduction of new technologies educational institutions have also experienced a rapid rise in enrolments and added revenue via the digital courses. Digital learning has made it possible for students to study as per their convenience and comfort level. Teachers find it convenient too as the new technology has helped them prepare for their learning plans.

According to Satish Bisla (2015), digital learning in India is the future of education. Various smart and rapidly changing technologies are substituting the overall educational framework in India. The penetration of online education into the rural market is also evolving rapidly. High speed internet and various other technological advancements have made it possible for rural students to study online courses and improve their knowledge, skill and competence.

Hitherto the rural sector in India has been facing many challenges, including outdated teaching methods and a shortage of proper teaching aids. But with the digitalization of education, students in rural areas are being taught with the help of latest technologies such as LCD screens, videos, etc. Digitalization will help in addressing the shortage of teachers in the country.

2.6.1 Trends in the Digitalization of Education in India

(1) **Social media** Nowadays teachers and students are using social media platforms as an integral part of their online teaching and learning experience. Such platforms have now become an important means to share information about various important issues. They have also become a source of networking opportunities.
(2) **Interactive learning resources** With the evolution of various technologies, learning is not confined to the traditional classroom setup and it is all because of the various interactive sources such as flipped classrooms, mobile apps etc.; learning has been enhanced with collaborative technologies. Now sitting in one place, students can join with others globally to work on their projects and assignments.
(3) **Massive open online courses (MOOCS)** MOOCS are an emerging trend in India's education system. Such courses are helping the young population in the country to enhance and upgrade their knowledge, qualifications and skills. The courses are also helping millions of students to improve their employability by gaining access to a variety of skill-based courses. MOOCS are also encouraging professionals and making it convenient for them to study at any place and at any time.

2.6.2 Some of the Indian Online Learning Portals

A study conducted by Sahitya Karra (2020) lists some of the online learning portals in India for students and teachers. They are:

(1) **Bharat Skills** Bharat Skills follows the National Skills Qualification Framework (NSQF) curriculum. Currently, it has videos available in 79 streams such as carpentry, plumbing, etc.
(2) **e-Skill India** This is a multilanguage portal which offers more than 400 courses in around ten regional languages.
(3) **NASSCOM FutureSkills** This is an online portal which helps students learn the future skills. It aims to reskill professional students and employees in industry.
(4) **Skills build** A new job role requires new skills. This portal provides various courses which include the study of the latest technology such as artificial intelligence, cyber security, etc. along with soft skills training.
(5) **TCS iON Digital Learning Hub** This is an online portal which provides a number of courses in different fields in collaboration with various organizations such as the National Skill Development Corporation (NSDC), NSC, etc. which provide digital training and job information to the aspirants within the skilling ecosystem.
(6) **SWAYAM** This digital portal runs on the principles of access, equity and quality. It runs courses for various standards from class nine to postgraduate level. If learners want a SWAYAM certificate then they have to attend an exam at a designated center and pay examination fees. However, the courses themselves are absolutely

free of cost. The marks and certificate should be approved by the college or university to which the student belongs.

(7) **NPTEL IIT (National Programme on Technology Enhanced Learning Indian Institute of Technology) Madras** is the coordinator of NPTEL portal in collaboration with other IITs present in India. The lectures are recorded by the professors and then provided to students for free access. NPTEL provides courses in around 23 areas and learners receive a certificate on completion.

(8) **SWAYAM PRABHA** 34 DTH (direct to home) channels run educational programs on the SWAYAMPRABHA portal. It provides courses from class nine to post-graduate level in multiple subjects including arts, commerce, science etc. There is new content every day which is repeated five times a day.

The content is provided by various educational bodies such as NPTEL (National Programme on Technology Enhanced Learning), IITs (Indian Institutes of Technology), UGC (University Grants Commission), CEC (Consortium for Educational Communication), IGNOU (Indira Gandhi National Open University), NCERT (National Council of Educational Research and Training) and NIOS (National Institute of Open Schooling).

(9) **ePathshala NCERT** has initiated this digital portal which is a storehouse of audios, videos, flipbooks, etc. It has a total of 3,868 resources and 504 e-textbooks.

(10) **Diksha** is built to host Open Education Resources (OER). It provides resources such as lesson plans, videos and worksheets mapped to the curriculum.

These web portals present a choice of free and paid courses and the certification of the programs differs on the basis of course.

2.7 The Rise of Digital Education during COVID-19

The COVID-19 pandemic has disrupted traditional education systems across the world. There has been a global shift to online teaching and learning as a safety measure to prevent coronavirus infection. Now a "digital" or "virtual" world is the reality due to the quick spread of the pandemic. After the outbreak of COVID-19, all colleges, universities and schools started teaching online as it is the only method offering an alternative to traditional classroom settings. The trend towards online teaching, learning, seminars, conferences, etc. has accelerated significantly.

It is observed that enrolments in online teaching and learning are growing at a faster rate as more colleges and universities are offering online courses. For example, MOOCS courses of UGC are very popular in India as students can download lessons, e-texts and videos. According to a survey it is estimated that 53.6 percent of schools and colleges will be adopting online education for the long run (Sudhakar Patra and Kabita Kumari Sahu 2020).

Due to the pandemic and enforced closure of schools and colleges, existing platforms like Google Classroom, Microsoft Classroom, Zoom, etc. are being used to deliver lectures. Various engaging resources such as the Khan Academy, TED-Ed and Minecraft: Education Edition are available for students.

While talking about India, to promote digital education the Ministry of Human Resource Development has released a directory of digital/e-learning which covers both schools and higher education in multiple subjects. To lessen the impact of the pandemic on education, the government has come up with various initiatives to support and benefit students – for example, Diksha and ePathshala, etc.

The efforts made by governments all over the world have helped revamp the overall education system during the crisis. Digitized education is changing the approach of learning with virtual classrooms and free education content, especially in various rural areas and semi-urban areas. Due to the pandemic and need for online learning the online assessment platforms and ed tech companies are working to improve their products and services with the help of various advanced technologies. Various plans have been made and more improvements are underway. The immense use of technology during the crisis will lead to a new era in the education sector as there is no doubt that the crisis of the coronavirus pandemic has accelerated the use of technology for teaching and education purposes. And this will definitely help to build up the country's digital teaching and learning infrastructure.

2.8 Advantages and Disadvantages of Digitalization of Education

In the current scenario digital learning seems to be beneficial for schools and colleges. According to Halina Ostancowicz (2016) and Viren Kapadia (2020) there are various advantages of digital learning which are as follows:

2.8.1 Advantages

(a) **Engagement** Due to engaging content and game-based strategies students find digital learning quite motivating and it also improves their learning.
(b) **Time** Students can learn at any time.
(c) **Location** Anywhere learning creates a new world of opportunity for students.
(d) **Content** In digital learning there is a presence of rich and up to date content.
(e) **Ownership** In e-learning students choose what to learn and how to demonstrate their learning.
(f) **Parent involvement** There is a presence of transparency between students, teachers and parents.

2.8.2 Disadvantages

(a) **Health related issues** Online learning requires the use of computer or laptops, etc. and this means that student may face eye strain, bad posture and various other health related issues.
(b) **Lack of social interaction** In a traditional classroom setting there is an interaction among students and teachers and there are lively group discussions which make learning easier. But in an online class there is lack of social interaction. For some, face-to-face interaction is essential to bring the material to life.
(c) **Practical skills are hard to pick up** The practical experience is essential for some students: for engineering and medical students practicals are a must. In online learning it is easy to share theoretical knowledge rather than practical knowledge. There is a lack of hands-on practice.

(d) **Lack of authenticity** Authenticity is also a major problem in online learning as in the online mode of education anyone can do the project set rather than the real student.

(e) **Focus on memorization** Online learning focuses more on memorization rather than learning core competencies, as compared to real-world classroom learning.

2.9 Issues and Challenges Faced by Students due to the Digitalization of Higher Education

Digital learning has many advantages and disadvantages for teachers and students as compared to the traditional classroom system. Teaching and learning can take place anywhere and anytime.

But still there are some issues and challenges which students are facing on digital platforms which are as follows:

(1) **Students' feedback is limited in online learning** In the traditional classroom, the feedback by the teachers is given in face-to-face mode. Students who face problems in any content can resolve their problems during the lectures or during office hours. Personalized feedback from the faculty staff leaves a positive impact on students.

On the other hand, in online learning students face a struggle with feedback. Students who complete their assignment on time becomes dissatisfied due to the lack of feedback from the faculty staff. So, the traditional method of giving feedback is not always successful in the online learning process.

(2) **Online learning can cause social isolation** Online learning makes students undergo remoteness and lack of interaction. As a result, the student who spends much of their time virtually starts experiencing signs of social isolation, as there is a lack of human interaction among students. Social isolation when integrated with lack of communication may lead to mental health issues such as stress, anxiety, negative thoughts, etc.

(3) **Technological obstacles** As we all know, today's generation are the first to have mobile devices. Not everyone has access to recent laptops and other devices. Many students rely on a smart phone for their online learning and study content. Some will have limited access to wi-fi or broadband connections and some of them use their mobile data to attend online classes.

So, it is important to choose which course material would be easy to access and choose on a smart phone and tablet, as well as on a laptop and desktop.

(4) **Lack of communication skills development in online students** The development of students' communication skills is often missing from online classes. Due to the lack of interaction between students and teachers in online mode, the students may feel that they are not able to work as a team. So, due to a lack of communication skills many graduates may give their best in theoretical knowledge, but can fail to pass on their knowledge to others and also fail in practical knowledge.

(5) **Focus on theory rather than practice** Although awareness of this particular challenge of online learning is growing, the problem has yet to be eliminated completely. Due to lack of personal interaction, the teaching staff choose to focus largely on developing theoretical knowledge, rather than practical knowledge. The reason behind this is that theoretical knowledge is easier to implement. So, to use

a workshop for practical projects in online learning requires advance planning for implementation in online mode.

(6) **Online learning lacks face-to-face communication** Lack of interaction and communication with the teaching staff inhibits students' feedback, causing student to feel a lack of pressure. Constant nudging by staff may not be desirable for students, but it is an effective way of improving student retention.

(7) **Online learning is better suited to certain disciplines** Not all educational streams are equal and not all fields of study can be effectively used in the online learning and teaching process. Online learning is useful for social science and humanities streams, rather than scientific and technical fields such as medical science and engineering which require practical experience and knowledge. No online lectures can restore an auto play for medical students and industrial training for building engineers.

(8) **Online learning is inaccessible to a computer-illiterate person** Despite various technological inventions and various online learning platforms, there is still a large gap in computer knowledge among people. Until such gaps cease to exist, online education will not be able to reach all citizens.

(9) **E-learning as a source of distraction** With the latest innovations social networking sites are ruling the world: the students and learners are busy checking their posts, counting the number of likes, checking their status on social media, etc. all the time. So, these activities are creating a huge distance between learners and their education.

2.10 Research Methodology

In order to gain a deeper understanding of the topic a survey has been done with the help of a questionnaire which was collected from the students in various institutions to examine students' attitude towards online learning and their perceptions regarding the gaining of knowledge in the context of online learning.

2.10.1 Participants

The population of the study comprised 317 students from various institutions. The percentage of female participants was 45.1 percent and male participants comprised 54.9 percent. The other variables are shown with the help of Table 2.1.

TABLE 2.1
Demographic Characteristics of Respondents

Variables	Category	Count	Percentage
Gender	Female	174	54.9
	Male	143	45.1
	Bachelor	199	62.8
Degree	Master	118	37.2
Age	18–22 years	226	71.3
	23–25 years	85	26.8
	Over 25 years	6	1.9

Source: Primary data

Data was collected in online mode via questionnaires. The questionnaire was sent to the group of institutes through Google Forms. The participants received the information regarding the purpose of the survey at the beginning of the questionnaire.

2.10.2 Quality of Online Learning

The survey also recorded the quality of the online education as experienced by students/ learners covering various aspects like understanding in the home environment, concentration at home, clarification of doubts, etc. Table 2.2 illustrates the responses as recorded by the survey.

The variables shown in Table 2.2 reflect various attributes of online learning: students' opinions regarding the mode of online teaching, the appropriateness of online learning, concentration level of students, understanding level of students through online learning, doubt clarification, interaction between teachers and students, information processing. Each of these attributes plays a significant role in the effectiveness of online learning for students.

Around 62 percent of the students find it comfortable to study in the home environment and find it easy to concentrate better at home. From this survey we can presume that this section of students does not face any issues when switching from the school to home environment. But it is also important to assess the quality and efficacy of the learning materials provided to the students. The second variable was the understanding of the subject through online learning materials: around 30 percent of the students agree that they find it easier to understand the subjects through online learning materials. On the other hand, 13.7 per cent of the students disagree.

The next variable is about the difficulty in understanding the subject without the presence of the teacher. There were mixed views about this: 27.8 percent of students agree that they find it difficult to understand the subject without the presence of the faculties and 10.1 percent disagree with this statement. Furthermore, 37.8 percent of students disagree with the statement that they are unable to clarify their doubts with their teachers and 18.1 percent state that they agree that they are unable to clarify their doubts with their faculties as represented in Figure 2.1.

A majority of the students report that they interact with the teachers through live answers in a video conference. Bonding activities such as interaction with friends, teachers and peers, etc. contribute to emotional adjustments between teachers, friends and students. It is the presence of teachers, friends and peers which motivate them to attend college. There is a requirement of specific guidance to replicate the connection between students and teachers in an online environment. On the other hand, a majority of the students – around 45.4 percent – find it easier to present their projects and seminars online. But the courses and specialties such as information technology, engineering and architecture are reliant on hands-on practice and applied teaching methods, so it becomes difficult to conduct practicals online. So the next variable is in connection with this: 38.7 percent of students find it harder to process information online as compared to offline teaching.

A majority of the students are neither satisfied nor dissatisfied with the online learning environment and 37.7 percent of students have a neutral attitude towards the online learning environment. So the new digital age gives us the capability to change the face of learning and everyone must leverage new forms of education and learning to create a customized learning environment for the students.

TABLE 2.2
Students' Opinions Regarding Quality of Online Education – By Percentage

Variables	Category	Percentage
Hours of teaching online	More than 5 hours	54.9
	3–4 hours	45.1
	1–2 hours	
My concentration is better studying at home	Strongly agree	62.8
	Agree	37.2
	Neutral	26.2
	Disagree	14.5
	Strongly disagree	12
I find it easier to understand the subject through online learning materials provided to me	Strongly agree	71.3
	Agree	26.8
	Neutral	1.9
	Disagree	17.3
	Strongly disagree	13.7
It is difficult to understand the subject without physical classroom	Strongly agree	13.9
	Agree	27.8
	Neutral	25.9
	Disagree	22.4
	Strongly disagree	10.1
I am unable to clarify my doubts from my teacher	Strongly agree	6.7
	Agree	18.1
	Neutral	25.4
	Disagree	37.8
	Strongly disagree	12.1
Interaction of students with teachers	Live answers in a video conference	64.3
	Offering an answer on chat/forum	27.3
	No answer	8.4
Level of presentation of seminar projects or exercises online	It is hard	16.5
	It is easy	45.4
	The same	38.1
Processing information is easier when the courses are being conducted	The course is carried out on audio	31.6
	On audio and video	64.5
	On the chat/forum	3.9
As compared to traditional teaching, online information processing is	Easy	38.1
	Hard	38.7
	The same	23.2
	Dissatisfied	17.5
General opinion of students towards learning in the online mode of teaching	Neither satisfied nor dissatisfied	40.3
	Very satisfied	11.7
	Satisfied	30.5
The online environment is appropriate for learning and understanding	Strongly agree	11.7
	Agree	23.4
	Neutral	37.7
	Disagree	15.5
	Strongly disagree	11.7

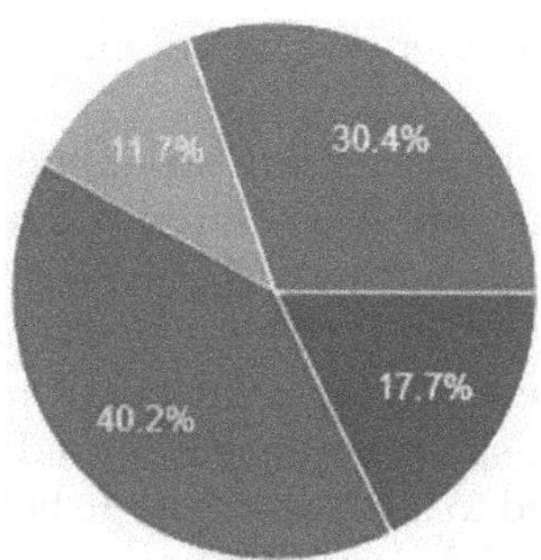

FIGURE 2.1
General opinion towards learning in the online environment (percentage of respondents).

2.11 Managerial Implications

The efforts to manage the challenges of the use of digital technology in higher education globally are not uniform. The need to address the challenges is based on the premise that there are a number of ways of using digital technology for learning and teaching processes. There are several measures that could be taken to meet the demands of the digital era which include:

(1) A combination of technologies like mobile applications, cloud solutions, etc. can be used to amplify the teaching and learning process.
(2) The institutions must plan various activities that allow students the opportunity for interaction and hands-on practices and experiential learning in the online environment.
(3) In an online class, the educators can try to enhance learners' motivational level and allow them to choose "how to learn". This is possible with the help of audio/video podcasts, presentations, surveys, quizzes, various mobile applications, etc.
(4) The educators can use platforms such as Google Docs, Google Drive, MS Teams, SlideShare, Skype etc. for learners so that they can collaborate, discuss, reflect and assess each other to make it an interactive learning experience.
(5) A "feed forward" model can be used to inculcate ideas about what a learner or teacher can do differently with the assignment.

With the advent of various technologies and mobile gamification the educators can successfully meet most of the needs in an online class. It allows learners to learn at their own pace and time.

2.12 Findings

The findings of the study have shown that no one can imagine the digitalization of education devoid of complications and challenges. A country like India still needs to determine its expectations of higher education. A large mass of the population in India is still illiterate and lacks technology. In the rural part of India, students and teachers accept the digital means of teaching and learning but there is a lack of infrastructure such as a reliable power supply, fast internet, etc.

The educational institutions which lack a clear vision of digitalization are unable to respond to the challenges of the twenty-first century (Coman et al. 2020). The findings also showed that reasons for digitalization in higher education facing challenges are that digital technologies are not reliable, people resist technological changes and new technology, and there is a lack of information about the global environment.

The findings from the survey show that there are advantages and disadvantages to learning. Students who responded to the questionnaire believe that it is easy to be focused online. Furthermore, students also observed that presentation of seminars and projects is easier online as they don't have the courage to speak publicly in a classroom situation. The study also showed that students get easily distracted in the online learning environment and also lack experience of this type of learning. In addition, environmental hindrances like noise and lack of adequate learning space make students get distracted while learning online.

2.13 Limitations

The study has some limitations as well as the sample in the study was non probabilistic and data was collected from only a few institutions. It would be useful to widen the sample in order to make comparisons according to different institutions, fields of study and previous experiences of universities with online learning. Furthermore, it can be seen that a longitudinal study could be conducted that would allow us to show how various colleges and institutions adapted to teaching and learning online, and how the students' attitudes towards online learning have changed.

2.14 Suggestions

The study and the survey provided a few suggestions that could be implemented in educational institutions, be it college or university. The suggestions are as follows:

(1) Integration of electronic media into everyday practice such as providing online assignments, sharing presentations, etc.
(2) The lectures could include some discussions which are indirectly related to the syllabus.
(3) Practical classes should be conducted in order to understand the topics easily.
(4) Organizing peer teaching and group projects will motivate the students to work in a team.
(5) There should be a use of positive communication techniques.
(6) Video lessons should be available offline in order to provide flexibility and to remove the necessity to attend live lessons.
(7) Regular classes should be conducted to clarify doubts and written notes for the classes taken by the teachers should be provided.

2.15 Conclusion

With the digital transformation, the education industry is trying to re-adjust itself in terms of how we learn as well as what we learn. In order to be successful in the e-learning environment students have to overcome the challenges with support of the teachers and faculties and best-practice solutions. The learners and educators must try to accept the transition from traditional classroom practices to an e-learning approach to education. Today's generation is technology-savvy but still the use of technology for learning provides challenges for student motivation. We can conclude that with the proper guidelines and support from the educators, the digital learners can be successful within the e-learning environment.

References

Admin. 2018. *Challenges of digitization in education industry user.* Techplus Education Technology 7 June. techplusmedia.com/education/2018/06/07/challenges-of-digitization-in-education-industry-users (accessed 11-01-2021).

Ali, Wahab. 2020. "Online and remote learning in higher education institutes: A necessity in light of COVID-19 pandemic." *Higher Education Studies* 10.

Bisla, Satish. 2015. *Digital education: Scope and challenges of a developing society.* eLearning Industry 24 May. www.elearningindustry.com

Bose, Ranjit. 2009. "Advanced analytics: opportunities and challenges." *Industrial Management and Data System* 109 (2): 8–9.

Chari, Rashmi. 2020. *Challenges of quality in online learning.* Times of India 6 May. www.google.com/amp/s/timesofindia.indiatimes.com/blogs/edutrends-india/challenges-of-quality-in-online-learning

Coman, Claudiu, Laurentiu Gabriel Tiru, Carmen Stanciu, and Maria Cristina Bularca. 2020. "Online teaching and learning in higher education during the coronavirus pandemic; Students' perspective." *Sustainability* 12 (24). www.mdpi.com/2071-1050/12/24/10367

Dabbagh, Nada and Anastasia Kitsantas. 2012. "Personal learning environment, social media and self-regulated learning: A natural formula for connecting formal and informal learning." *The Internet and Higher Education* 15 (1): 1–2.

Dhawan, Bulbul. 2020. *COVID-19: How smart classrooms are transforming India's education system.* Financial Express 5 May. www.financialexpress.com/education-2/covid-19-how smart-classroom-are-transforming-indias-education-system/1948670/

Dos Santos, Catia. 2019. *What are the leading countries in the eLearning industry?* DynDevice 27 March. www.dyndevice.com/en/news/what-are-the-leading-countries-in-the-elearning-industry-ELN-510/

Dua, Shikha, Seema Wadhawan, and Sweety Gupta. 2016. "Issues, trends and challenges of digital education: an empowering innovative classroom model for e-learning." *International Journal of Science, Technology and Management* 5 (5): 143–144.

Duderstadt, J. 2003. "Higher education in the new century: Themes, challenges, and options." University of Michigan.

Duffin, Erin. 2019. *Opinions of online college students on quality of online education.* Statista 26 October. www.statista.com/statistics/956123/opinions-online-college-students-quality-online-education/e-student.org

Gaebel, Michael. 2015. E-learning in the European Higher Education Area. European University Association.

Henderson, Michael, Neil Selwyn, and Rachel Aston. 2017. "What works and why? Student perceptions of useful digital technology in university teaching and learning." *Studies in Higher Education* 42 (8).

Hill, Rowena, Betts, Lucy R., and Gardener, Sarah E. 2015. "Older adults' experiences and perceptions of digital technology: (Dis)empowerment, wellbeing, and inclusion." *Computers in Human Behaviour* 48.

Hiranandani, Niranjan, Deepak Sood, and Charu Malhotra. n.d. *Digitalization of education; A readiness survey.* ASSOCHAM.

Jones, Chris, and Simon Cross. 2009. "Is there a net generation coming to University?" In *Alt 2009.* In dreams begins responsibility" – Choice, evidence and change. Conference Proceedings. 10–20. Available at: https://repository.alt.ac.uk/466/3/ALT-C_09_proceedings_091209_web.pdf

Jones-Kavalier, Barbara R. and Suzanne L. Flanningan. 2006. "Connecting the digital dots: Literacy of the 21st century." EDUCAUSE Quarterly 29 (2): 8–10.

Kapadia, Viren. 2020. *Top 6 Advantages and Disadvantages of E-Learning for Your Training.* Gyrus 24 January. www.gyrus.com/top-6-advantages-and-disadvantages-of-e-learning-for-your-training

Karra, Sahitya. 2020. *10 best online learning portals in India for students and teachers.* National Skills Network 26 June. www.nationalskillsnetwork.in/10-best-online-learning-portals-in-india-for-students-and-teachers/

Kennedy, George E., Terry Judd, Anna Churchward, and Kathleen Gray. 2008. "First year students' experiences with technology: Are they really digital natives?" *Australasian Journal of Educational Technology* 24 (1).

Kirkwood, Adrian and Linda Price. 2013a. "Missing: Evidence of a scholarly approach to teaching and learning with technology in higher education." *Teaching in Higher Education*, 18 (3): 327–337.

Kirkwood, Adrian and Linda Price. 2013b. "Examining some assumptions and limitations of research on the effect of emerging technology for teaching and learning in higher education." *British Journal of Educational Technology* 44 (4).

Lea, Mary R. 2013. "Reclaiming literacies: Competing textual practices in a digital higher education." *Teaching in Higher Education* 18 (1).

Loebeccke, Claudia and Arnold Picot. 2015. "Reflections on societal and business model transformation arising from digitization and big data analytics: A research agenda." *The Journal of Strategic Information System* 24 (3).

Margaryan, Anoush, Allison Littlejohn, and Gabrielle Vojt. 2011. "Are digital natives a myth or reality? University students' use of digital technologies." *Computers & Education* 56 (2).

Marks, Magic. 2019. *The future of effective digital learning and its role in the education system.* eLearning Industry 28 February. https://elearningindustry.com/the-future-of-effective-digital-learning-and-its-role-in-the-education-system

Ostancowicz, Halina. 2016. "Benefits and drawbacks of online education." *Benefits and Drawbacks of Online Education.* January.

Palvia, Shailendra., Prageet Aeron, Parul Gupta, Diptiranjan Mahapatra, Ratri Parida, Rebecca Rosner, and Sumita Sindhi. 2018. "Online education: Worldwide status, challenges trends and implications." *Journal of Global Information Technology Management* 21 (4).

Parker, Kim, Amanda Lenhart, and Kathleen Moore. 2011. "The digital revolution and higher education." *Social and Demographic Trends.*

Patra, Sudhakar and Kabita Kumari Sahu. 2020. "Digitalization, online learning and virtual world." *Journal of Humanities and Social Science Research* 45 (52).

Shoaibh, Abu Elnasr, Ahmad M. Hasanein, and Ahmad E. Abu Elnasr. 2020. "Response to COVID-19 in higher education: Social media usage for sustainable formal academic communication in developing countries." *Sustainability* 12 (16).

Teo,Timothy, Chwee Beng Lee, and Ching Sing Chai. 2008. "Understanding pre-service teachers' computer attitudes: Applying and extending the technology acceptance model." *Journal of Computer Assisted Learning* 24 (2).

Tyner, Kathleen. 2014 [1998]. *Literacy in a Digital World: Teaching and Learning in the Age of Information.* London: Routledge.

Vaquero, Luis M., Luis Rodero-Merino, Juan Caceres, and Maik Lindner. 2009. "A Break in the Clouds: Towards a Cloud Definition." *Computer Communication Review* 39 (1).

3

Pedagogies in Digital Education

Kulvinder Kaur Batth

Assistant Professor, Department of Commerce, K.C. College, Mumbai, India

3.1 Introduction

The transformations in society and the changing scenario have brought enormous opportunities and challenges. A dynamic higher education system needs to accommodate the

DOI: 10.1201/9781003203070-4

demands of the global knowledge society. The academic community all over the world has been rethinking and re-designing knowledge systems to innovate and create more engaging pedagogies via digital education. Changing norms and the "new normal" world have again put the focus on digital education. The pedagogies in digital education should accommodate the changing needs and challenges, as well as attitudes and perceptions, of the new-age learners. The needs, challenges, perceptions and attitudes of the trainers as well as learners play a significant role in the adoption of digital pedagogical tools and also vary across geographical territories and demographic characteristics. The innovative pedagogical tools need to meet the demands of the global society as well as the expanding expectations of the trainers and learners.

A number of studies have shown that digital tools in the pedagogical process generate far better student engagement as well as interactions. The technological approach assists and supports the learners and the learning process with the help of cognitive methods. The results also revealed that the digital pedagogical approach focuses on the learners and their needs. It encourages and nurtures student interaction, interest and involvement in their learning methodologies. The majority of the learners also were of the opinion that digital pedagogy is far more effective, flexible, wider in reach and more accessible as compared to the physical platforms of learning.

3.2 Objectives

This chapter aims to understand and explore the creative and innovative pedagogical tools of teaching and learning. It analyses the challenges faced by the trainers as well as learners in the digital pedagogical process. The attitudes and perceptions of the trainers and learners make a huge difference in understanding their expectations of as well as attitudes towards digital tools in the teaching-learning process. The meta-analysis research is based on data collected from a number of empirical studies of the innovative pedagogies available on digital education platforms. The combined effect of the empirical studies will provide a pathway for drawing interpretations and conclusions.

3.3 Digital Platforms in Learning

A large number of creative and innovative research studies have contributed towards a broad understanding of tools and techniques in the pedagogical journey of digital education. The various tools combine to achieve the objectives of digital technology. The digital platforms aim to provide a teaching-learning process which is effective, reachable and interesting as well as engaging. The wide range of platforms aim to accommodate the learners across diverse boundaries and from different backgrounds. Moreover, the digital platforms strive to overcome the challenges posed by the pedagogical approaches of the physical classroom that are faced by both trainers and learners. The innovative skills are significant for helping teachers to prepare for the tough challenges and competition of the twenty-first century. Even more than the teachers, it is important to prepare learners for the digital revolution and therefore the teaching pedagogies need to demonstrate the required skills. Digital pedagogies help to build learner engagement while equipping the learners with the competences required for the twenty-first century (Duffy and Ney 2015). The appropriate preparation of the learners will take place only with the required skill set, comprising communication skills, critical thinking and analytical skills. Blundell, Lee and Nykvist (2020) discussed the larger need to provide digital education as a part of schooling in the learners' initial years. The adoption of digital pedagogies is mainly determined by the teacher's attitudes to and experience of digital technology and the accompanying modes of learning. Globalization has brought immense challenges in the field of education. The globalized world demands an innovative pedagogical approach in order to prepare students for life. Innovative pedagogies should enhance critical thinking and analytical skills, as well as the integration of knowledge with insights from real life experiences (Apple, Kenway, Lang and Singh 2005).

Digital education needs to work together with needs to be combined with real-world, practical education, in order to provide a blended educational experience. Such an experience reflects the need for adaptation, for combining physical classroom learning with digital pedagogies. Digital technology could be adopted across the subjects including practical, hands-on education. Educators need to be equipped with the appropriate digital education and skills so as to integrate digital tools in the process of imparting practical knowledge. Koekoek and van Hilvoorde (2019) emphasise the changes in physical education. The biggest challenge is the selection of the right media to motivate and retain the young learners in the sports activities. Pedagogy plays an important role in the manner in which a subject is taught to the learners. The application of technology builds innovative pedagogies in the process of teaching and learning.

Some countries have shown remarkable growth in terms of their adoption as well as usage of digital teaching and learning skills. Moreover, during that time attention has turned towards the adoption of digital tools by teachers in the field of physical education. Sargent and Casey (2018) emphasized the adoption of digital technology in the field of physical education as prominent and suggested that the introduction of images and short videos can create a very positive framework and build morale as well as motivation among young learners. The use of innovative techniques in the teaching-learning process fosters student engagement. Innovative techniques work not only for learners in their early years but they also produce positive results for higher-education learners in their later years. Furthermore, the innovative pedagogies lead to student engagement, participation and motivation, in addition to developing analytical skills and critical thinking as well as reflective learning (Santos, Simões Figueiredo and Vieira 2019).

Mobile technology plays an important role in enhancing the digital pedagogical experience. The adoption of mobile devices in digital pedagogy enhances the learning experience, in addition to providing ease and comfort in accessing the digital learning tools. Mobile-supported pedagogies on the one hand enhance the knowledge of the learners and, on the other, allow the learners to reflect. The learners are able to break down their knowledge and widen their approach. Mobile-based learning also provides a plethora of opportunities for the learners enrolled in distance-learning programs. The mobile technology influences the teaching-learning process as well as the relationship between the teachers and the learners by offering broad avenues for different means of communication. Laurillard (2007) opined that mobile technology creates opportunities for the learners, by building different contexts as well as allowing different patterns of learning. The three important aspects analysed in the process were learners, the technological tools employed and the content to be delivered to the learners. The digital competence of the teachers is an important consideration in the adoption of digital technology. The two crucial criteria for assessing digital competence are the teachers' own knowledge and practical use of digital tools in the teaching-learning process. The important factors which determine teachers' digital competence are based on demographic characteristics: their age, gender and educational level. These three factors have been considered as salient in influencing the usage of digital tools by the teachers (Guillén-Gámez, José Mayorga-Fernández, Bravo-Agapito, Escribano-Ortiz 2020).

The digitalization of the learning environment is not only desirable but also the need of the hour. Digital learning platforms build critical thinking spaces for learners to analyse concepts; they foster a more transformative learning landscape. Digital education is a new awakening for education which transcends geographic boundaries. Moreover, it acts as a bridge across distance and can overcome other barriers to accessing high-quality education. The learning objectives are fulfilled when the learning takes place without any form of boundaries, creating a wider sphere of learning. Moreover, digital learning overcomes the challenges of distance education by presenting the real physical environment in the virtual world through the adoption of digital tools and techniques (Smith and Jeffery 2017).

The teaching and learning approach needs to be more results oriented while preparing the learners for the future. It should be able to prepare and nurture the learners to be problem-solvers in real-life situations and, most importantly, to transform the learners into happy, cheerful and healthy individuals. Apparently, deep-learning technological tools also promise to create a strong base for a moral education, which would inculcate the learners with the ethical values of honesty and self-regulation. The deep-learning technologies emphasize nurturing the human spirit by providing enriched experience. Fullan and Langworthy (2013) stated that digital learning aims to enhance individuals' creative skills by providing immense scope for imagination, collaboration and communication.

3.3.1 M-Learning

The spread of mobile technology has been witnessed all over the world. In fact, in the western world there is rarely a person without at least one such device. Herrington Guillén (2009) argued that the easy availability and accessibility of these devices have led to the weak positioning of personal computers. Furthermore, the hands-on experience and finger-touch options allow the users to complete any task within a fraction of seconds. The ease of use as well as portability add to the comfort of doing things from anywhere and anytime. Herrington et al. (2009) focused on the need for and importance of mobile technology in the pedagogical process. With technological advancement and also the vast spread of these devices across geographic and demographic boundaries, it has become much easier for the educational system to adopt digital teaching learning practices through the use of such mobile devices. The results of Demirbilek's study reflected that 76% of the adults showed positive interest in mobile learning methodologies (Demirbilek 2010).

Apparently, the adoption and usage of mobiles in teaching-learning processes have been faster in developing nations than in less developed nations. Additionally, keeping pace with the technological revolutions as well as digitization, it is much easier for the trainers as well as learners to make use of mobiles as compared to other devices due to their cost, accessibility and user-friendliness. While the use of mobile phones is considered to be effective in the teaching-learning process, the whole process becomes futile when some students are deprived of the mobile technology due to whatever reason (Al-Fahad 2009).

Mobile-based learning on the one hand aims to enhance learner engagement and increase inclusion in the teaching-learning process, and on the other it attempts to make the whole process full of fun and excitement. Digital platforms provide immense scope for exploring the physical environment. Further, the use of photos, videos, texts, locations, sharing of products, results and so on makes the learning experience memorable and even joyful (Laurillard 2007).

3.3.2 Information Communication Technology (ICT)

The so-called will, skill and tool model displayed a high amount of correlation in showcasing the teacher's willingness to adopt information and communication technology (ICT) in classroom teaching. Petko (2012) conducted a survey among 357 Swiss teachers and the findings revealed that a strong correlation exists within the will, skill and tool model while analysing the teachers' attitudes towards the adoption of ICT in the pedagogical process.

The Technological Pedagogical Content Knowledge (TPACK) model has been used to introduce games into the teaching-learning process. The introduction of games will help to improve teacher preparation as well as enhance the professional growth and development of the teachers. Apparently, along with the TPACK game-based learning approach, the research also evaluated an important aspect termed as ADGBL, i.e. Acceptance of Digital Game-Based Learning. The willingness of teachers and learners to adopt a game-based learning approach will provide a strong base for implementation of this technology.

3.3.3 Gaming Pedagogy

Gaming pedagogy aims to provide a holistic experience for the learners while ensuring that learning is coated with a large amount of fun and excitement. The mobile games were used as a way into the innovative pedagogical practices. Further, among all the mobile games, the opensource games were preferred by the learners due to their ease of availability, accessibility and use. The mobile games as an electronic mode were presented to the learners to increase their engagement in the pedagogical process and were considered a powerful learning approach. The game-based learning exposed the learners and the trainers to a different form of learning altogether (Hsu, Liang, Chai and Tsai 2013; Shin, Shin, Choo and Beam 2011).

A study conducted among eight European countries explored the adoption of innovative pedagogies. Apparently, few of the adult learners themselves made much use of the technology in the pedagogical process, but they agreed that it can play a significant role in the teaching of communication skills, cultural themes, computer literacy and problem-solving skills. The adult learners agreed that such topics could be taught more effectively with the help of mobile games (Demirbilek 2010).

The introduction of digital tools has been an important part of teaching of mathematics in the form of game-based learning. The multimedia approach has been considered effective in achieving the goals of the teaching-learning process. Perhaps, the game-based learning approach has been considered promising for teaching science and various languages. The integration of entertainment and education is gaining popularity across the world. Further, this has led to a huge market for gaming products promising to provide a game-based learning approach to teaching various subjects. The innovative tools aim to take a critical thinking approach by providing real-life problems in the virtual environment. The dire need for interventions in the pedagogical process of teaching mathematics paved the way for learner-engaged tools and techniques. Hwa (2018) believed that mathematics requires concept-building and problem-solving skills among the learners which would on the one hand develop their critical and analytical thinking ability and on the other would foster effective employability skills.

3.4 Students' Contribution to Pedagogy

The pedagogical process which involves students in order to engage them deeply is known as Contributing Student Pedagogy (CSP). In CSP, the students not only contribute to the teaching-learning process but also add a lot of value by enhancing the learning experience of their fellow learners (Hamer, Cutts, Jackova, Luxton-Reilly et al. 2008). The CSP approach is linked to two main theories known as communist theory and constructivist theory (Makarova and Makarova 2018). The involvement and engagement of the learners in the teaching-learning process is thought to contribute towards effective learning, as it will help to develop the learners as better individuals. The three important aspects analysed in the Makarovas' study aimed to equip the learners with a sense of self-dependence and confidence and a practical orientation towards their subjects.

The so-called flipped classroom is another process of enhancing student engagement in classroom teaching. In the flipped classroom, the focus of the teaching-learning process is at the learner. Lam (2020) conducted a study and the results of the study reflected that out of the three modes of teaching and learning comprising the traditional, digital and flipped classroom approaches, the latter weighed more in terms of learning outcomes and the overall learning derived by the learners.

The digital storytelling techniques help to understand and analyse the role of innovative pedagogies in teaching learning. The digital storytelling techniques help to decipher the effectiveness of the innovative pedagogical techniques (Smeda, Dakich and Sharda 2012). The innovative methodologies lead to building a connection with the learners, foster learner engagement and promote better learning outcomes as well as creating a constructive learning environment (Smeda, Dakich and Sharda 2012). In 2016, a new association was formed: the Association of Visual Pedagogies. The purpose of this organisation was the bringing together of the innovative work of the six institutes working in the area of visual pedagogies. The first conference, held in 2016 and focusing on visual pedagogical innovations, aimed to combine the role of physical and virtual classrooms (Jandric and Haynes 2017).

The aim of the visual pedagogical practices was to record the events in the form of videos during the teaching-learning process, in order to generate the educational content and create digital learning materials for the learners. The pedagogical tools focus on supporting factual knowledge through the use of innovative digital technologies. The research focused on the role of digital pedagogy and the intervention of digital technology in order to create a multi-literate world (Strobl et al. 2019; Henderson 2014).

The digital pedagogies help to reach out and cater to the needs of the learners belonging to diverse ethnic groups. The range of pedagogies also helps to meet the requirements of learners from diverse linguistic groups (Martín, Hirsu, Gonzales and Alvarez 2019). The use and application of the dynamic pedagogical practices play a significant role in effectively reaching out to the minds of the learners. The innovative pedagogical practices make a lot of sense, especially when the teacher is dealing with the learners across a diverse group of learners (Martín, Hirsu, Gonzales and Alvarez 2019).

The innovative pedagogical techniques are equally important and integral to the teaching-learning process of learners at higher educational levels (Petko 2012). The five important factors which contribute in digital pedagogy are: the teacher's confidence, competency, technology, availability of adequate infrastructure and the teacher's belief that technology will play an important role in the pedagogical process.

A number of revolutions have been taking place in the field of digital pedagogies. The digital revolutions have wrought immense change in the education sector. Its transformation has also been due to an emphasis on skills, digital literacy and the need to develop global competencies. Mason, Shaw and Zhang's research drew upon two case studies conducted in two different diverse backgrounds in Australia and Indonesia (Mason, Shaw and Zhang 2019). The results of the case studies showed that the usage of technological pedagogies is largely dependent on the teachers' level of content knowledge and ease with technology, as well as their willingness to use technological pedagogies in the teaching-learning process (Sachin, Celik, Akturk and Aydin 2013).

TPACK describes the technological content knowledge which the teachers require for an effective teaching-learning process. The technological content knowledge will aid the teachers in efficiently combining the content knowledge with the digital technology so as to give an impactful output to the learners. Researchers have measured the performance of TPACK by assessing the reliability and validity of the learning outcomes. The seven sub-scales of the TPACK model comprise technological knowledge, pedagogical knowledge, content knowledge, technological pedagogical knowledge, technological content knowledge, pedagogical content knowledge and the model itself. Further, to explore the variations in the sub-scales across languages, the study involved both English and Turkish (Ismail 2011; Koehler et al. 2014).

3.5 Attitudes towards Digital Education

The adoption of digital technology in the teaching-learning process largely depends upon the teachers' perceptions and attitudes. Though the take-up of digitization in education is also dictated by the financial, technological and educational constraints faced by the teachers at various levels, the infrastructural requirements and adequate training in methodology for the teachers also play a significant role in influencing their perceptions and attitudes towards adopting digital education experiences. Kreijns, Van Acker, Vermeulen and van Buuren (2013) revealed that digital training and skills will help in encouraging the teachers to focus on digital learning materials. Their research also found that previous use of digital learning materials as well as the use of learning materials by colleagues made a huge difference in building a positive attitude towards adopting pedagogies in digital education. It is important to understand and explore the intentions and attitudes of the teachers towards adopting digital technologies. Apparently, there are a number of factors that stimulate the interest and attention of the teachers towards adopting ICT in their pedagogical practice.

Further, in the same way that it is important to understand teachers' attitudes and perceptions, and to analyse their approach to digital education, similarly, it is important to understand the factors influencing the learners' attitudes towards digital education. The learners' attitudes to the digital learning process involve family norms, values and lifestyles (Darvin and Norton 2017). Further, Darvin and Norton's previous (2014) research focused on the digital divide among the rich and poor. They found that learners' attitudes are largely shaped by their social class positions as reflected in the capital required for the smooth conduct of the digital learning process. Also, apart from capital, the home environment, use of language at home, literacy level at home, and parents' education and work, also define the implications of pedagogical practices. Additionally, Jones and Vagle (2013) made a huge demand for a social-class sensitive pedagogy to provide a more inclusive approach within the teaching-learning process. The digital divide is much wider in poor countries as well as developing nations with little or no support for the education of children. In contrast, the majority of developed nations encourage and support their children's education, either financially or by ensuring adequate infrastructure in order to provide a better learning environment and a better future for the society. Education has been considered an important tool for future generations and therefore there is a need for a systematic and organised effort in order to provide better quality education.

The in-service teacher training programs play a significant role in transforming teacher attitudes towards the adoption of ICT in their classroom teaching-learning process. The results of George's research revealed that the majority of the teachers studied had a positive and moderate attitude towards using ICT in their classroom teaching (George 2015).

The lack of mobile devices dissuades some learners from the effective digital pedagogical process. In Al-Fahad's study, the majority of his 186 respondents used their mobiles for other purposes rather than for learning (Al-Fahad 2009). The respondents agreed that mobile learning is an effective mode of learning, though they considered it to be an expensive mode of digital learning. The attitudes and behaviour of students also varies with regard to the use of digital textbooks (Weisberg 2011). The digital platforms evaluated in the research were Amazon, Kindle, Sony E-reader, Apple iPad and CourseSmart. The learners' attitude towards digital learning largely depended upon their computer efficacy. Also, the mere knowledge of basic computer skills was not enough to attain the digital learning skills. Additionally, the computer self-efficacy level of the students varied according to gender. Similarly, the attitudes and perceptions of the music and computer teachers varied largely across male and female teachers. Moreover, the computer self-efficacy of the students also varied according to whether the students possessed computers at home. Further, the attitudes and perceptions of the students towards computer skills varied depending upon the earlier years in which the learners engaged themselves with digital learning technology (Gudek 2019).

Parents also play an important role in the digital learning process of their children. Parents are important stakeholders in ensuring and providing the right kind of education. Mikelić Preradović, Lešin and Šagud (2016) investigated parental attitudes to the digital learning process: 99% of the parents owned smart phones, laptops or computers, but mere possession of these digital devices didn't guarantee the development of computer or information literacy skills among children. Also, these device-owning parents were far more anxious about their children receiving digital education, despite their easy access to digital technology.

In another study, although medical students displayed a positive attitude towards M-learning, ironically when they were given the opportunity for M-learning, their use of M-learning skills was very limited. Apparently, their positive attitudes were not reflected in their learning process or their engagement with the pedagogical tools, either in terms of downloading the reference material or their level of participation in the class (Patil, Balaji, Mrunal et al. 2016). Demirbilek (2010) analysed the attitudes of adults towards educational mobile media and found that, though the majority of the adults showed positive interest in mobile education, their actual use of the same in the learning process was limited.

Kul Aksu and Birisci gave thirty pre-service teachers training in the form of interactions through web-based applications (Kul Aksu and Birisci 2019). The teachers who underwent the training showed far greater understanding of the TPACK model and subsequently, there was a significant relationship between their use of the model and their level of self-efficacy. The combination of digital pedagogical tools and an innovative pedagogical approach aims to provide learners with an enriched teaching and learning experience to the learners (Makarova and Makarova 2018).

3.5.1 Challenges in Adapting to the Pedagogies in Digital Education

The challenges of adopting the critical pedagogies in digital education have been a cause of concern for trainers as well as learners. Social class structures have created challenges for learners belonging to various social groups and also have hugely impacted the lives of learners in adapting to the dynamic infrastructural environment. Digital platforms have enabled resources which are flexible, accessible and accommodative. Learning materials and resources need to be created in more accessible digital environments, with immense scope for open access platforms and free sharing as well as permanency of information. The immense flexibilities will on the one hand make it possible to accommodate large numbers of learners, and, on the other, they will satisfy the different requirements of the learners.

The digital pedagogies are intended to make the teaching-learning process innovative as well as intensely engaging (Smeda, Dakich and Sharda 2012). The purpose of the technology-based pedagogy is to tap the advances being made in the digital world. Digital technologies are designed to engage the teacher and the learner in the teaching-learning process and to make that process fruitful. But the digital platforms are also shaped by social inequalities. These inequalities are reflected in the infrastructural limitations of the learners as well as trainers. The infrastructural restrictions comprise availability of computers, laptops, internet, connectivity or broadband speed (Darvin and Norton 2017).

The introduction of digital technologies into the classroom environment has paved the way for a digital divide among the students (Henderson 2011). The digital divide is also present within the classroom and school environment. Henderson's research looked at two classrooms in order to understand the digital divide and the diverse levels of multi-literate groups being created. The innovative and dynamic pedagogies are intended to create supportive student practices to assist the learners in the learning process (Henderson 2011).

Digital technologies are important in building opportunities for learners and encouraging student engagement. Digital technologies are also important for enabling a reliable marking system to be used in the online examinations. Such technologies could be further used to design and develop new examination systems in order to ensure consistency in the evaluation process (Penney, Newhouse, Jones and Campbell 2012). The digital pedagogical practices are largely dependent upon sustained computer usage as well as the amount of time the teachers have spent exploring internet and other digital resources. According to another study, the relationship between computer usage and pedagogical practices is much evident in the subjects of science and social studies (Becker and Ravitz 1999). The shift towards a knowledge-based economy is creating innumerable demands on society as a whole. Learners need to develop these skills in order to thrive in the competitive knowledge-based economy. Due to ICT, there has been a skills revolution which is developing cognitive, affective and social skill-based pedagogies. Such software tools lay a creative path to enhance collaborative skills for transforming global society (Clarke and Clarke 2009). Technology can be a challenge, as it requires preparedness and adoption, plus adaptation to the changing demands. The fast transformations in digital platforms require teachers to learn the skills, to prepare and adapt to the tools in their pedagogical journey. There are models designed to equip teachers as well as pre-service teachers, to train them with the necessary digital pedagogical content knowledge (Abbitt 2011).

3.6 Hypothesis

The need to inculcate and adopt digital pedagogical practices is the need of the hour. A number of institutions have been making systematic and concentrated efforts in order to accommodate their learners by using innovative digital pedagogical practices. The hypothesis in this chapter is based on a systematic review of the literature on the application of digital technology within innovative pedagogical practices.

3.7 Research Questions

- H_1: There is a significant association between the willingness and adoption of the digital pedagogical practices.
- H_2: There is a significant association between the factors influencing the attitudes and perceptions of the stakeholders towards adopting digital pedagogies and the demographics of gender and education.

3.7.1 Analysis and Hypothesis Testing Based on Meta-Analysis Technique

3.7.1.1 Introduction to Meta-Analysis

The hypothesis testing was done with the help of Meta-Analysis technique. The Meta-Analysis is a technique used in order to synthesize data (Suurmond, Henk and Hak 2017). The systematic presentation of data helps to analyse and present the same in a simple form through depicting and devising relationships across the variables. Therefore, hypothesis testing is considered to be a crucial aspect of data analysis. Meta-Analysis is the collaboration of a number of empirical studies revolving around the similar variables and analysing the relationships among the variables.

3.7.1.2 Assumptions of Meta-Analysis

Meta-Analysis is based on certain underlying assumptions. All the studies in Meta-Analysis are empirical studies with dependent and independent variables. The criteria for the employability of the technique requires the research to be comprehensive and clearly mention the number of responses which have been considered for the different studies. Also, it requires that all the associated studies should be collaborated while stating the results. Apparently, this assumption is to some extent difficult to fulfil, as there might be a number of studies in the area and the requirement to cover all of them becomes very difficult, especially when many of the studies in the related field may not even be published.

3.8 Results and Discussion

3.8.1 Meta-Analysis Model

The Meta-Analysis model is based on the secondary data. In the research analysis, the secondary data is being collected from a number of research studies on a similar area. The basis of meta-analysis model is number of subjects of the study as well as the correlation values. Meta-analysis is a research technique which collaborates the findings and the results of all the studies analysed and provides the combined results for better interpretations across the demographic and geographical boundaries.

Table 3.1 depicts the p-value of the z test. The p-value of the z test possesses a value less than 0.05, stating that the alternative hypothesis is accepted. Thus, there is a significant positive correlation between the attitudes and perceptions of the stakeholders towards adopting digital pedagogies and the willingness in the adoption of digital pedagogical practices. The main components comprising willingness, skill sets and the varied technology contributed towards the explained variance of the usage of technology in the pedagogical practices. The correlation of 0.78 describes the strong positive association between the variables of the study.

TABLE 3.1
Meta-Analysis Model

Model	**Random effects model**
Confidence level	95%
Presentation	
Sort By	Entry number
Order	Ascending
Combined Effect Size	
Correlation	0.78
Confidence interval LL	0.67
Confidence interval UL	0.86
Prediction interval LL	0.33
Prediction interval UL	0.94
Z-value	9.98
One-tailed p-value	0.000
Two-tailed p-value	0.000
Number of incl. subjects	1325
Number of incl. studies	10
Heterogeneity	
Q	107.82
p_Q	0.000
I^2	91.65%
T^2 (z)	0.09
T (z)	0.30

TABLE 3.2
Meta-Analysis Model

Between sub-group weighting	Random effects		
Within sub-group weighting	Random effects (Tau separate for subgroups)		
Confidence level	95%		
Combined Effect Size			
Correlation	0.77		
Confidence interval LL	0.73		
Confidence interval UL	0.80		
Prediction interval LL	0.73		
Prediction interval UL	0.80		
Number of incl. subjects	1325		
Number of incl. studies	10		
Number of subgroups	2		
Analysis of variance	**Sum of squares (Q*)**	**df**	**p**
Between / Model	0.33	1	0.568
Within / Residual	9.10	8	0.334
Total	9.43	9	0.399
Pseudo R^2	3.45%		

3.8.2 Sub-Group Analysis

Table 3.2 states the sub-group analysis among the variables used in the empirical studies. The correlation value of 0.77 states, the strong positive relationship between the attitudes and perceptions of the trainers in adopting digital pedagogies and the willingness in adopting digital pedagogical practices. The main components of will, skill and the technological interventions contribute towards the explained variance. The strong positive correlation reflects the positive attitudes and perceptions of the trainers towards the digital interventions in the pedagogical practices. Also, there is a significant association between the factors influencing the attitudes and perceptions of the stakeholders towards adopting digital pedagogies and the demographics of gender and education.

3.8.3 Moderator Analysis

3.8.3.1 Regression

Figure 3.1 depicts the strong positive relationship between the attitudes and perceptions of the trainers in adopting digital pedagogies and their willingness in the adoption of digital pedagogical practices. The dots represent a positive association between the x and y variables. The close association among the majority of the dots states the agreement among the results of the various empirical studies. It denotes that there exists a strong positive correlation among the variables of the studies. The association among the will, skill and the technological tools denotes the positive perception and attitude of the trainers in the adoption of digital technology in the pedagogical practices. Also, there is a significant association between the factors influencing the attitudes and perceptions of the stakeholders towards adopting digital pedagogies and the demographics of gender and education.

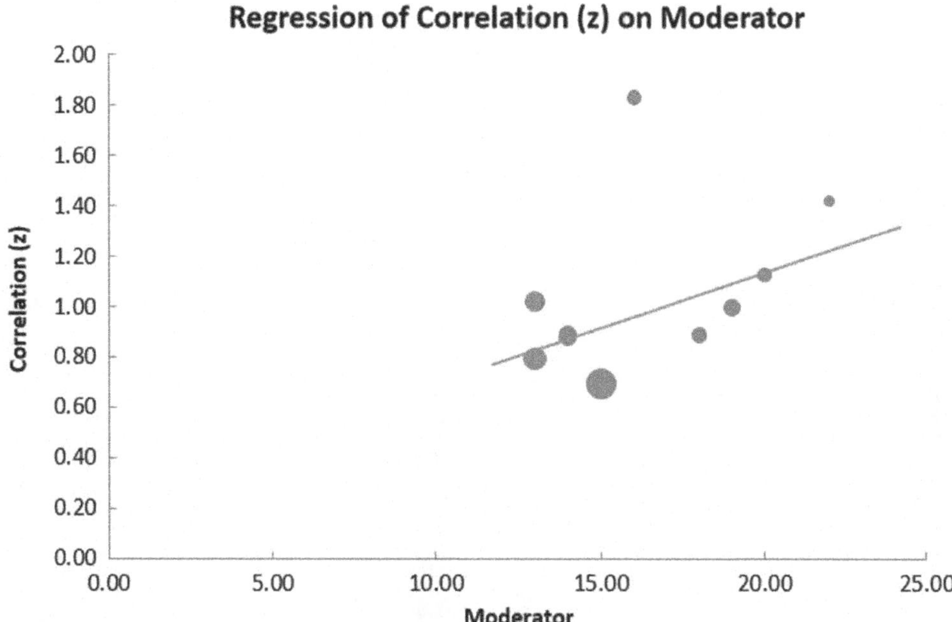

FIGURE 3.1
Regression.

TABLE 3.3
Moderator Analysis

	B	SE	CI LL	CI UL	β	-value	p-value
Intercept	0.26	0.17	-0.12	0.64		1.53	0.127
Moderator	0.04	0.01	0.02	0.07	0.40	4.11	0.000
Analysis of variance	**Sum of squares (Q)**	**df**	**p-value**		**Mean square**	**F-Value**	**p-value**
Model	16.90	1	0.000		16.90	1.49	0.257
Residual	90.92	8	0.000		11.37		
Total	107.82	9	0.000				
Combined effect size	0.95						
T^2 (method of moments estimation)	0.08						
R^2	15.67%						

3.8.4 Moderator Analysis

Table 3.3 states the moderator analysis and the p-value of the z test in the moderator analysis. The p-value is less than 0.05, leading to acceptance of alternative hypothesis. Also, the combined effect size is 0.95 stating the positive association between the attitudes and perceptions of the stakeholders towards adopting digital pedagogies and the willingness and the adoption of digital pedagogical practices. Further, there is a significant association between the factors influencing the attitudes and perceptions of the stakeholders towards adopting digital pedagogies and the demographics of gender and education.

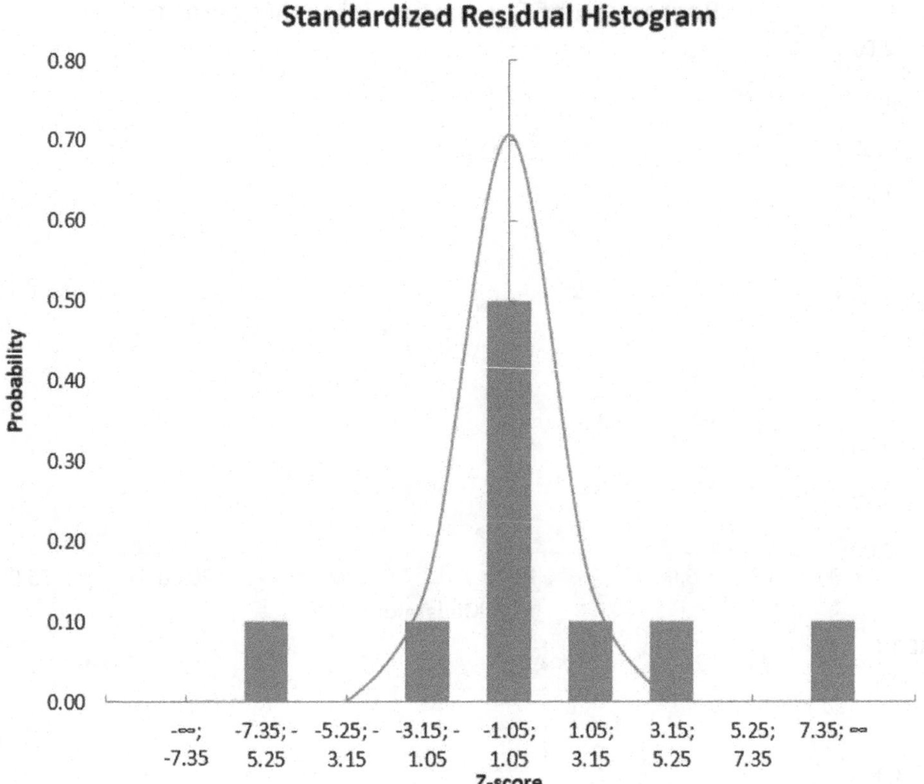

FIGURE 3.2
Histogram.

3.8.5 Publication Bias

3.8.5.1 Histogram

Figure 3.2 states the standard residual histogram values in the pictorial form. The histogram is the result of the z scores of the individual empirical studies analysed in the secondary data. The individual z scores are also known as standard residuals, therefore, the above figure is denoted as standard residual histogram. The individual z scores are forming a normal distribution. The results of the histogram denote a strong relationship among the variables of the study. The values of z score as compared to their probabilities depict a value of 0.71, stating a positive relationship between the attitudes and perceptions of the trainers in adopting digital pedagogies and their willingness in adoption of digital pedagogical practices.

3.8.5.2 Galbraith Plot

Figure 3.3 depicts the Galbraith plot by comparing the inverse standard error to the z score figures. The Galbraith plot is used to run the z scores on the inverse of standard error. The three lines indicate that 95% of the studies analysed in the secondary data fall within the area. The slope value of 0.000 depicts the positive relationship between the attitudes and perceptions of trainers in adopting digital pedagogies and their willingness in the adoption

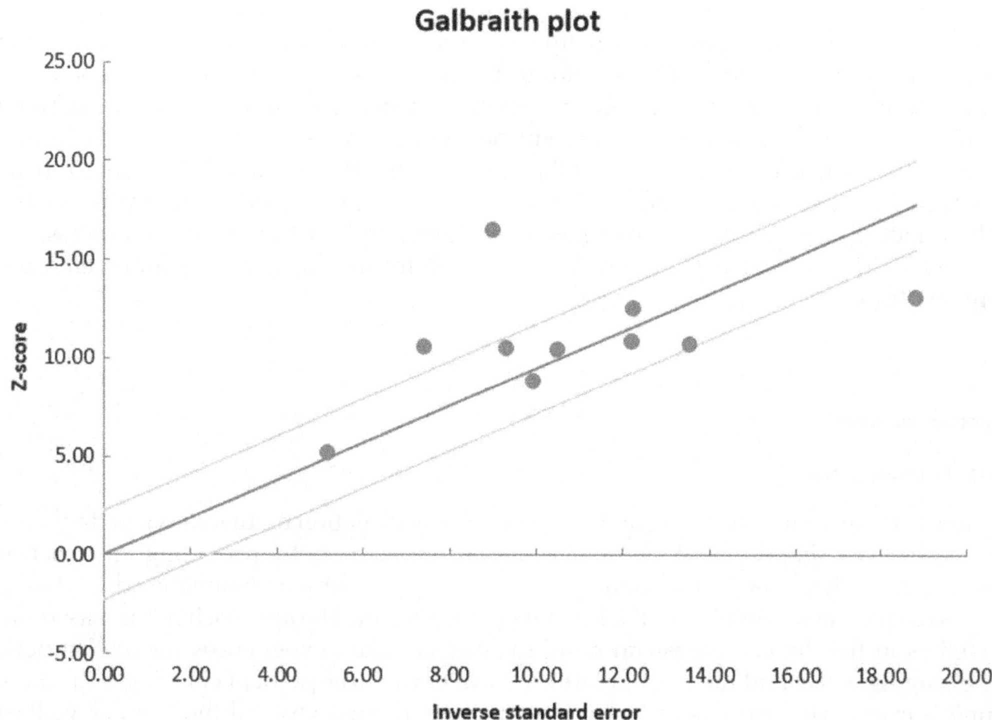

FIGURE 3.3
Galbraith plot.

of digital pedagogical practices. The dots falling within the area of the lines clearly indicate the strong relationship among the will, skill and the adoption of technological tools in pedagogies of digital education.

3.9 Conclusion

The outcome of the study clearly indicates that will, skill and the level of comfort with the technological tools play a very important role in the perceptions and attitudes of the trainers as well as in their interest in adoption of digital pedagogies. The analyses of the empirical studies in the secondary data analysis also point out the fact that though the majority of the trainers share positive attitudes and perceptions towards adoption of digital technology in the pedagogical process, their application of digital education was largely influenced by a number of variables comprising experience, prior knowledge and personality of the trainers as well as learners. Also, the significant association between the factors influencing the attitudes and perceptions of the stakeholders towards adopting digital pedagogies and the demographics of gender and education indicates the manner and the form in which the digital technology is being embraced by the people from different genders as well as educational backgrounds.

The application of digital technology based on TPACK (Technological Pedagogical Content Knowledge) of the trainers as well as learners emphasizes the need for imparting the technical knowledge for better and comfortable adoption of digital technology. The findings reveal that though infrastructure is paramount for digital education, it is not the only criterion for adoption of digital technology. The teachers are designers, being constantly involved with knowledge designing and delivery process and the learning has to be with purpose and full of life. Further, in the process of designing, it becomes pertinent for the teachers to understand their learners and build relations in order to create pedagogies which are more learner centric. The learning goals are primarily associated with an increased form of learner engagement during the teaching-learning process. An enriched learning experience will prepare the youth for the global transforming environment and the changing digitized world.

3.10 Implications

The teacher plays a highly significant role in the transformation of innovative pedagogies. The teacher can shape the whole perspective of the learners by providing an enriched experience. The knowledge and the adaptability of the teacher with innovative digital tools can lead to the transformation of the learning environment. The approach in the classroom as well as in the digital spaces can build lifelong enriched experiences for the learners. The changing world and the global platform have been posing a lot of challenges for these young learners. The learners of today have to be equipped with all the hard as well as the soft skills along with a rich character to live happier lives. The employability quotient needs to be systematically worked upon in order to bridge the gap between industry and academia. Digital education possesses the required platform to bridge the gap and create holistic and memorable experiences for the learners. It ignites and drives the passion of teaching and learning among all the stakeholders.

3.11 Application and Future Scope of Research

The results of the study would be applicable to a large number of academic and non-academic institutions in employing digital technology in the pedagogical processes. The attitudes and perceptions of the trainers as well as learners would be a guiding factor in exploring the acceptance level and adoption behaviour of digital technology. The teachers need to be equipped with the digital tools, so that they can design innovative tools for a varied classroom environment. The challenges faced in the digital technology, changing perceptions, attitudes and obstacles in adoption of digital technology could be further researched and explored across geographical and demographic segments. The future of innovative pedagogies will expand with the increase in remote teaching as a result of the pandemic. Technology expands the learning platform, allowing the learners to learn at their pace with different learning abilities as well as builds opportunities for the teachers, to enrich the classroom experiences and create insightful memories.

References

Abbitt, J. T. 2011. "Measuring technological pedagogical content knowledge in pre-service teacher education: A review of current methods and instruments." *Journal of Research on Technology in Education* 43(4): 281–300.

Al-Fahad, N. 2009. "Students' attitudes and perceptions towards the effectiveness of mobile learning in King Saud University, Saudi Arabia." *The Turkish Online Journal of Educational Technology – TOJET* 8(2).

Apple, M. W., Kellaway, J., Lang, P., and Singh, M. 2005. Eds. *Globalizing Education: Policies, Pedagogies, & Politics.* New York: Peter Lang Publishing Inc.

Becker, H. J., and Ravitz, J. 1999. "The influence of computer and internet use on teachers' pedagogical practices and perceptions." *Journal of Research on Computing in Education* 31(4). 356–384.

Blundell, C., Lee, K-T., and Nykvist, S. 2020. "Moving beyond enhancing pedagogies with digital technologies: Frames of reference, habits of mind and transformative learning." *Journal of Research on Technology in Education* 52(2). 178–196.

Clarke, T., and Clarke, E. 2009. "Born digital? Pedagogy and computer-assisted learning." *Education & Training* 51(5/6). 395–407.

Darvin, R., and Norton, B. 2017. "Identity, language learning, and critical pedagogies in digital times." *Encyclopedia of Language and Education* 6. 43–54.

Demirbilek, M. 2010. "Investigating attitudes of adult educators towards educational mobile media and games in eight European countries." *Journal of Information Technology Education: Research* 9(1). 235–247.

Duffy, K., and Ney, J. 2015. "Exploring the divides among students, educators, and practitioners in the use of digital media as a pedagogical tool." *Journal of Marketing Education* 37(2). 104–113.

Fullan, M., and Langworthy, M. 2013. *Towards a New End: New Pedagogies For Deep Learning.* Seattle, WA: Collaborative Impact.

George, A. 2015. "Attitude of teachers towards ICT implementation in classroom teaching and learning process." *Journal of Advanced Studies in Education and Management* 1(3).

Gudek, B. 2019. "Computer self-efficacy: Perceptions of music teacher candidates and their attitudes towards digital technology." *European Journal of Educational Research* 8(3). 683–696.

Guillén-Gámez, F. D., José Mayorga-Fernández, M., Bravo-Agapito, J., and Escribano-Ortiz, D. 2020. "Analysis of teachers' pedagogical digital competence: Identification of factors predicting their acquisition." *Technology, Knowledge and Learning.* 1–18.

Hamer, J., Cutts, Q., Jackova, J., Luxton-Reilly, A., McCartney, R. et al. 2008. "Contributing student pedagogy." *ACM SIGCSE Bulletin* 40(4). 194–212.

Henderson, R. 2011. "Classroom pedagogies, digital literacies and the home-school digital divide." *International Journal of Pedagogies and Learning* 6(2). 152–161.

Herrington, J., Herrington, A., Mantel, J., Olney, I., and Ferry, B. 2009. Eds. *New Technologies, New Pedagogies: Mobile Learning In Higher Education.* Faculty of Education, University of Wollagong, Australia. Available at: https://ro.uow.edu.au/newtech/

Hsu, C.-Y., Liang, J.-C., Chai, C.-S., & Tsai, C.-C. 2013. "Exploring preschool teachers' technological pedagogical content knowledge of educational games." *Journal of Educational Computing Research* 49(4). 461–479.

Hwa, S. 2018. "Pedagogical change in mathematics learning: Harnessing the power of digital game-based learning." *Journal of Educational Technology & Society* 21(4). 259–276.

Jandrić, P., and Hayes, S. "Editorial: Visual pedagogies and digital cultures." *Knowledge Cultures* 5(5). 11–13.

Jones, S., and Vagle, M. D. 2013. "Living contradictions and working for change: Toward a theory of social class–sensitive pedagogy." *Educational Researcher* 42(3). 129–141.

Koehler, M. J., Mishra, P., Kereluik, K., Shin, T. S., Graham, C. R. 2014. "The technological pedagogical content knowledge framework." In *Handbook of Research on Educational Communications and Technology.* New York: Springer. 101–111.

Koekoek, J., and van Hilvoorde, I. 2019. Eds. *Digital Technology in Physical Education: Global Perspectives*. London and New York: Routledge.

Kreijns, K., Van Acker, F., Vermeulen, M. and van Buuren, H. 2013. "What stimulates teachers to integrate ICT in their pedagogical practices? The use of digital learning materials in education." *Computers in Human Behavior* 29(1). 217–225.

Kul, U., Zeki, A., and Salih, B. 2019. "The relationship between technological pedagogical content knowledge and Web 2.0 self-efficacy beliefs." *International Online Journal of Educational Sciences* 11(1). 198–213.

Lam, S. 2020. "A review in our present teaching pedagogies: Traditional, digital and flipped learning." *Applied Communication eJournal* 2(26).

Laurillard, D. 2007. "Pedagogical forms of mobile learning: framing research questions."153–175. Available at: www.academia.edu/309117/Pedagogical_Forms_of_Mobile_Learning_Framing_Research_Questions.

Makarova, E. A., and Makarova, E. L. 2018. "Blending pedagogy and digital technology to transform educational environment." *International Journal of Cognitive Research in Science, Engineering and Education* 6(2). 57.

Martín, C. S, Hirsu, L., Gonzales, L., and Alvarez, P. A. 2019. "Pedagogies of digital composing through a translingual approach." *Computers and Composition* 52. 142–157.

Mason, J., Shaw, G., Zhang, D. 2019. "Shifting pedagogies and digital technologies: Shaping futures in education." In: Yu, S., Niemi, H., and Mason, J. Eds. *Shaping Future Schools with Digital Technology. Perspectives on Rethinking and Reforming Education*. Singapore: Springer. 201–223.

Mikelić Preradović, N., Lešin, G., and Šagud, M. 2016. "Investigating parents' attitudes towards digital technology use in early childhood: A case study from Croatia." *Informatics in Education* 15(1). 127–146.

Patil, R. N., Balaji, D. A, Mrunal, P., Amit, G., Supriya, D., Anuradha, R. P., and Shriram, G. 2016. "Attitudes and perceptions of medical undergraduates towards mobile learning (M-learning)." *Journal of Clinical and Diagnostic Research: JCDR* 10(10).

Penney, D., Newhouse, P., Jones, A., and Campbell, A. 2012. "Digital technologies: Enhancing pedagogy and extending opportunities for learning in senior secondary physical education?" In Thao Lê and Quynh Lê. Eds. *Technologies for Enhancing Pedagogy, Engagement and Empowerment in Education: Creating Learning-Friendly Environments*. IGI Global. 15–26.

Petko, D. 2012. "Teachers' pedagogical beliefs and their use of digital media in classrooms: Sharpening the focus of the 'will, skill, tool' model and integrating teachers' constructivist orientations." *Computers & Education* 58(4). 1351–1359.

Sahin, I., Celik, I., Akturk, O. A., and Aydin, M. A. 2013. "Analysis of relationships between technological pedagogical content knowledge and educational internet use." *Journal of Digital Learning in Teacher Education* 29(4). 110–117.

Sahin, I. 2011. "Development of survey of technological pedagogical and content knowledge (TPACK)." *Turkish Online Journal of Educational Technology–TOJET* 10(1). 97–105.

Santos, J., Simões Figueiredo, A., and Vieira, A. 2019. "Innovative pedagogical practices in higher education: An integrative literature review." *Nurse Education Today* 72. 12–17.

Sargent, J., and Casey, A. 2018. "Exploring pedagogies of digital technology in physical education through appreciative inquiry." *Digital Technology in Physical Education: Global Perspectives*. 69–87.

Shin, D., Shin, Y., Choo, H., and Beam, K. 2011. "Smartphones as smart pedagogical tools: Implications for smartphones as u-learning devices." *Computers in Human Behavior* 27(6). 2207–2214.

Smeda, N., Dakich, E., and Sharda, N. 2012. "Transforming pedagogies through digital storytelling: Framework and methodology." In *International conference on education and e-learning (EeL). Proceedings*, Global Science and Technology Forum. 206.

Smith, K. M., and Jeffery, D. I. 2017. "Critical pedagogies in the neoliberal university: What happens when they go digital?" *The Canadian Geographer/Le Géographe canadien* 57(3). 372–380.

Strobl, C., Ailhaud, E., Benetos, K., Devitt, A., Kruse, O. et al. 2019. "Digital support for academic writing: A review of technologies and pedagogies." *Computers & Education* 131. 33–48.

Weisberg, M. 2011. "Student attitudes and behaviors towards digital textbooks." *Publishing Research Quarterly* 27(2). 188–196.

4

Students' Perspective of Cloud-Based Digitalization of Higher Education

Renu Bala

Research Scholar, Chaudhary Devi Lal University, Sirsa, Haryana, India

4.1 Introduction

In the twenty-first century, people are addicted to the latest technology. This digitalization is playing a very significant role in people's lives, especially young people. As all of us know that every coin has two sides; similarly, there are many advantages to the latest technology but it also some disadvantages. The positive side of digitalization can enhance

DOI: 10.1201/9781003203070-5

students' lives, but the negative side of technology can adversely affect the future. When students use technology for study purposes, it provides many advantages, such as access to a wide, versatile knowledge base. However, students have to face many challenges due to the drawbacks of digitalization. Different kinds of issues in this field can affect students' study life or their career path. The main issues and challenges that students face in their education and the measures that can be adopted to overcome those challenges are discussed.

At present, the concept of cloud computing is gaining popularity day by day in student life. What is the actual meaning of this term? As in real-life situations, clouds represent the groups of water molecules, the term cloud computing and the term cloud denote different network collections. Cloud computing services are divided into three parts: infrastructure services, software, and platform services. Cloud computing provides many advantages to users in the form of security benefits, flexibility, and cost benefits. Good examples of cloud computing can be seen in, for example, Gmail, YouTube, and Facebook.

4.2 Literature Review

Jadhav (2011) showed how technology has changed the field of education's overall dimensions due to its advancements. Both primary and secondary data were collected from various sources to conduct the study. Kamble (2013) showed what kinds of classrooms will be generated in the future by using cloud computing as well as ways traditional education will be replaced by the modern education system. Olalere et al. (2013) described the cloud computing concept, features, and challenges faced by media in Nigeria. Nerurkar (2014) analyzed several challenges in online marketing associated with both consumers and companies. Companies use various kinds of fraud by using fake advertisements and exploiting the customers. Singh (2014) reviewed how cloud computing benefits the retail sector by labor-saving and the management of work in an organized way using technological equipment. Gupta and Arora (2015) highlighted the positive impacts of cloud computing on the Indian economy and discussed how the lives of rural Indian people are impacted by cloud computing. Khan et al. (2015) highlighted that cloud computing offers advanced preservation opportunities and provides wide access to information. Kumar (2015) highlighted the retail sector problems which occur due to the modernization of retailing services. During the study, it was observed that poor and uneducated people suffer various challenges due to the use of technology in the retail sector because they cannot adopt the new retailing system due to their lack of knowledge and financial issues. Nigam et al. (2015) presented the importance of cloud computing in various kinds of settings. The study defined how digitalization plays a significant role in the IT and education sectors, and in the research field. Jha and Shenoy (2016) described how the traditional education system has changed step by step due to the latest technology and institutions' efforts to maintain the technological environment. Midha (2016) presented the challenges that Indian people have to face in using the technology and suggested measures to solve such issues. Priyadarsini and Vijayaratnam (2016) presented the nine pillars of digital India and described how the lifestyles of Indian villagers have been changed due to such technological advancements. Gulati (2016) highlighted those challenges that occur during the successful implementation of cloud computing and offered various remedies to solve such issues. Shamim (2016) described the concept of digital India and the initiatives taken by the Indian government to promote digital pillars. Soni and Pandey (2016) highlighted the role of cloud computing in e-marketing. The study mentioned how customers are enjoying marketing servicers just by a click on their cell phones and how cloud computing has upgraded such kinds of marketing facilities for the buyer and seller both. Feibert et al. (2017) described the role of technology in shipping services. During the study, it was found that digitalization plays a very significant role in shipping services. Ignat (2017) showed the impact of digitalization at the global level and described how many changes have taken place in the global market due to advanced technology. Kaul and Mathur (2017) analyzed the challenges during the successful implementation of digitalization and how financial issues occur during the technological up-gradation. Maiti and Kayal (2017) presented the impacts of digitalization on the Indian services sector and the mirco, small and medium enterprises sector by including positive impacts, challenges, and remedies. Narual and Rana (2017) highlighted how India is trying to become one of the leading countries in digitalization and what strategies have been adopted by the Indian government to promote this. Neumeier et al. (2017) showed that digitalization presents a positive role not just in a single sector but in every sector of today's economy and highlighted various advantages of digitalization in the current scenario. Parviainen et al. (2017) expressed how digitalization challenges can be tackled and opportunities created. Sheokand and Gupta (2017) highlighted the impacts of the digital India campaign and its effects on the Indian economy. Shivasankaran (2017) discussed how digital marketing has changed youngsters' buying behavior. Now, young people compare items by using their internet services, and can easily shop around online before purchasing the items. Singh (2017) described the impacts of digitalization on small and medium enterprises situated in India. The study concluded that such enterprises are enjoying a high rate of productivity and profitability due to the positive impacts of digitalization. Valverde (2017) described how financial stability has affected digitalization and what changes have taken place in the banking stream due to technological advancements. Pari and Giri (2018) highlighted the impacts made by digitalization of the rural economy and of the banking system in rural areas. The study concluded that digital banking has changed the banking sector's overall scenario by providing several kinds of facilities. Gobble (2018) highlighted many challenges in the digitalization world, detailing that these challenges need to be solved to generate innovation in this area. Hema and Suma (2018) defined what kinds of challenges must be faced by the Indian government to make India digital and what kinds of hurdles must be faced by the people of rural areas during digital payments. The study was carried out in the area of Hyderabad and included 183 respondents. The study found that digital payments should make the transactions process very easy and time-saving, but instead, rural people are still facing various problems. Neeraj (2018) highlighted the role of digitalization in human resource management and described the importance of digitalization in managing human capital in the workplace. Kumar et al. (2018) mentioned the role of technology in the retail sector. Secondary data was gathered using various kinds of articles, newspapers, magazines, journals, blogs, and reports, and the analyzed data demonstrated that technology has created very fruitful results for both buyer and seller in the retail sector. Pawadi (2018) described how technology has changed the banking sector's working and how useful it is for bankers. The study analyzed how technology reduced workers' burdens due to easy access of data, as now customers can also use banking facilities from their own home. Srivastava and Khan (2018) highlighted the concept of cloud computing by defining different aspects of its advantages and services. Sujata (2018) highlighted the role of digitalization in the banking sector. The study found that digitalization is considered a boon in the banking sector due to its results. Kumar (2018) presented the impacts of digitalization trends on the Indian economy based on previous literature. Matt et al. (2019) described how cloud computing helps researchers position their work, and define synergies and similarities with others. Rachinger et al. (2019) showed that while digitalization has gained importance in current times, new innovations are constantly appearing. Rastogi (2019) analyzed the views of faculty members in educational institutions and found that education is worthless without ICT knowledge in this technological era. Shallu et al. (2019) presented the impacts of digitalization on the Indian economy, society, and environment and mentioned the challenges faced by the Indian government to resolve the issues related to technological up-gradation. Nadkarni and Prugl (2020) described what kinds of opportunities exist in the cloud computing world and what kinds of steps can be initiated to exploit that opportunity. Komala et al. (2020) highlighted the role of ICT in higher education and described what kinds of challenges have to be faced by the higher authority of institutions during the implementation and installation of technological equipment and cloud computing.

4.3 Research Questions

1. What are the main issues and challenges students face in the digital education system or cloud computing?
2. What are the required strategies to deal with students' and teachers' issues and challenges in the digital education system or cloud computing?

4.4 Research Objectives

1. To identify students' main issues and challenges in the digital education system or cloud computing.
2. To analyze the required strategies to deal with students' and teachers' issues and challenges in the digital education system or cloud computing.

4.5 Data and Methodology

For the purposes of the study, both primary and secondary data were used. The pre-structured questionnaire was framed for the primary data to collect students' and teachers' views. The sample included 220 students and 100 teachers in different colleges and universities situated in Haryana and the Punjab state. Data were collected through an online survey due to the limitations of the COVID-19 period. Collected data were analyzed with the help of percentage analysis. Following that, for the secondary data, various research papers, articles, and newspapers were explored.

4.6 How Technology Facilitates Learning

Cloud computing plays a very substantial role in the education system. The following details provided by students and teachers during the study highlight the contribution of cloud computing in the educational stream:

1 In the traditional education system, students often face a lack of resources in the classroom. However, due to the latest technology, many teaching resources are more easily available for students.
2 The digitalized classroom provides more effective and fruitful teaching to the students.
3 Students get better engagement opportunities in high-tech classes.
4 The cloud computing education environment facilitates students' interactive charts, pictures, videos, and audios, which help improve learning and remembering.
5 Use of cloud computing in education saves faculty time in conducting various kinds of educational activities and makes them entertaining and engaging.
6 At the authority level, cloud computing helps capture and store a large amount of data related to students such as fees, attendance, and results.

4.7 Difficulties Faced by Educational Institutions

To build the cloud computing system in the education system, institutions have to fulfill a large variety of requirements, as presented by teachers during research:

a) Development of sustainable as well as sufficient funding model
b) Creation of efficient staffing model
c) Proper contribution of institutional leadership
d) Enthusiastic and operational support from faculty members.
e) Provide proper training to operators
f) Engage the whole institution community
g) Align with the strategies of the institution

Based on these aspects, it is clear that educational institutions have to make various adjustments to provide the cloud computing environment to students and meet high financial outlay.

4.8 Issues and Challenges Reported by Students

As per the analyzed data, students have to face many challenges due to cloud computing, which cover:

4.8.1 Adoption of Technology

To learn in addition to navigating cloud computing is a complicated task. It becomes challenging for students to learn minute details about the technology for their study purpose. In general, people resist change, so it becomes challenging for organizations to make them and their families aware of the benefits of technology in education.

4.8.2 Lack of Motivation

Students feel a lack of motivation towards digitalized learning as machines do not motivate them to study and succeed. Due to this lack of motivational feedback, students feel disappointed and do not like to learn just from the technological world. As students feel enthusiastic when teachers guide them or encourage them, this is a big reason that students avoid high-tech learning.

4.8.3 Maintenance of Self-Discipline

Cloud computing study demands self-discipline on students' behalf. However, it becomes complicated to maintain classroom discipline in the absence of a teacher because not all students take the study seriously, and disturb the class's environment by making noise, and so on. Due to this, all the students have to tolerate the noisy classroom and disturbance in their study.

4.8.4 Lack of Interaction with Teacher

The teacher's physical appearance plays a very significant role in the classroom as teachers resolve students' queries and make efforts to help students learn concepts quickly. Teachers use their voice, and the density of volume affects the mind of the learner. Students understand things rapidly and in a short period when they listen to the words from a teacher's mouth, irrespective of a machine. So, based on this fact, it is considered that teacher learning is more fruitful than machine learning.

4.8.5 Lack of Accessibility

Maintaining a proper cloud computing environment for study sometimes becomes a complicated task for the students. Some students who belong to village areas do not get a good internet connection and due to this lack of connectivity, they face many hurdles during study time. Attending online classes demands high bandwidth, but often becomes impossible for rural area students.

4.8.6 Security Issues Faced by Students

Students also have to face various kinds of security issues. As some learning sites demand the students' email addresses and primary biodata, the application can potentially misuse that data for another kind of purpose. Some areas require a large amount of money to access the application, and after the payment, students find out that the app was a fraud. Such kinds of websites misguide the students and exploit financially.

4.9 Strategies to Deal With the Issues and Challenges

Based on students' and teachers' collected data, the following suggested strategies can be adapted to better implement the education stream's cloud computing concept.

4.9.1 Adaptability

Technology offers many advantages to students in their study life. So students should not focus on the negative aspects of digitalization and should pay attention to its benefits. Students should adopt the technology as per the time requirement and try to create a positive change in society by concentrating on its beneficial aspects.

4.9.2 Maintenance of Proper Infrastructure

Educational institutions should set up high-tech infrastructure to provide digital educations to the students, so that students can learn from the technology with continuity and without any network issues.

4.9.3 Pay Attention towards Security Issues

Students must consider the security issues and should not share their private details on social media sites like Facebook and Twitter, as such kinds of mistake can create massive problems in the future. Students should avoid social connectivity and focus on study material.

4.9.4 Provide Proper Training to Staff

Educational institutions should provide proper training to faculty members to operate the technology-related projects. Only if teachers have the right knowledge can they accurately run the gadgets and guide students in their operation.

4.10 Research Gaps

Previous studies have described the basics, advantages, and limitations of cloud computing in general. However, the current study focuses on the education perspective by considering various students' and teachers' views.

4.11 Conclusion

Cloud computing plays a key role in the life of a student. Students should focus on the positive aspects of cloud computing and avoid its potentially harmful sites. Overcoming the challenges of various kinds of technological educational issues can lead to positive outcomes. If we consider the advantages of cloud computing, then we find that it is a boon for society, and with its proper utilization, a bright future can be built not just for students, but for the whole of society. A combination of classroom learning and online learning is the best way to produce good results, rather than one or the other. Cloud computing plays a significant role not just in a single sector but in every area of daily life. Today, a person can survive without basic necessities but cannot live without using technology. Simply put, the younger generation has become addicted to technological gadgets. Addiction to anything is not beneficial, so human beings should use the technology wisely. Humans made technology, so we should not be addicted to gadgets; otherwise, the day will come when there will be a saying that technology made humans. So by adopting the positive side of digitalization, humans should use it in a productive way.

4.12 Implications of Study

This study will offer guidance to educational institutions based on the data discussed; academic institutions can easily access students' views and find out what kinds of difficulties students can face due to the lack of digital services. Various measures have also been mentioned in the study. By accessing or implementing such standards, a range of hurdles can be avoided by faculty members and higher education institutions' authority.

4.13 Limitations of Research

During the research, data were collected from a limited number of students and teachers and limited areas by including Haryana and the Punjab state.

4.14 Future Research

In the future, research could be extended to include a greater number of students and teachers and also areas. Different states could be included in collecting the views of students and teachers.

References

Feibert D. C. 2017. "An Integrated Process and Digitalization Perspective on the Shipping Supply Chain: A Literature Review." *IEEE Conference on Industrial Engineering and Engineering Management IEEE* 1–6

Gobble, MaryAnne M. 2018. "Digitalization, Digitization, and Innovation." *Research-Technology Management* 6(4): 56–59.

Gulati M. 2016. "Digital India: Challenges & Opportunities." *International Journal of Management, Information* 10(4): 1–4.
Gupta N. and Arora K. 2015. "Digital India: A Roadmap for the Development of Rural India." *International Journal of Business Management* 2(2): 1333–1342.
Ignat V. 2017. "Digitalization and the Global Technology Trends." *IOP Conference Series: Materials Science and Engineering* 227(1): 1–5.
Jadha V. 2011. "ICT and Teacher Education." *International Educational E-Journal* 1(1): 64–69.
Jha N. and Shenoy V. 2016. "Digitisation of Indian Education Process: A Hope or Hype." *IOSR Journal of Business and Management* 18(10): 131–139.
Kamble A. D. 2013. "Digital Classroom: The Future of the Current Generation." *International Journal of Education and Psychological Research* 2(2): 41–45.
Kaul M. and Mathur P. 2017. "Impact of Digitalization on the Indian Economy and Requirement of Financial Literacy." *Proceedings of International Conference on Recent Innovations in Engineering and Technology*: 100–105.
Khan et al. 2015. "Digitalization and its Impact on Economy." *International Journal of Digital Library Services* 5(2): 138–149.
Komala R. et al. 2020. "ICT in Higher Education: Its implementation and Challenges." *IOSR Journal of Research & Method in Education* 10(4): 55–57.
Kumar R. 2015. "Online Retail in India – A Disruptive Force." *Samvad* 9(1): 45–48.
Kumar S. et al. 2018. "Proliferation of Digitalization in Retail Sector: A Review in Indian Context." *Review of Business and Technology Research* 15(1): 40–45.
Maiti M. and Kayal P. 2017. "Digitisation: Its Impact on Economic Development & Trade 'With Special Reference to Services and MSME Sector of India.'" *Asian Economic and Financial Review* 7(6): 541–549.
Matt C. et al. 2019. "The Digitalization of the Individual: Conceptual Foundations and Opportunities for Research." *Electronic Markets* 29(1): 315–322.
Midha R. 2016. "Digital India: Barriers & Remedies." *International Conference on Recent Innovations in Sciences, Management, Education and Technology*: 256–261.
Nadkarni S. and Prugl R. 2020. "Digital Transformation: A Review, Synthesis and Opportunities for Future Research." *Management Review Quarterly* 20(1): 1–109.
Narual T. and Rana, S. 2017. "Digitalization in India." *International Journal of Emerging Technologies* 8(1): 298–303.
Neeraj 2018. "Role of Digitalization in Human Resource Management." *International Journal of Emerging Technologies and Innovative Research* 5(1): 284–288.
Nerurkar A. 2014. "Online Marketing – Challenges in Future." *International Journal of Research in Humanities, Arts and Literature* 2(4): 183–188.
Neumeier A. et al. 2017. "The Manifold Fruits of Digitalization – Determining the Literal Value Behind." *Proceedings Der Wirtschaftsinformatik und Angewandte Informatik* 3(1): 484–498.
Nigam A. et al. 2015. "Digitising Education: A Cost Benefit Analysis." *Asian Journal of Information Science and Technology* 5(1): 1–5.
Olalere A. Q. et al. 2013. "The Challenges of Digitization on the Broadcasting Media in Nigeria." *Arabian Journal of Business and Management Review* 3(5): 88–98.
Paria I. and Giri A. 2018. "A Literature Review on Impact of Digitalization on Indian Rural Banking System and Rural Economy." *Research Review International Journal of Multidisciplinary* 5(2): 56–62.
Parviainen P. et al. 2017. "Tackling the Digitalization Challenge: How to Benefit from Digitalization in Practice." *International Journal of Information Systems and Project Management* 5(1): 63–77.
Pawadi A. B. 2018. "Digitalization in Banking Sector." *International Journal of Trend in Scientific Research and Development* 1(1): 45–47.
Priyadarsini K. and Vijayaratnam N. 2016. "Digitalization of India: Smart Villages towards Smart India." *International Journal of Innovative Research in Information Security* 9(3): 33–37.
Rachinger M. et al. 2019. "Digitalization and its Influence on Business Model." *Journal of Manufacturing Technology* 30(8): 1143–1160.
Rastogi H. 2019. "Digitalization of Education in India." *International Journal of Research and Analytical Reviews* 6(1): 160–167.

Shallu et al. 2019. "Digitalization in India: An Innovative Concept." *International Journal of Engineering Development and Research* 7(1): 452–456.
Shamim 2016. "Digital India – Scope, Impact and Challenges." *International Journal of Innovative Research in Advanced Engineering* 12(3): 90–93.
Sheokand K. and Gupta N. 2017. "Digital India Programme and Impact of Digitalization on Indian Economy." *Indian Journal of Economics and Development* 5(5): 1–13.
Shivasankaran S. 2017. "Digital Marketing and Its Impact on Buying Behavior of Youth" *International Journal of Research in Management & Business Studies* 4(3): 35–39.
Singh J. 2014. "A Review of Impact of Information Technology in Retail Sector." *International Journal of Management Research & Review* 4(11): 1047–1055.
Singh P. 2017. "Impact of Digitalization on Small and Medium Enterprises in India." *Paripex-Indian Journal of Research* 6(4): 468–469.
Soni V. and Pandey, B. 2016. "Impact of Digitalization in E-Marketing." *International Journal for Innovation Research in Science & Technology* 3(5): 120–123.
Srivastava, P. and Khan, R. (2018) A Review Paper on Cloud Computing. *International Journals of Advanced Research in Computer Science and Software Engineering* 8: 17-20
Sujata M. 2018. "Digitalization in Banking Sector." IJRAR 5(3): 333–337.
Suma K. and Hema K. 2018. "A Study on Digital Payments in India with Perspective of Consumer's Adoption." *International Journal of Pure and Applied Mathematics* 4(4): 34–44.
Valverde S. 2017. "The Impact on Digitalization on Banking and Financial Stability." *Journal of Financial Management, Markets and Institutions* 6(4): 64–72.

5

Digitalization of Higher Education using Cloud Computing: Issues and Challenges Faced by Teachers

Abhaya Ranjan Srivastava

Department of Management, Birla Institute of Technology, Mesra (Lalpur Extension Centre), Ranchi, Jharkhand, India

DOI: 10.1201/9781003203070-6

5.1 Introduction

Education is the process of facilitating learning, or the acquisition of knowledge, skills, values, morals, beliefs, and habits. Educational methods may include teaching, imparting training, discussion, or storytelling. It generally takes place under the guidance of educators; however, learners may also impart education. Education is the gradual process of acquiring knowledge. It is one of the important pillars in the development of a civilized society. Education develops the thinking and behavioural process of the people.

5.1.1 History

The word 'education' is derived from the Latin word *'educatio'*, which means an activity of breeding, bringing up, or rearing through training (wikipedia.com 2021). In the prehistoric era education was imparted by passing life skills from one generation to another through observations, oral instructions, and imitation (etymonline.com 2021). Adults used to train younger members on the skills and knowledge which they felt necessary in their society. Storytelling has also been used as an important method to pass on skills, knowledge, and values from one generation to another (wikipedia.com 2021). The Sumerians of Mesopotamia were the first to develop the art of writing in 3000 B.C. As cultures extended beyond basic skills 'script' evolved. A script is a form of writing. The Egyptians developed a script called 'hieroglyphics', which conveyed messages in the form of pictures. As time passed, the pictures and signs took the form of letters (ancient.eu 2021). Greek and Roman alphabets evolved from these scripts. The same scripts were also the source of English alphabets. Egyptians made twenty-four letters from the pictures (Kalra, et al. 2019). As societies and communities developed – and cultures started to extend their knowledge beyond the skills which could be learned through imitation – formal education evolved.

5.1.2 Contemporary

Education can be imparted both formally and informally. Most countries have made education compulsory for every child up to a certain age. In the upcoming 30 years UNESCO estimates that the initiative of compulsory education, along with population growth, will see more people receiving formal education than in all of human history to date (UNESCO

2020). The methodology of education has witnessed drastic change from the prehistoric era to the ancient age, then to the medieval period, and now to the present form. Today education is mostly imparted through a formal process, which is generally divided step-by-step into the stages of preschool, primary school, secondary school, followed by college and university education. The majority of countries have recognized the 'right to education' and this is also promoted by the United Nations (wikipedia.com 2021). Various reforms have been witnessed in the education system, including formal, informal, self-learning, distance learning with physical classroom support and with the support of information and communication technologies. Digitalization has already entered our present system of education but to a limited extent.

5.1.3 Future

Organisations and businesses are changing themselves in line with changes in the beliefs and values of people, society, and nations. Developments in technology are making products, processes, and systems better, faster, more efficient, and more effective. Knowledge transfer is found to be difficult when compared to product transfer. It is generally said that 100% knowledge transfer does not happen. Some part of it is lost in the transfer process due to the fault of the teacher, student or the medium of transfer. Technological application has made the transfer of knowledge and information faster today compared to earlier times. In the present 'knowledge era or the information age' we are bombarded with information due to the application of technology. Technology can act as an important tool to make this knowledge transfer precise, accurate, and faster with the support of digitalization. Cloud computing has emerged as an important tool to share knowledge and information.

The present education system is supported by digital technologies but with certain limitations. A more widespread, better, and advanced application of digital technologies would help in making the present education system faster, more accurate, and accessible. The present weaknesses in the education systems could be removed to a large extent with digitalization. Reforms in the education system and developments in internet and communication technologies indicate that the education system would improve on the digital platform.

5.2 Digitalization

Digitalization is the conversion of text, picture, or sound into digital form, which can be read or processed by a computer (Oxford Dictionary 2021). Integration of digital technologies into our daily life through digitization of all those things which could be digitalized is termed as digitalization (Ochs and Riemann 2018) (igi-global 2021). Digitalization is transforming the world of work according to Brooking's report (Muro, et al. 2017). According to the Gartner's glossary "Digitalization is the application of digital technologies to change business models which could generate new revenues and value-producing opportunities" (Bloomberg 2018). Digital platforms have been effective in providing knowledge and information to a wider audience, which could be accessed through a computer, tablet, smartphone, or some other electronic device.

5.3 Cloud Computing

Cloud computing is an important terminology today in the IT sector but is applicable to various industries including the education sector. Cloud computing delivers a different value when compared to the traditional IT environment. It is being defined in a number of ways by authors and researchers. One simple definition defines cloud computing as a cluster of distributed computers that provide on-demand resources and services over a network medium (usually the internet) (Lin, Fu and Dasmalchi 2010). A definition from IBM describes cloud computing as a pooling of computing resources that are virtual in nature and can be delivered through the web. The driving force behind cloud computing has been the increasing use and application of electronic gadgets like tablets, smart phones, and laptops in our offices and homes (Almajalid, n.d.).

Cloud computing ensures a global reach of information and services using a computing environment which allows on-demand scalability and minimal initial investment. It can also provide pre-built services and solutions together with the required skills for running and maintaining them, hence reducing the risk and the need for the institution to maintain a group of staff that is highly skilled and hard to find. Depending on the type of resources and the services offered through it, the major types of cloud computing are:

Infrastructure as a Service (IaaS): The basic storage and computing capabilities are provided as standardized services over the network in IaaS. These are self-service models for accessing, monitoring and managing remote datacentre infrastructures, such as computer (virtualized or bare metal), storage, networking, and networking services (e.g. firewalls) which are managed on behalf of the client. Common characteristics of IaaS are dynamic scaling, internet connectivity, platform virtualization and automated administrative tasks. It offers the benefit of lower ownership costs resulting in lower capital requirements. Common examples are Amazon, Flipkart, Google and eBay.

Platform as a Service (PaaS): In this category, a layer of software or development environment in totality is offered as a service upon which other higher-level services can be built or created. They are used for applications and other types of development while providing cloud components to software. It is a framework in which clients can design, develop, test, deploy, customize, and host applications but cannot control the hardware, OS, and the network infrastructure. Its provider offers a combination of predefined Operating System (OS) and application servers, like LAMP platform (Linux, Apple, MySQL, and PHP), Ruby, Googles App Engine, salesforce.com, and Microsoft Azzure.

Software as a Service (SaaS): Currently this is the biggest market of cloud computing and is growing very fast. SaaS uses the internet to offer applications which are managed by a third-party vendor and whose interface is accessed on the client side. However, clients cannot control its hardware, OS, or the network infrastructure. Most of the SaaS applications can be run directly using through a web browser without the requirements of any downloads or installations. However, some may require plugins. It ensures functional applications such as web conferencing, CRM, and ERP as well as email among the common applications. Some popular offerings are Meet from Google, Teams from Microsoft, and Salesforce.

Clouds can be offered as a service by a third party and also can be developed and deployed internally in an organization. Based on the type of resources which are shared and delivered to customers, clouds are classified in four types as:

Private Cloud: This is also considered as an internal cloud. The environment on which this cloud computing deployment model lies is protected by a firewall which is managed and monitored by the information technology department of a particular organization. It is available and could be accessed only by authorized clients. It is generally adopted by educational institutions.

Community Cloud: This type of cloud hosting is mutual and shared among several organizations of a particular community such as banks, insurance companies, trading firms, or gas stations. The users of the specific community should have similar computing comprehension.

Public Cloud: The cloud services in the public cloud are delivered through a network that is accessible to the public. It is considered as an ideal representation of cloud hosting. The service provider offers infrastructure and services to a wide range of clients in this type of hosting.

Hybrid Cloud: This represents an integrated model of the cloud computing environment. It usually consists of two or more cloud servers, which could be either private, public, or community clouds. The different servers are interconnected with each other although each remains as a separate entity. Hybrid clouds are highly beneficial as they can overcome boundaries and decrease isolation, but cannot be categorized as private, public, or community clouds.

Cloud computing has become highly acceptable because it is simple in usage and user friendly. Some other advantages of adopting cloud computing include: a cost effective solution, wider reach, 24-7 availability of resources.

5.4 Digitalization and Education

Technology is a primary driver of most of the innovations happening in the present era (Fenwick, Kaal and Vermeulen 2017). Over the past half century, different and subsequent waves of digital innovation have ensured that 'digitalization' – the diffusion of digital technologies into probably every business, workplace, and pocket – has been reshaping the US economy and the world of work (Muro, et al. 2017). 'Digitalization of everything' has become a hallmark of what technology promises to individuals and has led to business empowerment. In the current era, acquisition of digital skills has evolved as a prerequisite for individual, industry, regional, and global success. The influence of digitalization can also be seen in the education system around the world. Digitalization in the education system could be credited to the USA which was a pioneer in introducing online teaching in the education system (Cull 2018). In the USA, digital education evolved during the 1990s; this later spread in other developed countries and then in developing countries. The beginning of the 21st century witnessed the launch of online teaching in the education system in many countries around the globe. Online education operates without any physical boundaries of nations and this advantage has resulted in internationalization of education quickly, conveniently, and comfortably.

The modern form of education also has both formal and informal methods, as seen in earlier ages. It is said that we are in the knowledge era today, which is also referred as the information age. The present knowledge era/information age signifies that learners have fast and vast access to knowledge today through various sources which could be formal as well as informal, and physical as well as digital. This vast access to knowledge today has been possible due to the growth in the computer and information technology. Developments in information and communication technologies have further supported it and made it readily available to the learners.

The education system in the modern era is now powered by digitalization. Today education is supported and powered by e-learning (the convergence of the internet and learning) (Awodele, et al. 2011). Digitalization in education is the combined application of technology, knowledge, human skills, and instructions to make it more reachable, accessible, effective, and productive for all stakeholders involved in the process (Dneprovskaya, Komleya and Urintsov 2019). Digitalization in higher education was emerging slowly as an alternative and as a support element to traditional classroom teaching. Digitalization of education was happening in universities, colleges, and schools at the same time but generally at a slow pace.

5.5 Digitalization, Cloud Computing and Education

Educational institutions are continuously in search of new opportunities to improve the digitalization of education. In an attempt to deliver and support imparting of education through the digital platform, academic institutions have redesigned their IT infrastructure. They have always upgraded their hardware and software to support their students and teachers and kept up with the pace of rapid developments in information technologies (Ismail 2011). These regular upgrades in hardware and software are not always free and require a financial commitment on the part of educational establishments (Alfrod 2009). This commitment is not always possible in the budget and can be a big challenge, especially for small academic institutions. Such upgrades need to be affordable, and there are various technologies available which may support educational institutions in achieving their objectives (Ismail 2011) (Hayes 2008), but at the same time the IT industry is being forced to come up with new ways to support the rising demand of educational institutions. Cloud computing has emerged as an important computing tool in supporting the digitalization of education in the present economic context.

Cloud computing is a very good option which can add value to the present higher education system. The use of digitalization in higher education is well supported with cloud computing along with other available technologies. Cloud computing offers a good chance for reconsideration and re-design of IT services in the education system. Its usefulness and capability have already been considered and recognized by a number of higher education institutions globally. To name a few: Washington State University, University of California, IIT's, NIT's and many other higher education institutes of India, the UK, China, Malaysia, Australia, and New Zealand (Ajith and Hemalatha 2012). Cloud computing has emerged as a good option for educational institutions in order to reduce their costs and increase their reach in the present economic slowdown. It also offers the options of improved efficiency, business flexibility, reduced IT problems, and access to wider business applications 24-7 from anywhere.

5.6 COVID-19 and its Impact on Digitalization of Higher Education

The outbreak of COVID-19 was unexpected and slowed or closed most economies globally in its early phase. Later, economies went for a planned unlocking as per their local circumstances. Sixty-one countries in Africa, Asia, Europe, the Middle East, North America, and South America announced or implemented school and university closures and most universities enforced localized closures (UNESCO 2020) (Bao 2020). The spread of COVID-19 has fueled the process of digitalization in various sectors and the same was witnessed in the education system. Institutions in higher education have geared themselves up for increasing the role of online methods in educating their students and researchers. Various reforms were implemented by schools, colleges, and universities to minimise the effect of COVID-19 as far as possible (Blundell, et al. 2020). Cloud computing has supported digitalization efforts in the higher education system due to its better capability and efficiency in sharing learning resources among learners, teachers, researchers, and staff at any time and anywhere (Al-Rousan and Al Ese 2015).

5.7 Digitalization and Higher Education

Digitalization in higher education is the need of the hour and will be a necessity in the near future. The ease and convenience delivered by digital education is highly appealing to people who lack time. For learners who are trying to seek a balance between work, family, and other obligations while completing an education programme, digital learning has emerged as an opportunity just like distance learning programmes.

Today, digital technologies are no longer just an additional instrument, but are becoming a necessity and a condition for the existence of a modern education system (Rab, MacDonald and Riaz 2019). They directly affect higher education. The presence of digital technologies in higher education demands revisions and improvement in its content, forms, and methods. The digitalization process also requires a planned rethinking about the role of faculty members. They need to bring changes to their style of teaching, and the contents to be shared keeping in mind the need of students and of their respective colleges and universities. Teachers should have a high degree of motivation for adapting, in correspondence to the needs, styles, and strategies of the topics and subjects (Moe and Katz 2020).

As mentioned, some of the countries who have already taken prominent steps towards digitalization in higher education are the USA, UK, China, India, Malaysia, South Korea, Japan, South Africa, Australia, and New Zealand. Digital technologies have not only helped in reaching a wider population in their own country but also spreading and targeting students and learners around the globe. Many prestigious universities around the world are offering courses online which are supported by digital technologies like cloud computing. In the USA, universities are offering at least some courses online, and some universities are creating fully developed online degree programmes, even at postgraduate and doctoral levels (Bolliger and Halupa 2012) (Tompkins-Stange 2016). Asians have been the major targeted students and learners through digitalization and internationalization of higher education. India is one the countries which plays a very major role in promoting the growth of online learning opportunities that are popping up throughout Asia (Clinton 2011).

In the UK, increasing tuition costs have been turning students away from higher education. The UK government hopes that a more convenient and cheaper education option could break this trend. The government felt that online education would be the right medium to attract students towards higher education and would be highly accessible, so they funded it.

In China around 70 online colleges are running, and the online learning industry is expected to grow manyfold in the near future. The expected growth has been steady since 2018 and it seems that it is able to meet the expectations of learners (Tomlinson 2014).

Reasons for digitalization in higher education have been many. Countries seek various benefits through digitalization of education. Some of these are:

1) Increased reach
2) Convenience
3) An affordable education with rising tuition costs in many European countries
4) Opportunity to continue education without putting a career on hold
5) Internationalization of education
6) Option of specialized courses tuned to the needs of learners.

Digitalization in education has been supported through developments in internet technologies in terms of evolving new generations of internet, cloud computing, and so on. These developments have offered benefits such as lower costs, wider reach, increased smart phone acceptability, affordable education, and initiatives taken by the government in guiding, promoting, supporting, and implementing digital education (Moonsun, Glassman and Dean 2017). Various types of study material in the form of videos and texts available online are also motivating and attracting learners towards online education.

5.8 Digitalization and Difficulties Faced by Teachers

Digitalization in education has brought many benefits to its recipients. It has also benefited the respective organisations and governments involved in education and training at the same time; however, various types of challenges have also been encountered. Some of the difficulties faced by faculty members in teaching and delivering training in higher education are listed below:

5.8.1 Hurried Implementation Causes Stumbling Blocks and Limitations

Educational institutions were either slowly involving digital education in their programmes or were thinking of including it. The unexpected situation caused by COVID-19 forced educational institutions to move to a fully-fledged digital platform in the middle of their academic year. Most of these institutions were not ready for it and many had not even thought of it previously. This hurried implementation has meant many obstacles but due to the need of the hour and with no other option, educational institutions have had to adopt it. Faculty members in higher education who are experiencing limitations in terms of e-books, improper training, new software platforms, and so on, but trying to perform at their best in this pressured situation, must be applauded for their efforts.

5.8.2 Poor Internet Infrastructure, Especially in Rural Areas, Causes Connectivity Problems

The internet is the primary driver of digitalization of education and has spread quickly but still there are many areas it has not reached. So, these areas, especially the rural ones which lack the infrastructure needed for the internet, cannot benefit from it.

There are also many areas where the internet has marked its presence but there is very poor connectivity. Frequent interruptions mean faculty members face difficulties imparting education to students and learners residing in these areas because they cannot utilize the full potential of digital education. Sharing of data and information with the use of cloud computing and other technologies is still a challenge. The recent problem of COVID-19 has elevated this problem as students who were often forced to return to their native homes in small cities and rural areas now face lots of problems in their studies.

5.8.3 Software Compatibility Issues When Implemented without Testing

In the present evolving and changing environment due to COVID-19, institutions implemented online education in the middle of the academic session without full planning and testing of the online platforms. They were and are able to meet the minimum requirements but could not execute this in an optimum manner. Many challenges have been faced, one of them being the compatibility issue between existing software and the new online platforms on which they are teaching their students. Since proper training was also not received, resolving the software compatibility issue is an exercise which is still evolving and continuing. However, cloud computing technologies reduce the need for new software and hardware upgrades.

5.8.4 Network and Bandwidth Issues

Places with poor internet infrastructure and older generations of internet have a common problem of network issues. Students living in remote areas have taken admission in online courses but due to the network issues are not able to fully benefit from their classes on digital platforms.

Faculty members are not able to deliver classes in fully-fledged video and audio mode with internet generations of 2G or 3G as they present a lot of bandwidth issues. The 4G internet has been able to eliminate the bandwidth issue to some extent but putting a class of around 40–50 students with audio and video on from both sides remains a challenge. The video has to be switched off many times in order for the class to continue uninterrupted.

5.8.5 Attendance Could not Be Properly Downloaded/Recorded

Regular attendance of a class is required by faculty members, but software problems or network issues sometimes restrict them in taking/downloading/recording attendance – which needs to be taken care of by the technology in future for fulfilling academic norms. A full proof tested software is required for ensuring the above feature.

5.8.6 Lack of Face-to-Face Interaction

With the limited bandwidth availability of internet in most areas, online classes are generally conducted in audio mode, keeping the video mode off or utilizing a one-sided video mode. This has led to lack of face-to-face interaction, which is limiting the growth opportunities of students as well as restricting the efforts of faculty members in imparting education. It has also limited faculty members in understanding whether students have really understood what has been taught.

5.8.7 Seriousness of Students

This has been another major issue for faculty members to tackle. They have been trying their best to increase the involvement of students in the classes by use of audio and video modes but still the seriousness of students is limited which is a demotivating factor for faculty members.

The advantage of judging and accordingly taking corrective measures to involve the students in class was easy in the physical mode but is challenging in the online mode. The available speed of internet does not offer the autonomy to view all the students at the same time on the screen of smart phones, PCs, or laptops. In future 5G internet speed could help faculty members in improving this issue.

5.8.8 Feedback System Is not Adequate

Since digitalization in education is new and is continuously evolving, a standard way of giving feedback is not yet available. Sharing and feedback are possible using cloud computing but feedback norms in universities and colleges differ and in many cases are not clear to faculty members and students. Educational institutions should define a standard way of providing feedback and its parameters and should communicate this with their students and faculty members. This would help and guide faculty members in planning their lectures and other elements of feedback. It would also be helpful for faculty members in delivering in the right tone to the learners and opening a gateway for improvement if required.

5.8.9 Awareness among Teachers Is Lacking

Hurried implementation of the digital medium by most educational institutions around the globe due to COVID-19 is posing challenges to the teachers as they lack proper training about it. Awareness levels among teachers is limited regarding the hardware, software, and skills necessary for online education. They are continuing with it despite their limited knowledge and skills, but are not able to deliver to the best of their ability as many new problems arise with which they are not acquainted.

5.8.10 Creativity Is not at its Fullest

As digitalization in higher education is in its nascent stage and is evolving, both students and faculty members are unable to exploit it to its full potential. Faculty members are generally not fully aware of the provisions in the software through which they are delivering online education. Some of the teachers/trainers who are aware of these provisions lack the hardware and other skills needed to present through the digital medium. The above reasons restrict faculty members in using their creativity to the fullest. It is even restricting students in utilizing their creativity at its best due to lack of knowledge and the supporting hardware and software elements. Creativity is also lacking and seems to be underutilized when group activities are organized and presented by students.

5.8.11 Facing the Audience Is Lacking

Educational programmes and courses which involve the development of personality traits, presentation skills, and other skills to handle and face the audience in a physical mode could not be trained properly through the digital mode. Digital technologies and the present situation of COVID-19 are posing serious obstacles in imparting these skills as the audience is not faced physically. Students enrolled in MBA, BBA, Mass Communication, Hotel Management, and other such programmes cannot be trained to face the audience and handle the sales and other public dealing activities through these digital platforms.

5.8.12 Body Language

This is an important skill imparted to students in educational programmes of higher education such as Mass Communication, Business Management, and so on. It is a challenge for teachers and instructors to train students with the right body language skills through the digital medium while interacting with customers, general public, and their colleagues. The digital medium can be used as an additional tool but it is creating difficulties for students in developing such skills on the digital platform. Increasing confidence of dealing with people in a live physical set-up is limited.

5.8.13 Unfair Means during Tests and Exams

If you are not using a properly tested digital platform then conducting tests and exams is a challenge. Organisations conducting competitive exams like NEET, TOFEL, CAT, and JEE have the right infrastructure to ensure fair examinations. The situation of COVID-19 has forced all types of educational institutions to adopt the digital platform in a limited time period. They have adopted it but without full knowledge and proper testing, which is posing a challenge to conducting fair examinations. Use of unfair means are used during online tests and exams, which could not be properly monitored by teachers with the present limitations of internet technology plus limited knowledge and training on digital platforms.

5.8.14 Monitoring and Evaluation Is Tough and Challenging

This is another area which is raising questions. For delivering and sharing, cloud computing can be used but monitoring whether every student is learning and is involved in the class is a serious challenge. The virtual presence in the class needs to be supported by the right set of monitoring tools with faculty members. Responses by students in the online class are very limited. Students are not keen at asking questions despite the continuous encouragement by teachers to do so. This is leading to an unsatisfactory situation for teachers and trainers who are continuously adapting and retraining themselves on the digital platform but then also are not able to get the right outputs. A lack of standard evaluation procedure is leading to varied evaluation methods, which is also an issue faced by teachers in applying the right grades to the students.

5.8.15 One-to-One Student Handling Is Time Consuming and Difficult

The digital medium boasts of one-to-one student handling, which is possible but very challenging and time consuming. Expectations of the institute and students are high on this parameter but with the limited facilities available it is very tough for teachers. It requires a lot of effort, which is not at all appreciated by the teachers because it gives limited benefits for a very large amount of extra time contributed by them. Proper recognition for their extra efforts is also not shown either by students or the institute.

5.8.16 Teachers Involved in Non-Teaching Activities

The set-up of the digital mode of education involves many activities such as monitoring, attendance keeping, preparing assignments, uploading assignments and tests, downloading assignments and tests, data entry after evaluations, and preparing educational videos. The effort and time given by teachers is increasing in non-teaching activities, which is less productive for imparting education and is disliked by faculty members because it is taking up time which they could have devoted to teaching and research activities.

5.8.17 Increased Screen Time Has Led to Medical Issues

In using the digital mode for education, a lot of time is spent by faculty members on the screen. This extra time on the screens of smart phones, personal computers, laptops, and tablets, is leading to medical problems for the human body. Since people in general are not used to this digital medium the large increase in screen time on electronic devices has led to medical issues for the eyes, neck, spine, and other body parts for both students and faculty members.

5.8.18 Students in Government Schools and Colleges Are Poor and Cannot Afford the Digital Medium

This is another issue in the implementation of digital education, as smart phones, televisions, personal computers, and laptops cannot be afforded by underprivileged students who are enrolled in higher education, especially in government institutions. Governments are trying to broadcast teachers' lectures on free television channels, and make them available in the form of free videos on YouTube and other digital platforms but are not able to reach every student. Cloud computing can share but some basic infrastructure needs to be developed to deliver the contents. It has been a challenge for faculty members and the government to impart and continue education with these students who belong to the lower sections of society.

5.8.19 No Standard Method of Evaluation

As digitalization in education is still evolving, there is not yet a standard method of evaluation in higher education which is recognized by the Department of Education and/or Ministry of Human Resources and Development. Proper guidelines, procedures, and rules have still to be finalized and formalised. Each college and university has its own evaluation procedure. This loophole needs to be eliminated and is a concern for the education system, faculty members, and even the students. Since the education system will increasingly be embracing the digital platform in the future, an improved evaluation procedure is required for its successful implementation and acceptance.

5.8.20 Cannot Do Courses that Require Labs/Workshops

Courses which require laboratory and/or hands-on workshops can be supplemented through the digital mode but cannot be completed fully – such as Engineering, Hotel Management, Science, and Business Management. Also, in courses like MBA, students miss the chance of professional networking or overseas experience on the digital platform. Cloud computing is making resources available anywhere and at any time but conducting science, engineering, and other such subjects online is still under development. It has been a challenge for faculty members to design and develop a curriculum for such courses. In the present situation of COVID-19 faculty members of such courses are able to deliver only a part of such courses and are trying to find ways to deliver them fully.

5.8.21 Ethical Values Are under Threat

The present environment of COVID-19 is very challenging and has created many limitations in the functioning of organizations. Educational institutions went for an immediate and hurried shift on the digital platform for imparting education and supporting students. Both teachers and students have adjusted and upgraded themselves to the digital medium of education, but it has raised some ethical issues which need to be addressed. The first issue is when faculty members are taking classes and students join them, but are frequently only digitally connected with no actual involvement in the classes.

The second issue is that when exams are taken by students, unfair means are used by many of them. This practice applies more to college students and less to school students. This is also hampering the creativity and development of students as they are more involved with 'copy and paste' activities rather than writing the answers in their own words. When teachers point this out, students do not accept it, which raises questions and concerns, and threatens ethical values. Cloud computing can share resources, but this has to be utilized for the growth and development of students, and not for unethical practices. This rightly has to be addressed by both teachers and parents to build the right ethics among students. The role of parents will be important in instilling and ensuring the right ethical behaviour in their children.

5.8.22 Security of Data and Resources

The data and resources of faculty, researchers, students, and the academic institutions shared on the cloud may be under threat. If powerful devices and instruments are installed, this data could be protected through verification, information classification, and trustworthiness on the cloud computing platform; otherwise it may become a big issue for stakeholders. The potential of digital media in education can be rightly exploited to the full extent if data protection laws are revised and robustly framed. Copyright reforms would help teachers, researchers, and students to develop online teaching materials which could be used, updated, and edited continuously (hochschulforumdigitalisierung.de 2020).

5.9 Conclusion

It is an undoubted fact that digitalization of education has led to increasing the scope of education at all levels. It has also led to internationalization of education and made it more reachable, convenient, and affordable. Cloud computing technologies are supporting these developments when backed with powerful tools. The need of digitalization in education has been seen as more necessary and promising in the COVID-19 pandemic by countries across the globe. It has emerged as a sigh of relief to learners, educators, educational institutions, and governments. Researchers agree that e-learning is easier and effective and is helpful in developing the skills of students as well as faculty members (Tunmibi, et al. 2015) but at the same time, some limitations and issues have been faced in implementing it and imparting education through the digital mode. The hurried implementation of digitalization in course curriculums by all types of educational institutions, with lack of the right infrastructure and appropriate policy and guidelines, has been an area of concern. If issues are handled properly by the educational institutions, then it will be beneficial for students and will also help in increasing the productivity of faculty members.

New technological developments like 5G internet and appropriate software and hardware and other information technology tools may eliminate problems in the future. The future scope of digitalization in education is bright and promising and would make it more affordable, reachable, convenient, and productive. It should be supported by rich course material in the online mode, proper training of teachers and trainers, and the right infrastructure. Digitalization of education may be the means of fulfilling the idea of 'right to education for everyone', which is promoted by most of countries and the United Nations.

5.10 Suggestions

A holistic approach by educational institutions, regulatory bodies, and governments in framing policies and guidelines for digitalization of education and development of the right infrastructure can bring exemplary changes in the education system. Proper training to teachers and use of tested digital and online platforms would be able to deliver better results for teachers, researchers, and students as well as other stakeholders.

5.11 Limitations

The present study is restricted to the information available from secondary sources and the real-life professional experience of the researcher and his peers who are teachers in higher education institutes using the offline and online mode.

5.12 Future Scope

The problems faced by teachers in organising and conducting classes through the digital mode and the concerns of other stakeholders will emerge as an important area of research in the future. Ways to remove the shortcomings of cloud computing in digitalization of education would also attract the attention of researchers. Primary research on the topic could deliver more valuable information and is a concern of future development.

References

Ajith, S. N., and M. Hemalatha. 2012. "Cloud Computing for Academic Environment." *International Journal of Information and Communication Technology Research* 2 (2): 97–101.

Al-Rousan, Thamer, and Hasan Al Ese. 2015. "Impact of Cloud Computing on Educational Institutions: A Case Study." *Recent Patents on Computer Science* 8 (2): 106–111. https://doi.org/10.2174/2213275908666150413215916.

Alfrod, T. 2009. *The Economics of Cloud Computing*. New York: Booz Allen Hamilton.

Almajalid, Rania Mohammedameen. n.d. "A Survey on the Adoption of Cloud Computing in Education Sector," 1–12.

www.ancient.eu/Egyptian_Hieroglyphs/ (accessed January 23, 2021).

Awodele, O., S. O Kuyoro, A. K. Adejumobi, O. Awe, and O. Makanju. 2011. "Citadel E-Learning: A New Dimension to Learning System." *World of Computer Science and Information Technology Journal* 1 (3): 71–78.

Bao, Wei. 2020. "COVID-19 and Online Teaching in Higher Education: A Case Study of Peking University." *Human Behavior & Emerging Technologies.* 113–115. doi:10.1002/hbe2.191.

Bloomberg, Jason. 2018. www.forbes.com/sites/jasonbloomberg/2018/04/29/digitization-digitalization-and-digital-transformation-confuse-them-at-your-peril/?sh=4ebdf40e2f2c (accessed January 24, 2021).

Blundell, Richard, Monica Costa Dias, Robert Joyce, and Xiaowei Xu. 2020. "COVID-19 and Inequalities." *Fiscal Studies* 41 (2): 291–319. doi:10.1111/1475-5890.12232.

Bolliger, D. U., and C. Halupa. 2012. "Student Perceptions of Satisfaction and Anxiety in an Online Doctoral Program." *Distance Education* 33 (1): 81–98. doi:10.1080/01587919.2012.667961.

Clinton, Hilary. 2011. "'America's Pacific Century' Foreign Policy 189." 56–63.

Cull, Nicholas J. 2018. "The Long Road to Digitalized Diplomacy 2.0: The Internet in US Public Diplomacy." International Studies Review, 15 (1), March 2013: 123–139.

Dneprovskaya, Natalia V., Nina V Komleya, and Arkadiy I. Urintsov. 2019. "The Knowledge Management Approach to Digitalization of Smart Education." In *Advances in Artificial Systems for Medicine and Education II*, 641–650. Springer. doi:10.1007/978-3-030-12082-5_58.

www.etymonline.com/word/educate (accessed January 21, 2021).

Fenwick, Mark D., Wulf A. Kaal, and Erik P. M. Vermeulen. 2017. "Regulation Tomorrow: What Happens When Technology is Faster Than the Law?" *American University Business Law Review* 6 (3): 561–594.

Hayes, B. 2008. "Cloud Computing." *Communications of the ACM* 51 (7): 9–11. doi:10.1145/1364782.1364786.

https://hochschulforumdigitalisierung.de/en/20-theses-Digitalization-higher-education/ (accessed August 22, 2020).

igi-global. 2021. www.igi-global.com/dictionary/it-strategy-follows-digitalization/7748 (accessed January 24, 2021).

Ismail, N. 2011. "Cursing the Cloud or Controlling the Cloud." *Computer Law and Security Review* 27 (3): 250–257.

Kalra, Ashok, S. Latha, B. Vijaylakshmi, and Abiya Chelliah. 2019. *Crystal Curated: An Integrated Semester Series.* Noida: Pearson India Education Services Pvt. Ltd.

Lin, G., D. Fu, and G. Dasmalchi. 2010. "Cloud Computing: IT as a Service." *IT Professional* 11 (2): 10–13.

Moe, Angelica, and Idit Katz. 2020. "Emotion Regulation and Need Satisfaction Shape a Motivating Teaching Style." *Teachers and Teaching* 1–18. doi:10.1080/13540602.2020.1777960.

Moonsun, Choi, Michael Glassman, and Cristol Dean. 2017. "What it Means to be a Citizen in the Internet Age: Development of a Reliable and Valid Digital Citizenship Scale." *Computers & Education* 107: 100–112.

Muro, Mark, Sifan Liu, Jacob Whiton, and Siddharth Kulkarni. 2017. *Digitalization and the American Workforce.* Brookings.

Ochs, Thomas, and Ute A. Riemann. 2018. "IT Strategy Follows Digitalization." In *Encyclopedia of Information Science and Technology*, 15. IGI Global (accessed January 25, 2021). doi:10.4018/978-1-5225-2255-3.ch075.

Rab, M., S. MacDonald, and N. Riaz. 2019. "Digital Globalisation of Knowledge and the Impact on Higher Education in South Asia." *EDULEARN 19 Proceedings 11th International Conference on Education and New Learning Technologies.* Palma, Spain: IATED. 547–557. doi:10.21125/edulearn.2019.

Tomlinson, C. A. 2014. The Differentiated Classroom: Responding to the Needs of all Learners. 2nd edn. ASCD.

Tompkins-Stange, M. E. 2016. *Policy Patrons: Philanthropy, Education Reform, and the Politics of Influence.* Cambridge, MA: Harvard Education Press.

Tunmibi, Sunday, Ayooluwa Aregbesola, Pascal Adejobi, and Olaniyi Ibrahim. 2015. "Impact of E-Learning and Digitalization in Primary & Secondary Schools." *Journal of Education and Practice* 6 (17): 53–58. www.iiste.org (accessed August 24, 2021).

UNESCO. 2020. *COVID-19 Educational Disruption and Response.* UNESCO. https://en.unesco.org/themes/education-emergencies/coronavirus-school-closures (accessed August 24, 2021).

Wikipedia 2021 Wikipedia https://en.wikipedia.org/wiki/Education (accessed January 23, 2021).

6

Cloud-Based Digitalization in Higher Education: Issues and Challenges Faced by Students

Isha Gupta
Research Scholar, Amity University, Noida, Uttar Pradesh, India

Nandita Mishra
Universitetslektor, Department of Management
Linköping University, LINKÖPING, Sweden

Deepak Tandon
Professor, International Management Institute New Delhi, India

6.1 Introduction

The pandemic that emanated from the seafood market in Wuhan, China in December, 2019 has caused shudders and set alarm bells ringing in economies worldwide. This was

DOI: 10.1201/9781003203070-7

substantiated in the studies of (Huang et al., 2020) and also (Li et al. 2020; Paules et al. 2020; Wang et al. 2020) who observed in their clinical studies that the virus spread through person-to-person contact. The disease outbreak has pushed all educational institutions to move to digital platforms and has compelled worldwide physical closing of them. The educational institutions have also been shaken up by this catastrophe and this anxiety is expected to echo globally all around education institutions. The COVID-19 outbreak was supposed to hold several schools and colleges locked. Globally, countless places have been impacted and the entire current curriculum for six months or so has been taught online, with and a much greater risk to the following years. Learning opportunities may also suffer in future, with the imposing of social distancing. Educational institutions are trying to find alternatives to cope with this terrible situation.

In online learning, the internet and many other technologies are used to design instructional content and distribution and programme managements (Fry 2001). (Hrastinski 2008) divides online learning into two categories: synchronous and asynchronous online. Teachers, organisations and institutions need a thorough understanding of the advantages and disadvantages to make online learning successful and productive. E-learning has numerous obstacles, presenting problems for students, problems for educators, and issues with content. This is a concern for learners and for organisations participating in the process of teaching and learning. There is no explicit stipulation by the government for policies of education concerning e-learning facilities. There seems to be a dearth of consistency, quality control, e-resource creation and e-content distribution norms. E-learning was never really implemented by students and teachers at several universities. Since the start of the pandemic, the pace of online education has greatly increased in India (Saxena 2020). The majority of educational institutions seem to be apathetic and trapped within conventional teaching styles. Digital devices, the internet, and wi-fi are not open to all teachers and students. The lack of sufficient digital resources, internet connectivity or wi-fi connections has created a lot of issues, and many learners have missed opportunities to learn. The disparity in connectivity, from power and internet connections to devices such as computers or smartphones, is the key challenge of remote learning. Although a computer for online classes would be preferrable, the requirements could also be fulfilled by a smartphone. However, though the phone could be convenient for applications, it would not be suitable for long assignments or analysis. In India only 24% of the population (Krishan 2019; IMAI 2019) own a smartphone and the ratio of households who own a computer is 11%, including desktop computers, laptops, notebooks, netbooks, palmtops or tablets (Ministry of Statistics and Programme Implementation 2019). Thus, the purpose of this chapter is to study the issues and challenges faced by students in taking classes online, especially in the context of India.

6.2 Literature Review

Digitalization is not a modern invention, and for several years now it has supplemented traditional teaching in institutions of higher education (Leszczyński et al. 2018; Kopp et al. 2019). The study (Paudel 2021) examined the learner's and teacher's perception on online education with relation to its challenges, benefits and strategies after and during the COVID-19 in the education sector of Nepal. The study concluded that participants prefer blended learning. A key issue in the digitalization of academic institutions is that stakeholders need to consider the requirements of digitalization. The willingness to incorporate ICT across all facets of life will be at a nascent stage, thus educational institutions need to be willing to take on the challenge of mentoring new professionals to overcome difficulties and provide solutions, as the battle of the planet is to eliminate the pandemic (Sandkuhl & Lehmann 2017; Bond et al. 2018). To respond to the changes introduced by new technologies (Abad-Segura et al. 2020) and the recent outbreak, the incorporation of sustainable management has proposed this paradigm shift. In existing literature there are numerous studies that analyse the quality of different aspects of online education. Critical problems affecting the productivity of e-learning such as technology, connectivity, pedagogy, time management and evaluation have been documented (Conaway et al. 2005; Bassoppo-Moyo 2006; Ko & Rossen 2017). E-learning is a type of learning conducted digitally via electronic media typically using the internet. Online learning can be described as "educational experiences through various devices (e.g. mobile phones, laptops etc.) with internet connectivity in synchronous or asynchronous environments". In such ecosystems, learners could understand and communicate with teachers and other leaners from anywhere (independently) (Singh et al. 2019). Online platforms are required to meet the following conditions in the midst of such a fatal disease where (a) video conferencing software in which contact with at most 30–50 learners is possible, (b) student discussions could be conducted to retain classroom interactivity, (c) strong internet connectivity exists, (d) lectures can also be viewed on mobile phones, not just laptops, (e) the ability exists to view lectures for students already registered and (f) it is possible to receive immediate feedback from students and take assignments (Basilaia et al. 2020). During this challenging period, the question is not whether online teaching and learning strategies will provide the necessary standard of education, but how academic institutions can implement online learning to such a large extent (Carey 2020). (Dhawan 2020) has studied SWOC (Strength, Weakness, Opportunity and Challenges) of e-learning modes in the time of crisis and also ed-tech start-ups. The study also provides guidelines for educational institutions on how to deal with online learning issues. There seems to be a great deal of bewilderment among all the possibilities. In a programme developed in Indonesia called School from Home during the COVID-19 Pandemic, this research examines the perceptions of primary school teachers regarding online learning. This study contributes to online collaborative learning literature among teachers, parents and schools that impact student success (Aliyyah et al. 2020). A substantial part of the Indian population lives in remote regions and does not have ample resources to be part of mainstream education. The challenges perceived by students in online learning have been documented by researchers.

Several studies have shown the overall complexities of the blended learning mode of instruction holistically, and yet there is no common articulation of the challenges that occur in the online component of blended learning. A systematic literature review (Rasheed et al. 2020) was therefore carried out in order to recognise the problems in the online aspect of blended learning from the perspectives of students, teachers and educational institutions. (Muilenburg and Berge 2005) believed that academic skills, technological skills, social interactions, administrative issues, encouragement for learners, support and time for research, costs and internet connectivity and some of the difficulties associated with online learning have involved technological issues. In addressing the reception of technology by students (Keller and Cernerud 2002) have recognised variables such as gender, age, previous computer experience, individual styles of learning and technology acceptance as major explanatory factors. The objective is to create a theoretical framework that illustrates the factors which influenced the adoption of online education during the

COVID-19 outbreak. To better understand the elements that led to the acceptance of online teaching, this research used a time-series approach. The study presents and validates a theory-driven paradigm for online teaching that emphasises the factors that affect it. This study adds to the unified theory of technology adoption and usage by validating three new constructs: facilitative leadership, regulatory support and project team capacity (Mittal et al. 2021). This paper aims to determine how satisfied and accepting Ukrainian lecturers are with online education, as well as the challenges and benefits they have identified. The technological aspects of online education have also been examined. The findings state that instructors provided varying levels of technical support and used a variety of resources to organise online education. The key benefit was time productivity, with internet access and technical issues being the most common problems. Another finding was that lecturers were partially satisfied with online education (Bakhmat et al. 2021). The study by (Aboagye et al. 2021) found that in this pandemic period, students were not prepared for an online learning experience. Students may think that by studying online they would encounter a multitude of challenges, or believe that the outbreak period is family time for discussions on how to get essentials, not for academic study. Another significant factor can be based on the argument that learners are still usually connected to traditional methods of teaching. Studies conducted in countries such as the United Kingdom (Green & Hannon, 2007), the United States (Kvavik 2005; Caruso & Salaway 2007) and Australia (Kennedy et al. 2006) have concluded that students generally have ready access to internet-enabled personal computers and web features. But in India, students do not have ready access to these resources.

In online learning, existing literature had reported both favourable and unfavourable views of students. The authors specifically analysed the literature on possible barriers for students to online education and, broadly, on possible challenges to learning for students. The aim was to recognise challenges, problems and factors of success from the viewpoints of the learners, which may influence learning attainment (i.e. learner performance, learner perspective and motivation). In the context of India, the studies on challenges and issues faced by students in online learning are mainly very limited. The objective of the present study is to bridge the gap in existing studies by exploring the challenges faced by students in India in e-learning during the COVID-19 period and to identify factors that are the most significant regarding challenges and issues faced by students in the framework of online learning. Thus, they would be able to reimagine education vis-à-vis digital technology.

6.3 Theoretical Framework

The study of online learning is associated with many theories and models. The theories discussed in this study, in terms of their suitability for the digital world, are: "community of inquiry", "connectivism" and "online collaborative learning".

The community of inquiry theory introduced by (Garrison et al. 1999) for online instruction is focused on the idea of three major "presences", that is, cognitive, social and teaching. It became one of the most popular models for online and blended courses designed to be highly collaborative through discussion forums, blogs, wikis and web conferencing among faculty and students. One of the early massive open online courses pioneers, George Siemens, was the key proponent of connectivism, a learning paradigm that recognises significant changes in the flow, growth and change of knowledge and information due to large data communication networks. Online collaborative learning is a concept developed by (Harasim 2017) that relies on the internet's resources which provide collaborative and knowledge-building learning environments.

The purpose given by the authors for using online collaborative learning is to provide a better model to explain how technology for learning and teaching is embraced and used by students and educational institutions (Demuyakor 2020).

(Muilenburg and Berge 2005) established the fundamental constructs that include roadblocks to learning in the online mode for students. The eight parameters listed were (a) administrative challenges, (b) social connections, (c) academic skills, (d) technical skills, (e) encouragement of learners, (f) study time and support, (g) internet costs and access, and (h) technical issues. These barrier factors included independent variables that conclude student ratings were significantly affected by gender, ethnicity, age and form of learning institution.

6.3.1 Issues Related to Students

Issues related to students in online education can be summarised into learners' readiness, expectations, participation and identity. Students' expectations can be difficult to manage, and they can also make it difficult to teach online courses effectively (Li & Irby 2008; Luyt 2013). One of the main problems addressed in the literature is learners' readiness to take online courses (Smith et al. 2003; Hung et al. 2010). Not all students are able to complete online courses successfully. It can be difficult for students to identify and follow the learning styles and skills needed to engage in online courses (Mayes 2011; Luyt 2013). According to the literature, learners' technological skills impact on their computer usage as well as their views and attitudes toward the internet (Tsai & Lin 2004; Peng et al. 2006). In online classes, learners can feel alienated and isolated, which can impact learning (McInnery & Roberts 2004). The sense of identity and students' learning is influenced by their affiliation with the learning group (Koole 2014). It is essential to support students in developing a sense of mutual identity, purpose and norms (Lapadat 2007; Koole 2014). Another major concern raised by researchers is the extent of learners' involvement and interaction in online environments. Some researchers indicated participation by writing through the interaction with instructors and peers while others suggested that learners who spent more time reading than writing were still engaged in learning (Romiszowski & Mason 2004; Vonderwell & Zachariah 2005). Additionally, research suggests that combining audio or video conversation with online text discussions will improve learners' engagement in online discussions (An and Frick 2006; Ice et al. 2007; Hara and Hew 2007; Olesova et al. 2011; Ching and Hsu 2015).

6.3.2 Issues Related to Effective Teaching

The evolving position of the teacher is one of the major challenges of online education (Collins & Berge 1996; Coppola et al. 2001; Syverson & Slatin 2010). Online teachers have four distinct roles: pedagogical, psychological, managerial and professional (Berge 1998). Pedagogical functions are concerned with instructional methods; social roles are concerned with how instructors form relationships with students; managerial roles are concerned with administrative and organisational tasks; and professional duties are concerned with the technical assistance that instructors offer to students. The majority of online teaching's educational goals are met by completing pedagogical activities (Doll 1993; Robertson 2000).

Other research supports the instructor's change in function by emphasising the ability to deliver content, transition from teacher-centered to student-centered education, better interaction and technology use (Doll 1993; Collins & Berge 1996; Robertson 2000; Coppola et al. 2001; Fein & Logan 2003; Yang & Cornellius 2004; Choi and Park 2006; Tucker & Neely 2010; Syverson & Slatin 2010; Juan et al. 2011). Furthermore, online delivery differs from conventional face-to-face education in that students engage with faculty, peers and technology in an offline mode with no physical presence (Anderson et al. 2011; Juan et al. 2011). As seen, the technology and curriculum developers must support this change in the instructor's role.

6.3.3 Research Question

The research question that has led this study is to solve the problem and shape a combined classification of the above mentioned issues for online education: what are the main types of issues and challenges that education institutions in India face while teaching online?

6.4 Research Objective

The objectives of the study are

1. To examine the challenges and issues faced by students in online learning.
2. To identify the factors that define the characteristics of students' challenges and issues.
3. To give plausible inferences and future scope for the success of online teaching in this crisis-like period of stress and tension.

6.5 Methods

This research used the descriptive design of the survey method to understand the challenges faced by respondents in online teaching. Online teaching is the new method of teaching that has taken over the offline mode of teaching and has been embraced by almost every educational institution after the pandemic. The study focuses on identifying variables that take a lead in online teaching.

Students affiliated with the education sector are targeted as respondents for data collection. The participants are invited to participate in the research via google form. They found a connection to the questionnaire through emails, WhatsApp groups and other social media channels. The data was gathered randomly from respondents, primarily from the Delhi-NCR and Haryana geographical area. To test the efficacy of the survey questions, a pilot study was carried out. Surveys were distributed to 10 respondents who fitted the description of the target participants of the study. The researchers obtained input from this pilot group about the terminology and procedures for the survey. The responses of the pilot community offered general features of a possible sample. The survey was based on a total of 154 completed questionnaires. During this research with the participants, there was no face-to-face interaction or observation.

In the questionnaire, there are 6 demographic questions and 23 statements dealing with online teaching and learning. On the 5-Likert scale, each question is framed, with 1 taken as "strongly disagree" and 5 taken as "strongly agree". The data collected were evaluated in relation to the research questions and the research concluded the three key factors that contribute most to their satisfaction based on data analysis.

The pitfalls of administering internet surveys include a limited response rate, and even though the survey is randomly distributed, it is difficult to identify the survey environment and avoid selection bias. The surveys are self-reported for this study, which may have the following validity problems: 1) research depends on the integrity of participants; 2) while they may be true, they may lack contemplative ability; 3) respondents may vary in their understanding of specific questions; 4) respondents may view and use scales differently; 5) respondents' responses may not reflect the participants' actual actions; and 6) there may be a reaction bias, that is, a person's propensity to answer in a certain way.

For an observed data matrix $Y_{n}{\times}_{p}$ with p continuous variables, conventional factor analysis theory states that it can be restructured as a linear combination of d continuous latent factors $z_1, z_2, \ldots z_d$ plus a noise term ϵ.

$$Y = WZ + \epsilon, \quad Z \sim N(0, I_d), \epsilon \sim N(0, \sigma I_p)$$

But ordinal data variables violate the continuity assumption of the classical factor analysis and, therefore, it is important to determine a scale distance measurement to linearise ordinal data. The assumption in the case of a polychoric approach is that for categorical response, the ordinal responses are made on a continuously distributed attribute and levels. Therefore, it is possible to obtain a measure of association between these continuous characteristics, referred to as the polychoric correlation (tetrachoric correlation in the binary case). Then, on the polychoric correlation, classical factor analysis can be conducted, and the same has been applied in this study to get the results.

6.6 Findings

Most of the respondents are from Delhi NCR and Haryana states of India, as the convenience sampling method was used and also Delhi NCR and Haryana geographically are a strong mix of urban and rural areas, justifying the objective of the study. The questionnaire was sent to 450 respondents, of whom 154 took part in the study. The results are divided into subsections: response rate, descriptive statistics and analysis of polychoric factors.

6.6.1 Empirical Results

A similar survey by (Varenova et al. 2013) recorded a response rate of 17%, which is sufficient for the continuity of the research. In addition, the response rate of our study is 34.22% which is assumed to be acceptable, as seen in Table 6.1. Therefore, statistical evaluation can be carried forward with this response rate.

From Table 6.2, it can be inferred that most respondents in the survey are male. The largest group education-wise is graduate students, as they are the most exposed in the community to online teaching in the current scenario. This is good as it will give more

TABLE 6.1
Response Rate

Category	No of Questionnaires	Questionnaire Responses	Response Rate
Respondent wise	450	154	34.22%

Source: Author's estimation, 2020.

TABLE 6.2
Demographics of Respondents

	Response in Numbers	Response in %
Gender		
Female	63	40.9
Male	91	59.1
Prefer not to say	0	0.0
Total	154	100
Education		
10th	1	0.6
12th	21	13.6
Graduate	103	66.9
Postgraduate	29	18.9
Doctorate	0	0
Others	0	0
Total	154	100
Age		
15–25	145	94.2
25–35	09	5.8
35–45	00	0.00
45 & above	00	00.0
Total	154	100

Source: Author's estimation, 2020.

precise outcomes that will help in generalisation. The majority of respondents, generally, are students, with the highest response rate in the 15–25 age group.

The Eigenvalue of the study variables are shown in Table 6.3. A factor with an Eigenvalue of more than 1 should be extracted by the law of Kaizer extraction. There are three factors that have more than 1 value.

The result of factor analysis shows that there is 42.6% of variance explained overall. (Tinsley and Tinsley 1987) reported that often less than 50% of the total variance is explained by a factor solution. F1 captures 20.9% of total variance, which consists of primarily the variables related to efficiency of online classes, better connectivity, better interaction with faculty, efficiency in conducting theory and practical subject classes and better options for the long term. Overall, it can be interpreted as a factor defining "efficiency and interaction". F2 accounts for 15.2% of the overall variance and consists of variables that emphasise work life balance, time management, isolation and boredom while studying, health effects, and online learner experience. This factor may be categorised as "work life balance". F3 explains 6.3% of the total variance and consists of variables like emotional and physical support from colleagues, family and friends. A possible name of F3 can be "family support" as shown in Table 6.4.

The factors are named after grouping the key variables in explaining a typical attribute of challenges and issues in online education. Table 6.5 shows that the first

TABLE 6.3
Eigen Values

x1	5.957495
x2	2.781593
x3	1.059778
x4	0.620408
x5	0.467688
x6	0.357676
x7	0.315354
x8	0.22138
x9	0.168384
x10	0.060003
x11	0.027809
x12	–0.00255
x13	–0.05643
x14	–0.07593
x15	–0.12425
x16	–0.15977
x17	–0.16147
x18	–0.21037
x19	–0.2372
x20	–0.24301
x21	–0.29434
x22	–0.31755
x23	–0.35583

Source: Author's estimation, 2020.

factors identified with online classes are: effective; better for theoretical and practical subjects; interaction with faculty is smooth and proper; software used for imparting online education is effective; parents have better access to information about their child; and respondents are confident that no compromise occurs. These attributes can be grouped under factor-I and termed as "efficiency and interaction". This factor indicates that in online education, students are confident that there is no compromise in imparting education through online mode and there is no communication barrier between faculty and student. Thus, online education is acting as a panacea in times of this pandemic (Mishra et al. 2020).

The second factor is designated as work life balance. The attributes to these factors are: online education affects balance between work and life; has bad impact on physical health; time is difficult to manage; lack of support resources; lack of technical know-how and poor infrastructure; and learning environment lacks enjoyment. This factor concludes that many technological problems that obstruct and slow the teaching and learning process can be faced by users (Favale et al. 2020). While flexibility is a benefit of online learning in time and place, all such facets are unpredictable and lead to difficulties. Not every learner and educator are alike, and individuals vary in ability levels and degree of confidence. While studying online, some may not feel comfortable, contributing to increased agitation and confusion. Respondents may consider online teaching for a short time only because these online courses will help them to gain more information and maximise their time in the lockdown period, but they are not optimistic for the long term.

The third factor has two attributes viz. professional and emotional support from family, friends and colleagues. Thus, the third factor is named as "family support". The study

TABLE 6.4
Polychoric Factor Analysis

	F1	F2	F3
x1	0.275038	–0.02954	–0.12798
x2	0.122638	–0.03885	–0.08575
x3	0.187752	–0.04608	–0.11287
x4	0.11852	0.016698	0.011462
x5	0.081173	0.014787	0.029768
x6	0.183634	–0.07531	–0.11806
x7	0.016909	0.037627	–0.09085
x8	0.075608	–0.03191	0.062476
x9	0.087322	–0.01398	0.097807
x10	–0.01693	0.042726	–0.05163
x11	–0.04715	0.068208	0.007761
x12	0.105171	–0.01249	0.087333
x13	–0.03143	0.10658	0.061494
x14	–0.05287	0.358203	0.059751
x15	–0.01055	0.126793	0.017542
x16	–0.03408	0.113659	0.023549
x17	–0.0235	0.170776	–0.02822
x18	0.002163	0.217367	–0.03069
x19	–0.01094	0.009789	0.387392
x20	–0.04452	–0.01105	0.439383
x21	0.039951	–0.09311	–0.02526
x22	0.022907	0.035545	0.004916
x23	0.048419	0.055109	0.059372
SS loadings	4.828089	3.503773	1.467005
Proportion Variance	0.209917	0.152338	0.063783
Cumulative Variance	0.209917	0.362255	0.426038

Source: Author's estimation, 2020.

TABLE 6.5
Summary of the Factor Categorisation

F1	F2	F3
Efficiency and interaction	Work-life balance	Family Support
Effective online classes	Classroom teaching is more desirable	Adequate professional support from family, friends and colleagues
Better for theoretical subjects	Students lacks one to one interaction with Faculty	Adequate emotional support from family, friends and colleagues
Better for practical subjects	Effect on work life balance	
Proper faculty interaction	Difficulty in managing time	
Software used is effective	Effect on physical health	
Parents have better access to information about their child	Lack of support resources (mobile phones, laptops)	
Students are confident that no compromise occurs in online learning	Learners lack online learning experience	
Enjoyed remote learning	Lack of technical know-how and poor infrastructure (i.e. internet connectivity)	
Students have good skills to learn through online learning	Feel bored and lonely in online learning	

Source: Author's estimation, 2020.

found that friends, family and colleagues lack support (Muilenburg and Berge 2005) and (Kapasia et al. 2020) also stated that most students suffered from stress, anxiety and depression (42.0%). The causes of these can be associated with the lack of family, friends and colleagues' professional and emotional support.

In the factor analysis graph, the identified factors are plotted, which displays the three factors vividly. The three variables and their associated variable and their rounded off loads with an absolute value greater than 0.3 are shown in the cluster analysis plot in Figure 6.1. Polychoric factor analysis is an ideal approach to the identification of hidden structures in ordinary data with minimum assumptions and better performance. Polychoric factor analysis provides a simple preliminary guide and eventual confirmation of the choice of the number of factors and a better outcome of the latent structure.

6.7 Discussion of the Results

Finally, it can be inferred that the three factors identified in the study are: efficiency and interaction, work life balance and family support. In these three factors, all the challenges and issues faced by students in the era of digitalization have been summed up. The questions related to online learning effectiveness, in which respondents were asked how well they learned in a traditional classroom as compared to online learning. The respondents were asked how much they enjoyed digital learning as compared to their learning in a traditional classroom. Overall efficiency and productivity of online learning is mainly based on the design, the content of the course, the outline of the content of the course, the correspondence between the student and the teacher, and the accessibility of learning resources and internet infrastructure. The study argued that internet infrastructure in India and health problems that developed due to online learning hampered the learning process. On the basis of our study it can be concluded that faculty and family provide a lot of support during the digitalization of education. At both individual and group levels, faculty facilitate discussions. They respond to the questions asked by the students, develop projects, and evaluate students' learning. It is important to note that technology may not be capable of replacing a teacher's work and classroom learning.

It is evident that in educational technology, as a multi-sub-division research area, the impact of COVID-19 on educational practices has played a crucial role by acting as the only tool for assessment platforms, instructional design and distribution (Wang et al. 2020). The goal is to establish pandemic prevention and control strategies; contemporary research results need to be shared with a view to facilitating communal investigation and technical networking to ensure viable studies during the pandemic. Online education is based on appropriate preparation and instructional designs with many hypotheses and models available, but because of the pandemic, universities' migration process to online education is uncertain due to the lack of adequate planning, design and development of online instructional programmes. The crisis-response migration approaches implemented by academic institutions are restricted to distribution media, and lack knowledge of successful online education models and theories. Therefore, owing to the outbreak, it is not appropriate to compare crisis-response migration with successful online education or the scope of digital transformation in university education. This is also substantiated by the studies of (Adedoyin and Soykan 2020) emphasising online education as remote emergency teaching platforms.

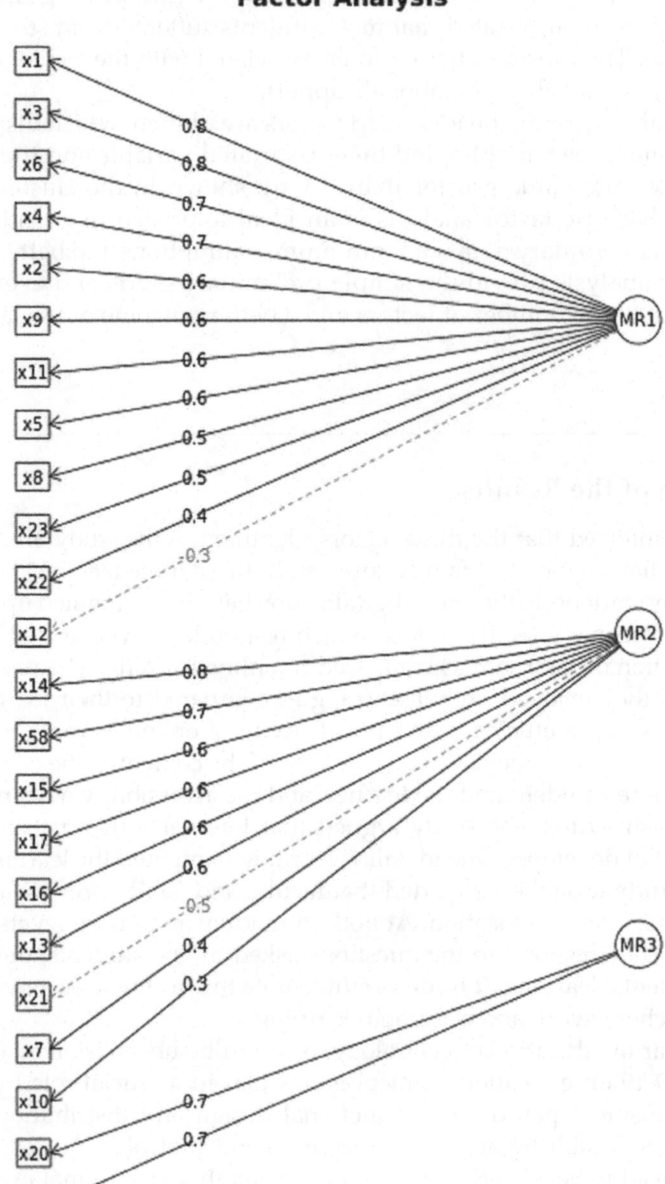

FIGURE 6.1
Factor Analysis
Source: Author's estimation, 2020.

6.8 Conclusions

Over the years, e-learning has acquired tremendous prominence. Massive open online courses have increased dramatically and their services provide students with economical courses. A number of institutions in India are still hesitant to teach and learn online. However, the changes wrought by the coronavirus disease outbreak meant institutions were transformed into a new paradigm of remote teaching and online learning. Many networks for communication and social collaborations, like Microsoft Teams, Zoom, Adobe connects and GoTo Meeting, have facilitated the educators who have engaged themselves in online teaching (Kapasia et al. 2020). This chapter concentrated on finding the challenges and issues faced by students in the phase of digitalization of teaching. A survey method through questionnaire was adopted to gain inputs from the respondents. The questionnaire mainly focused on questions which show respondents' issues and challenges in online teaching. Polychoric factor analysis was performed on the data collected and the results identified three major factors which define students' satisfaction. The first factor was "efficiency and interaction", which overwhelmingly indicates that respondents feel that online classes were conducted efficiently, and they are very well connected with their faculty members (Mishra et al. 2020). The second factor was "work life balance". It was found that online teaching has affected work life balance and physical health, due to long hours sitting in front of devices, and learners' lack of online education experience. The results are in sync with the study (Muilenburg and Berge 2005). Respondents feel that there is a lack of support resources (e.g. mobile phones, laptops) and technical know-how and poor infrastructure (i.e. internet connectivity). Because of power cuts and inadequate online access, students from remote areas and marginalised groups primarily rejected online learning. In this unwanted crisis era, poverty further exacerbates problems with the digital learning process (Kapasia et al. 2020). The third factor identified in the study was "family support", which demonstrates that during online teaching there is adequate professional and emotional support from faculty, friends and family. This support sends a positive signal and allows students to focus on and pursue studies in a completely new framework. (Muilenburg and Berge 2005) found that there is a lack of support from friends, family and colleagues and the study by (Kapasia et al. 2020) reported that most students were suffering from depression, anxiety and stress (42.0%). The reasons for this can be attributed to lack of professional and emotional support from family, friends and colleagues.

Respondents feel pessimistic about online systems and are not confident that they will continue with this remote learning and learn over the long term. They feel that only in the short term these online courses will help them to gain more knowledge and optimise their time in the lockdown period. Overall, the chapter concluded that respondents face many issues and challenges in learning online, but the respondents do not feel that online teaching has led to any compromise in their learning process. Furthermore, there is a need for a systematic, well organised approach to online learning, which might empower the overall learning process.

6.8.1 Recommendations

The COVID-19 pandemic has taught lessons to all developed and developing economies, including in online education, which has involved a steep learning curve. New pedagogical tools like simulation, role play and case study methodology have to be included in the programme objectives and evaluation of these is imperative. Goal formulation and accomplishment have become an uphill task for all educators. It is recommended that focus-based education be combined with outcome-based education so that there is no loss of content to pupils.

To keep abreast of current changes in digitalization, open-source digital solutions and learning software have to be accessible. Employability, health and wellbeing are crucial in these testing times.

6.9 Implications of the Study

This chapter provides theoretical and practical implications to higher education institutions and policy makers. For educational institutions, the study provides a clear view of students' perceptions. Institutions should make sure that they provide resources to their students to avoid problems related to lack of resources. Also, they should try to apply a more user-friendly mode of teaching. A focused model should be built to provide support to vulnerable students in society and measures should be taken to eliminate the digital gap. This study provides factors which educational institutions should focus on to support students in this tough time by outlining recommendations for teachers. This will improve the quality of educational process in this new environment. The study also provides a clear view to policy makers about students' perspectives. There is a need for concrete action in order to improve the process of online teaching. Policy makers can design training programmes for teachers on online teaching and the way they interact with students. Disasters and pandemics such as COVID-19 will generate a lot of uncertainty and frustration, so in the middle of these emergencies, there is a significant need to research the technology thoroughly and with due diligence to negate these uncertainties and conflicts.

6.10 Limitations and Future Scope

The study has its own limitations. Firstly, it is confined to the geographical area of Delhi NCR and Haryana, which does not represent the entire population of India. This might not be very effective in reflecting the challenges and issues faced by the students in distance learning during the COVID-19 pandemic, so there is future scope to study more regions of India, to discern greater understanding on distance learning challenges and issues. Furthermore, the learners' background characteristics and demographics are not taken into account in the analysis, which could be different and influence their experience. Online education is not suitable for hearing-impaired students, and there is a need to study the ways in which students are managing this.

The study can be extended in future by including variables like number of courses completed, number of courses dropped during lockdown and, in relation to this, the likelihood of taking future online classes and the type of learning institution attended which may be compared to identify education level. The current study emphasises only the relationship between the variables, but no causal relationship was identified. Future research may study the causes of these relationships. For this, possibly some qualitative techniques need to be used to enable the researcher to establish the causation between these relationships.

References

Abad-Segura, Emilio, Mariana-Daniela González-Zamar, Juan C. Infante-Moro, and Germán Ruipérez García. (2020). "Sustainable management of digital transformation in higher education: Global research trends." *Sustainability* 12(5): 2107. https://doi.org//10.3390/su12052107

Aboagye, Emmanuel, Joseph Anthony Yawson, and Kofi Nyantakyi Appiah. (2021) "COVID-19 and e-learning: The challenges of students in tertiary institutions." *Social Education Research* 2(1): 1–8. doi.org/10.37256/ser.212021422

Adedoyin, Olasile Babatunde, and Emrah Soykan. (2020). "Covid-19 pandemic and online learning: The challenges and opportunities." *Interactive Learning Environments*: 1–13. www.tandfonline.com/action/showCitFormats?doi=10.1080/10494820.2020.1813180 (accessed 11 October 2020)

Aliyyah, Rusi Rusmiati, Reza Rachmadtullah, Achmad Samsudin, Ernawulan Syaodih, Muhammad Nurtanto, and Anna Riana Suryanti Tambunan. (2020). "The perceptions of primary school teachers of online learning during the COVID-19 pandemic period: A case study in Indonesia." *Journal of Ethnic and Cultural Studies* 7(2): 90–109. http://dx.doi.org/10.29333/ejecs/388

An, Yun-Jo, and Theodore Frick. (2006). "Student perceptions of asynchronous computer-mediated communication in face-to-face courses." *Journal of Computer-Mediated Communication* 11(2): 485–499. https://doi.org/10.1111/j.1083-6101.2006.00023.x

Anderson, Derek, Sandra Imdieke, and N. Suzanne Standerford. (2011). "Feedback please: Studying self in the online classroom." *International Journal of Instruction* 4(1): 3–15. e-ISSN: 1308–1470

Bakhmat, L., O. Babakina, and Ya Belmaz. (2021). "Assessing online education during the COVID-19 pandemic: A survey of lecturers in Ukraine." *Journal of Physics: Conference Series,* 1840(1), 012050

Basilaia, Giorgi, Marine Dgebuadze, Mikheil Kantaria, and Girshel Chokhonelidze. (2020). "Replacing the classic learning form at universities as an immediate response to the COVID-19 virus infection in Georgia." *International Journal Research Applied Science Engineering Technology* 8(3): 101–108. ISSN: 2321-9653

Bassoppo-Moyo, Temba C. (2006). "Evaluating eLearning: A front-end, process and post hoc approach." *International Journal of Instructional Media* 33(1): 7–23

Berge, Zane L. (1998). "Barriers to online teaching in post-secondary institutions: Can policy changes fix it." *Online Journal of Distance Learning Administration* 1(2): 1–12

Bond, Melissa, Victoria I. Marín, Carina Dolch, Svenja Bedenlier, and Olaf Zawacki-Richter. (2018). "Digital transformation in German higher education: Student and teacher perceptions and usage of digital media." *International Journal of Educational Technology in Higher Education* 15(1): 1–20. https://doi.org/10.1186/s41239-018-0130-1

Carey, Kevin. (2020). "Everybody ready for the big migration to online college? Actually, No." *The New York Times* 13

Caruso, Judith Borreson, and Gail Salaway. (2007). "The ECAR study of undergraduate students and information technology". www.csplacement.com/downloads/ECAR-ITSkliisstudy.pdf (accessed 12 October 2020)

Ching, Yu-Hui, and Yu-Chang Hsu. (2015). "Online graduate students' preferences of discussion modality: Does gender matter?" *Journal of Online Learning and Teaching* 11(1). https://scholarworks.boisestate.edu/cgi/viewcontent.cgi?article=1114&context=edtech_facpubs (accessed 10 Ocotber 2020)

Choi, Hee Jun, and Ji-Hye Park. (2006). "Difficulties that a novice online instructor faced: A case study." *Quarterly Review of Distance Education* 7(3): 317–322

Collins, Mauri, and Zane Berge. (1996). "Facilitating interaction in computer mediated online courses." In *Proceedings of the FSU/AECT Conference on Distance Learning. June 20–23, Tallahassee, FL*

Conaway, Roger N., Susan S. Easton, and Wallace V. Schmidt. (2005). "Strategies for enhancing student interaction and immediacy in online courses." *Business Communication Quarterly* 68(1): 23–35

Coppola, Nancy Walters, Starr Roxanne Hiltz, and Naomi Rotter. (2001). "Becoming a virtual professor: Pedagogical roles and ALN." In *Proceedings of the 34th Annual Hawaii International Conference on System Sciences*, IEEE

Demuyakor, John. (2020). "Coronavirus (COVID-19) and online learning in higher institutions of education: A survey of the perceptions of Ghanaian international students in China." *Online Journal of Communication and Media Technologies* 10 (3): e202018. https://doi.org/10.29333/ojcmt/8286

Dhawan, Shivangi. (2020). "Online learning: A panacea in the time of COVID-19 crisis." *Journal of Educational Technology Systems* 49(1): 5–22. https://doi.org/10.1177%2F0047239520934018

Doll Jr, William E. (1993). "A post-modern perspective on curriculum." Teachers College Press. eISBN: 978-0-8077-7439-7

Favale, Thomas, Francesca Soro, Martino Trevisan, Idilio Drago, and Marco Mellia. (2020). "Campus traffic and e-learning during COVID-19 pandemic." *Computer Networks* 176: 107290. https://doi.org/10.1016/j.comnet.2020.107290

Fein, A. D., and Logan, M. C. (2003). Preparing instructors for online instruction. New Directions for Adult and Continuing Education, 2003(100), 45–55.

Fry, Kate. (2001). "E-learning markets and providers: Some issues and prospects." *Education+ Training* 43(4/5): 233–239. https://doi.org/10.1108/EUM0000000005484

Garrison, D. Randy, Terry Anderson, and Walter Archer. (1999). "Critical inquiry in a text-based environment: Computer conferencing in higher education." *The Internet and Higher Education* 2(2–3): 87–105. https://doi.org/10.1016/S1096-7516(00)00016-6

Green, Hannah, and Celia Hannon. (2007). "Their space: Education for a digital generation." ISBN 1 84180 175 5

Hara, Noriko, and Khe Foon Hew. (2007). "Knowledge-sharing in an online community of health-care professionals." *Information Technology & People* 20(3): 235–261. https://doi.org/10.1108/09593840710822859

Harasim, Linda. (2017). "Learning theory and online technologies." Routledge. ISBN: 0415999766

Hrastinski, Stefan. (2008). "Asynchronous and synchronous e-learning." *Educause Quarterly* 31(4): 51–55

Huang, Rui, Li Zhu, Leyang Xue, Longgen Liu, Xuebing Yan, Jian Wang, Biao Zhang. (2020). "Clinical findings of patients with coronavirus disease 2019 in Jiangsu province, China: A retrospective, multi-center study." *PLoS Neglected Tropical Diseases* 14(5): e0008280. https://doi.org/10.1371/journal.pntd.0008280

Hung, Min-Ling, Chien Chou, Chao-Hsiu Chen, and Zang-Yuan Own. (2010). "Learner readiness for online learning: Scale development and student perceptions." *Computers & Education* 55(3): 1080–1090. https://doi.org/10.1016/j.compedu.2010.05.004

Ice, Philip, Reagan Curtis, Perry Phillips, and John Wells. (2007). "Using asynchronous audio feedback to enhance teaching presence and students' sense of community." *Journal of Asynchronous Learning Networks* 11 (2): 3–25. ISSN-1939–5256

IMAI (Internet and Mobile Association of India). (2019). *Digital in India: Round 2 Report*. (https://cms.iamai.in/Content/ResearchPapers/2286f4d7-424f-4bde-be88-6415fe5021d5.pdf) (accessed 16 October, 2020)

Juan, Angel A., Cristina Steegmann, Antonia Huertas, M. Jesus Martinez, and José Simosa. (2011). "Teaching mathematics online in the European Area of Higher Education: An instructor's point of view." *International Journal of Mathematical Education in Science and Technology* 42(2): 141–153. https://doi.org/10.1080/0020739X.2010.526254

Kapasia, Nanigopal, Pintu Paul, Avijit Roy, Jay Saha, Ankita Zaveri, Rahul Mallick, Bikash Barman, Prabir Das, and Pradip Chouhan. (2020). "Impact of lockdown on learning status of undergraduate and postgraduate students during COVID-19 pandemic in West Bengal, India." *Children and Youth Services Review* 116: 105194

Keller, Christina and Lars Cernerud (2002). "Students' perceptions of e-learning in university education." *Journal of Educational Media* 27(1-2): 55–67. https://doi.org/10.1080/1358165020270105

Kennedy, Gregor, Kerri-lee Krause, Kathleen Gray, Terry Judd, Susan J. Bennett, Karl A. Maton, Barney Dalgarno, and Andrea Bishop. (2006). "Questioning the net generation: A collaborative project in Australian higher education." Annual Conference of the Australasian Society for Computers in Learning in Tertiary Education: 413–417

Ko, Susan, and Steve Rossen. (2017). Teaching Online: A Practical Guide. Routledge. ISBN: 978-0-415-83242-7

Koole, M. (2014). "Identity and the itinerant online learner." *The International Review of Research in Open and Distributed Learning* 15(6). https://doi.org/10.19173/irrodl.v15i6.1879

Kopp, Michael, Ortrun Gröblinger, and Simone Adams. (2019). "Five common assumptions that prevent digital transformation at higher education institutions." *INTED2019 Proceedings*: 1448–1457

Krishan, Varun B. (February 08, 2019). 24% of Indians have a smartphone, says Pew Study. www.thehindu.com/news/national/24-pc-of-indians-have-a-smartphone/article26212864.ece (accessed 18 October 2020)

Kvavik, Robert B (2005). "Convenience, communications, and control: How students use technology." *Educating the Net Generation* 1: 7–1. www.educause.edu/research-and-publications/books/educating-net-generation/convenience-communications-and-control-how-students-use-technology (accessed 15 October 2020)

Lapadat, Judith. (2007). "Discourse devices used to establish community, increase coherence, and negotiate agreement in an online university course." *International Journal of E-Learning & Distance Education* 21(3): 59–92

Leszczyński, Piotr, Anna Charuta, Beata Łaziuk, Robert Gałązkowski, Arkadiusz Wejnarski, Magdalena Roszak, and Barbara Kołodziejczak. (2018). "Multimedia and interactivity in distance learning of resuscitation guidelines: A randomised controlled trial." *Interactive Learning Environments* 26(2): 151–162. https://doi.org/10.1080/10494820.2017.1337035

Li, Chi-Sing, and Beverly Irby. (2008). "An overview of online education: Attractiveness, benefits, challenges, concerns and recommendations." *College Student Journal* 42(2): 449–458

Li, Qun, Xuhua Guan, Peng Wu, Xiaoye Wang, Lei Zhou, Yeqing Tong, and Ruiqi Ren. (2020). "Early transmission dynamics in Wuhan, China, of novel coronavirus-infected pneumonia." *New England Journal of Medicine*. https://doi.org/10.1056/NEJMoa2001316

Luyt, Ilka. (2013). "Bridging spaces: Cross-cultural perspectives on promoting positive online learning experiences." *Journal of Educational Technology Systems* 42(1): 3–20

Mayes, Robert. (2011). "Themes and Strategies for Transformative Online Instruction: A Review of Literature." *Global Learn Association for the Advancement of Computing in Education (AACE)*: 2121–2130

McInnerney, Joanne M., and Tim S. Roberts. (2004). "Online learning: Social interaction and the creation of a sense of community." *Journal of Educational Technology & Society* 7(3): 73–81. www.jstor.org/stable/pdf/jeductechsoci.7.3.73.pdf (accessed 15 October 2020)

Ministry of Statistics and Programme Implementation. (2019). Key Indicator of Household Social Consumption on Education in India, NSS 75th Round 2017–18, 18 October 2020. http://mospi.nic.in/sites/default/files/publication_reports/KI_Education_75th_Final.pdf

Mishra, Nandita, Deepak Tandon, Neelam Tandon, and Isha Gupta. (2020). "Online teaching perceptions amidst covid-19." *JIMS8M: The Journal of Indian Management & Strategy* 25(3): 46–53. https://doi.org/10.5958/0973-9343.2020.00023.X

Mittal, Amit, Archana Mantri, Urvashi Tandon, and Yogesh K. Dwivedi. (2021). "A unified perspective on the adoption of online teaching in higher education during the COVID-19 pandemic." *Information Discovery and Delivery* Forthcoming. https://doi.org/10.1108/IDD-09-2020-0114

Muilenburg, Lin Y., and Zane L. Berge. (2005). "Student barriers to online learning: A factor analytic study." *Distance Education* 26(1): 29–48. https://doi.org/10.1080/01587910500081269

Olesova, L., J. Richardson, Donald Weasenforth, and Christine Meloni. (2011). "Using asynchronous instructional audio feedback in online environments: A mixed methods study." *MERLOT Journal of Online Learning and Teaching* 7(1): 30–42

Paudel, Pitambar (2021). "Online education: Benefits, challenges and strategies during and after COVID-19 in higher education." *International Journal on Studies in Education* 3(2): 70–85. https://doi.org/10.46328/ijonse.32

Paules, Catharine I., Hilary D. Marston, and Anthony S. Fauci. (2020). "Coronavirus infections – more than just the common cold." *Jama* 323(8): 707–708. https://doi.org/10.1001/jama.2020.0757

Peng, Hsinyi, Chin-Chung Tsai, and Ying-Tien Wu. (2006). "University students' self-efficacy and their attitudes toward the internet: The role of students' perceptions of the internet." *Educational studies* 32(1): 73–86. https://doi.org/10.1080/03055690500416025

Rasheed, Rasheed Abubakar, Amirrudin Kamsin, and Nor Aniza Abdullah. (2020). "Challenges in the online component of blended learning: A systematic review." *Computers & Education* 144: 103701

Robertson, Donald Alexander. (2000). "Teaching and learning in the computer-mediated conferencing context." PhD Dissertation, University of Toronto

Romiszowski, Alexander, and Robin Mason. (2004). Computer Mediated Communication Handbook of Research for Educational Communications and Technology. Routledge: 397–431

Sandkuhl, Kurt, and Holger Lehmann. (2017). "Digital transformation in higher education: The role of enterprise architectures and portals." In Alexander Rossmann, Alfred Zimmermann (eds.), Digital Enterprise Computing. 2017 Lecture Notes in Informatics (LNI), Gesellschaft für Informatik, Bonn 2017, 49–60

Saxena, Kavita. (2020). "Coronavirus accelerates pace of digital education in India." EdTechReview. http://library.ediindia.ac.in:8181/xmlui/bitstream/handle/123456789/10145/EdTechReview%20by%20Dr.%20Kavita%20saxena%2017Apr2020.pdf?sequence=1&isAllowed=y (accessed 16 October 2020)

Singh, Vandana, and Alexander Thurman. (2019). "How many ways can we define online learning? A systematic literature review of definitions of online learning (1988–2018)." *American Journal of Distance Education* 33(4): 289–306. https://doi.org/10.1080/08923647.2019.1663082

Smith, Peter J., Karen L. Murphy, and Sue E. Mahoney. (2003). "Towards identifying factors underlying readiness for online learning: An exploratory study." *Distance Education* 24(1): 57–67. https://doi.org/10.1080/01587910303043

Syverson, M. A., and John Slatin. "Evaluating learning in virtual environments." (2010). www.learningrecord.org/caeti.html (accessed 15 October 2020)

Tinsley, Howard E. A., and Diane J. Tinsley. (1987). "Uses of factor analysis in counseling psychology research." *Journal of Counseling Psychology* 34(4): 414–424. https://doi.org /10.1037/0022-0167.34.4.414

Tsai, Chin-Chung, and Chia-Ching Lin. (2004). "Taiwanese adolescents' perceptions and attitudes regarding the internet: Exploring gender differences." *Adolescence* 39(156): 725–734

Tucker, Jan P., and Patricia W. Neely. (2010). "Unbundling faculty roles in online distance education programs." *International Review of Research in Open and Distributed Learning* 11(2): 20–32. https://doi.org/10.19173/irrodl.v11i2.798

Varenova, Daria, Martin Samy, and Alan Combs. (2013). "Corporate social responsibility and profitability: Trade-off or synergy: Perceptions of executives of FTSE All-Share companies." *Sustainability Accounting, Management and Policy Journal* 4(2): 190–215. https://doi.org/10.1108/SAMPJ-May-2012-0020

Vonderwell, Selma, and Sajit Zachariah. (2005). "Factors that influence participation in online learning." *Journal of Research on Technology in Education* 38(2): 213–230. https://doi.org/10.1080/15391523.2005.10782457

Wang, Chuanyi, Zhe Cheng, Xiao-Guang Yue, and Michael McAleer. (2020). "Risk management of COVID-19 by universities in China": 36. https://doi.org/10.3390/jrfm13020036

Yang, Yi, and Linda F. Cornelius. (2004). "Students' perceptions towards the quality of online education: A qualitative approach." *Association for Educational Communications and Technology*: 861–877 https://files.eric.ed.gov/fulltext/ED485012.pdf (accessed 15 October 2020)

7

Pathways for an Internet Equitable Higher Education in India

Jency Treesa

Assistant Professor in Commerce, St Teresa's College (Autonomous), Ernakulam, Kerala, India

7.1 Introduction

Digital equity among learners and instructors is a prerequisite for quality online learning. The pandemic period witnesses an unprecedented quest for digital equity in higher education. The objective of this paper is to trace out the levels of digital inequity in Indian higher education and identify practical pathways to bridge them. A template for strategising for an internet-equitable institution with specified parameters for each student is provided in this research work.

Responses to the sudden shift to online learning were illustrated by many. One of the true reflections was from Chantal Ladias, Lecturer at Dublin Business School (Ladias 2020):

> Between the four walls of my lecture room, I felt safe; all that was shared inside those walls stayed there. Suddenly, with the pandemic threat, the walls were torn down. Our homes were now our offices. Zoom, Panopto, and WhatsApp became our lifelines for maintaining a connection with students who were dealing with lost jobs, overcrowded accommodations, and homesickness. Sometimes students did not even own the right equipment or have the stable internet connections necessary to hold a conversation, let alone show their face on Zoom.

DOI: 10.1201/9781003203070-8

Ladias resonates with most teachers around the globe. Being late adopters of technology, the intensity of its impact will be much more severe in developing countries like India. Educational institutions in developed countries are assumed to be better off as they have better equipped online delivery channels in place. Pre-existing experience with the online mode of teaching also came in handy during the pandemic, and made the transition to online smoother. In India, however, most educational institutions, except some premiere institutions, were unprepared or underprepared to manage this crisis. The transition from on-campus to online has proved equally challenging for educators and students. One of the reasons for this is the disparity in access to the information and communication technology (ICT), which is generically referred to as the 'digital divide'.

Digital equity in higher education is on the political agenda of governments around the globe. Ranges of modes in higher education (full-time or part-time; on-campus or at a distance) require different usage rates of internet for accessing the course content and course activities. But access to technology is unfortunately denied to many student cohorts. Historically marginalised groups like women are gradually being included into the mainstream with progress being made in access and participation in higher education.

7.2 Research Questions and Methods

The paper starts with two research questions. Firstly, it tries to understand what the responses are to digital inequity from different quarters, in the wake of the COVID-19 pandemic. It attempts to build on the existing literature of digital equity to understand how the pandemic and digital inequity enact together to amplify existing inequities. The second objective is to suggest practical pathways to bridge the digital inequity in the educational context in general and institutional context in particular.

This is a conceptual paper supported by literature review and reflective analysis. The author has reviewed more than 120 papers from leading databases like Ebsco, Proquest, and Elsevier and selected the most relevant four dozen papers from which ideas, themes, concerns, solutions, and insights are configured for the current paper. The author has used a reflective approach to briefly share what her institution has done in similar situations. In professional learning settings, critical reflection is widely used to enhance the quality of practice (Fook 2011). The reflection is a result of the author's engagement in addressing digital equity in the institutional context since March 2020.

7.3 Theoretical Framework

The role of modern communication technologies in the formation of 'knowledge economies' and 'network societies' are well researched (Reich 1991). Use of ICT will 'empower' individuals (D'Allesandro and Dosa 2001), by enabling better social interaction and civic involvement, thereby enhancing access to education and other services (Katz et al. 2001).

At the same time, an equally prominent theme of research focused on unequal access to the use of technology and new media, which has the potential to nullify the stated benefits of ICT, if unaddressed. This was referred to as digital divide. Prior to the 1990s, the term was largely used in a generic sense referring to information inequality, information gap, knowledge gap, or information asymmetry related to computer or media literacy. Ferrari (2012) suggests that digital competence is a combination of information skills, communication skills, content creation skills, safety skills, and problem-solving skills.

(Sen 1992) instructs that every investigator studying any problem related to equality has to answer the most pertinent question: 'Equality of what?' Accordingly, the first question that should be answered would be: What inequality does the concept of digital divide refer to? A superficial glance through the social-scientific and economic literature produces answers that can be grouped as technological, immaterial, material, social, and educational types of inequality.

7.3.1 Digital Divide

The term 'digital divide' was coined by Larry Irving, Jr., former US Assistant Secretary of Commerce for Telecommunication and Communication in the mid-1990s. This term was added to caution the public on the gap in access to information services between those who can afford to purchase the computer hardware and software necessary to participate in the global information network and those who cannot (Boje and Dragulanescu 2003).

The digital divide is the variance existing between different demographics on access to information technology. Wilson (2004: 300) defines the digital divide as 'inequality in access, distribution, and use of information and communication technologies between two or more populations.' He identified eight aspects of the digital divide: 'physical access, financial access, cognitive access, design access, content access, production access, institutional access, and political access'. It is the gap between the haves and the have-nots (De Munster 2005). The term 'digital inequity' is also used to refer to the digital divide (Straubhaar 2012).

Problems of digital inequity are pointed out by many researchers. 'The knowledge gap between the information-rich and the information-poor has caused excluding certain parts of the world from enjoying the fruits of the global village' (Iskandarani 2008). The determinants and dimensions of digital inequity are wide and varied (Yuen et al., 2018). Bridging this divide is shown as a solution. Facilitating the provision of ICT skills and access helps to bridge the disparities in information, education, income, and gender (Heeks, 2006).

7.3.2 Layers of Digital Inequity

In the 1990s the main topics of mainstream political discussion were focused on 'information haves' and 'information have-nots' (Wresch 1996), 'information and communication poverty' (Williamson et al. 1991) and most importantly digital divide. The concept of divide shall be focussed on content rather than technological platform. The term 'access' is also highly debatable and often related to technology and information. According to Wise (1997) 'access' refers to making ICT resources available to all citizens and thus it simply refers to the availability of the physical infrastructure.

Van Dijk (1999) distinguishes four kinds of barriers to access: mental, material, skill, and usage. Firstly, mental access is the end result of the absence of interest, computer anxiety, and unattractiveness of the new technology. Secondly, material access represents the lack of possession of computers and network connections. Material access to digital technologies is the next level of inequality. Socio-economic differences between people and between countries are the main reason for this inequity. Economically and socially impoverished people and regions are affected more by this. Thirdly, skill access means the lack of digital skills caused by insufficient user-friendliness and inadequate education or social support. Lack of digital skills impedes the handling of technology and widens the divide between people who can use digital skills and those who cannot. This may further impact on the pre-existing gender disparities too. Finally, usage access denotes lack of significant usage opportunities or exposure. Quality of use gap is the inability to use the skills to get good results. The difference in the expertise of using the required phrase or key-words while using a search engine is an example of this inequity.

The digital split arises from a plethora of social, geographic, and economic factors. The digital divide operates across geographic location (whether it be rural-urban), income (whether it be rich-poor), gender (whether it be male-female) and language (whether it be English–vernacular) (Kenniston 2003). Digital inequity was considered to be a temporary phenomenon, which was expected to be bridged as people gained physical access to devices. But over time and as more technologies evolved, it increased. There is a general misconception that the digital divide is bridged when people have equal access to computers and internet connectivity (Van Dijk and Hacker 2003). The mental barrier is often ignored as a type of digital divide and viewed as being confined to elderly people, some categories of homemakers, people who are illiterate, and those who are unemployed. Similarly, the skills gap and usage gap are also given little attention while confronting the problem of the digital divide. In many societies there is inequality of access to both the technology and information and this often creates a digital divide between different social groups (Selwyn 2002). It is often argued that when individuals and groups are deprived of using ICT, they are also deprived of the various potential benefits that ICT can bring to their lives. The participation in ICT and connectivity helps to acquire economic advantage (Parker 2000). Digital technologies offer an opportunity to minimise and manage social disparities, to tackle social exclusion, to enhance social and civic rights, and to promote equity (Ruiu Ragnedda 2020).

7.3.3 Ensuring Digital Equity

Of late, the theory on digital access and the digital divide has started to focus on how to bridge the divide. The units of study for such enquiries varied, like individuals, communities, nations, and the world as a whole. In general, the theory revolved around themes like promoting digital literacy, developing and making available relevant and local content, and promoting innovations for overcoming the digital divide.

A spike in the execution part of digital inequity and subsequent research was triggered by the rapid increase in mobile subscriptions across the globe. Yet there are groups of digitally excluded peoples within and across countries. Most countries were striving to address connectivity issues, digital technology, teacher training, and associated learning concerns within local contexts and beyond (Resta and Laferrière 2015) even before the pandemic.

The primary difference between attempts before and after the pandemic was institutional involvement. Institutions of higher education started facing the ill effects of digital inequity directly during the pandemic. This forced them to rethink and devise ways to address the issue at first hand, when previously it would have been considered generally as an issue for the state. Many institutions were quick to respond.

Discussing the online teaching-learning modes adopted by the Mizoram University during the lockdown, Mishra et al. (2020) points out that some of the students did not have essential resources to join online, which further pushes the digital divide. The study reiterates a lack of devices and unstable internet connection as difficulties faced by students.

7.3.4 Addressing the Inequity

Countries of the world responded differently to bridge the digital divide that became more apparent due to the shutting down of educational institutions during the COVID-19 pandemic. Innovative methods were used to improve access to the internet and help students and teachers in online teaching-learning. The common methods deployed were: using broadcast media (video and audio), distributing printed study materials; broadcasting videos through websites, portals, social media (Facebook, YouTube, WhatsApp); video lessons on CDs and memory cards. Table 7.1 details some of the practices followed in different countries as noted by the World Bank from March 2020 to June 2020.

Srinivas and Salil (2020) provide a set of affordability focused, access focused, support focused and system focused measures to bridge the digital inequity, as given in Table 7.1. Though the classification suggested is subjective, the framework is useful in understanding various efforts to solve digital inequality.

TABLE 7.1
Preparing the Baseline Data for Strategising at the Institutional Level

No.	Dimension	**Details** *To be collected from each student for baseline data*	**Institutional Strategies** *To be devised as per the need and relevance*
1	Device	i. Availability ii. Quality iii. Usage iv. Power	• Affordable computing devices • Common wifi zones • Community PCs and televisions • Solar-powered PC units • Low-cost educational tools
2	Connectivity	v. Infrastructure vi. Reliability vii. Power	• Zero-rating arrangements • Asynchronous data saving lessons • Compressed data-saving video lessons • Free high-speed internet for students • Shared learning spaces • Community controlled learning centres with power back-ups
3	Affordability	viii. Price ix. Choice x. Payment terms	• Pay-it-forward loans • Rent-a-device • Lend-a-device • Instalment sharing arrangements like library-of-things • Institutionally subsidised services • Seller subsidised services • Bankers' subsidies • Government subsidies
4	Relevance	xi. Content form xii. Content level xiii. Context xiv. Language	• Focus on design • Bundling from OER • Sharing content/language • Translation services • Customising content in the relevant language
5	Support	xv. Educator support xvi. Technical support xvii. Maintenance load xviii. Digital leadership	• Faculty-student groups and apps • Open-source support systems in the campus • Time-based voluntary support groups • E-buddies and mentoring • Data privacy and security assurance

7.4 Methodology

7.4.1 Discussion: Indian Responses and Pathways

There are many governmental and non-governmental efforts to bridge the digital inequity in India. The micro-chitty laptop scheme under the Pradhan Mantri Dhan Yojana offers laptops or the required monetary help through the state. These laptops are priced under Rs.15,000 and laptops costing more than 2 lakh are expected to be distributed in the current year. Some states like Punjab and Karnataka have launched the distribution of smartphones or laptops to youths. Some of the schemes come with free data and talk time.

The Ministry of Education and University Grants Commission had made widely available more than two dozen useful resources in higher education to the academic community even before the pandemic. This is in addition to the online platforms like SWAYAM. The top hundred universities of the country have allowed online education to start. A system for multi-mode access to digital education is envisaged under the e-Vidya programme through which a selection of Television Channels, more e-content, QR coded energised books, and special e-content for those with disabilities are being made available.

There are other institutional attempts. The team in IIT Mumbai, India, led by Dr Kannan Moudgalya has come-up with an affordable, compact and high-performing laptop with an 11.6-inch screen, Intel Atom processor, 4GB RAM, 64GB storage space, 10000 mAH battery power and Linux Operating System, all for Rs 10,000. Initially piloted among IITB students, it is reported that this model is sold in bulk of 100s (Nath, 2019). St Teresa's College (Autonomous), Kerala, India has initiated a laptop lending project to less privileged students. The college has mobilised funds from the Alumni, staff, students, parent-teacher association and its other stakeholders for this project. The college has also launched an e-buddy programme wherein senior students are allotted to help the newly admitted students in their journey of coping with the online education system and other related issues.

There are many non-governmental organisation initiatives too. 'Support our students' is a Bengaluru based organisation that provides refurbished laptops, desktops, and tablets to underprivileged students (Mathew, 2020). The venture collects old devices, refurbishes them, and provides them to deserving students.

Zero-rating is a practice in which certain services or applications are exempted from data charges. It enables users who cannot afford expensive data plans to access a few applications without charges towards the individual's data cap. This means that learners on low incomes will get more data for their money, as some data applications are not charged. Citing examples from different developing countries, West (2015) argues that zero-rating programmes are effective ways to bring people on low incomes into the digital era and promote innovation in the internet sector. Many mobile operators around the world offer some type of zero-rating services. However, the zero-rating approach raises many questions about internet neutrality. Firstly, it goes against the principle that internet service providers should treat transmission of all data equally. Second, is the issue of long-term cost. The zero-rating service launched in India by Facebook under the tag *Free Basics* was banned by the Telecom Regulatory Authority of India in 2016 because of the above reasons. But in many countries, similar schemes still exist. The literature shows mixed results on the impact of the zero-rating practice. Saenz de Miera (2016) shows that consumers are better off with zero-rating in terms of estimated consumer surplus and that it brings socially desirable outcomes, though the practice may have the potential for adverse consequences. Criticisms on zero-rating services are relevant when the application selected is of commercial value, as in the case of Facebook in India. The demographic potential needs to be explored where educational applications from the government may come under zero-rating practices. In many countries, like Argentina, Korea, and South Africa, educational websites are zero-rated. This is yet to be explored in India.

Subsidised internet plans are a commonly used but less studied way of facilitating a programme. Internet service providers can also offer their assistance to families on low incomes. One such programme in the US is Lifeline where a monthly discount is provided on telephone service, broadband internet service, or bundled voice-broadband packages purchased from participating wireline or wireless providers. A similar programme is available with BSNL in India where the discount ensures that low-income consumers can afford broadband access. However, studies are yet to be conducted on the educational impact of such offers in India. Similarly, reimbursement of internet packages is another method to extend attempts to address inequity.

Fee waivers for devices are yet another approach, which generally comes as part of selected educational loans for eligible students. No-tax connections for the deserving is also already implemented in India.

Pay-it-forward programmes involve a no-fee, no-cost loan offered to students to address the affordability barrier. It is suitable for those who do not have credit back-up or a proven track record. Borrowers are kept accountable to either pay it back sooner or later to someone equally eligible, thus creating accountability and a support framework.

Though there are corporate bodies who attempt to bridge the digital divide through their funds for corporate social responsibility, the practice is not widespread in India despite its potential. According to the Corporate Social Responsibility Policy (Section 135 of the Companies Act, 2013), every company with a net worth of five hundred crores rupees or specified turnover or net profit should spend at least two per cent of the average net profits on a cause of social responsibility. Using such funds in a coordinated way in the areas surrounding the company or where its bottom-of-the-pyramid customers, if any, are located will provide a big push in bridging the digital divide.

7.4.2 Addressing Inequity at the Institutional Level

We are unsure of the containment possibility and potential recurrence of biothreats like COVID-19. Preparing for instructional disruptions is a priority for all institutions. The following template provides for strategising for an internet-equitable institution in more specific detail, showing IT policies, system and preparedness at the institution level. Strategising for digital equity at the institutional level starts by collecting learner information from each student, which will serve as baseline information. Exploring all options to address the gaps in baseline data will open up possible community-links, industry-links, and related solutions which may lead to restructuring IT policies to be more inclusive. Apart from the top-down approach, there are possible bottom-up approaches too. This may include identifying the local governance member from the student's home town and intimating the requirements. This was partially done in certain remote panchayats in the state of Kerala during the lockdown situation. Such approaches can ensure better community support and awareness.

In practice, this author's institution took stock of device and data access for all its students in the initial days of the lockdown, which helped to design ubiquitous connectivity and device availability for all its 3000 plus students, thus taking care of the first three dimensions in the template through a scheme, *Sumanusu*. Reworking the learning management system – in the author's case, Moodle – with more asynchronous sessions followed by short interactions helped to address many contextual and discipline-related changes required in the fourth dimension. Among others, a program named e-buddies, in which each first-year undergraduate student is paired with a senior for e-learning and personal support, was used to address the fifth dimension. Finally, the institution can develop transition protocols for each segment of the institution and integrate this into the institution as a whole to ensure sustained digital leadership.

Ensuring *digital trust* among teachers and students is a priority as problematic internet behaviours are high in Asia compared to European countries. Balhara et al. (2019) uses the term 'problematic internet usage' to encompass all potentially problematic web-related behaviours including gaming, gambling, purchasing, pornography viewing, and unwanted social networking. Differences in technological and economic advances between countries leading to differential smartphone ownership, internet penetration, bandwidth availability, and pricing offered by local providers could also be responsible for these differences observed in the pattern of *problematic internet usage* (Mak et al. 2014). Therefore, the strategy of ensuring meaningful connectivity shall also pre-empt the potential problematic internet usages by infusing digital trust. Srinivas and Salil (2020) say that digital trust among teachers and students is beyond regulations.

7.5 Conclusion

At a basic level, the benefits of digital access are obvious. From an economic point of view, citizens of the country can easily network, learn new areas, and find better employment or business opportunities and increase their earnings. In educational parlance this assigns higher importance to our moral responsibility to provide a better learning experience for students. As several authors point out (Bayne 2014; Ito et al. 2013), digital technology supports and improves the educational situation.

At a deeper level, as suggested in the template in this study, we need to work from the institutional baseline data on all forms of student access in order to address various layers of digital inequity. A bottom-up institutional plan and top-down governmental plan can cohesively co-exist, which perhaps is the only way to resolve the inequity issues in education in India. Using the template given in this work will increase the preparedness for emergencies and enhance institutional resilience. While large scale IT infrastructure and long-term solutions need more resources, the template suggested is relatively easily to implement in a learning community. More studies are required on each of the paths and how they converge. The significance of cultural capital and parental background in middle-income groups in India should be subjected to further scrutiny while designing digital assistance programmes.

References

Ani, 2020. Businessworld. www.businessworld.in/article/Punjab-CM-to-launch-scheme-to-distribute-free-smartphones-to-youth-on-Aug-12/11-08-2020-307272/ Accessed date 21 September 2020.

Balhara, Y. P. S., Doric, A., Stevanovic, D., Knez, R., Singh, S., Chowdhury, M. R. R., & Arya, S. 2019. "Correlates of Problematic Internet Use among college and university students in eight countries: An international cross-sectional study". *Asian Journal of Psychiatry*, 45, 113–120.

Bayne, Sian. 2014. "What's the matter with 'technology-enhanced learning'? "*Learning, Media and Technology* 40 (1): 5–20. Informa UK Limited. doi:10.1080/17439884.2014.915851.

Boje, C. & Dragulanescu, N. G. 2003. "Digital divide in Eastern European countries and its social impact". In Proceedings of the 2003 American Society for Engineering Education Annual Conference & Exposition.

D'Alessandro, Donna M. & Dosa, Nienke P. 2001. "Empowering children and families with information technology". *Archives of Pediatrics & Adolescent Medicine* 155 (10): 1131. American Medical Association (AMA). doi:10.1001/archpedi.155.10.1131.

De Munster, Irene L. 2005. "The digital divide in Latin America: a case study". *Collection Building* 24 (4): 133–136. Emerald. doi:10.1108/01604950510629309.

Ferrari. A. 2012. Digital Competence in Practice: An Analysis of Frameworks. Sevilla, JRC IPTS.

Fook, Jan. 2011. "Developing critical reflection as a research method". *Creative Spaces for Qualitative Researching*: 55–64. SensePublishers. doi:10.1007/978-94-6091-761-5_6.

Heeks, R. 2006. "Social outsourcing: creating livelihoods". Information for Development (i4d), 17–19 September.

Iskandarani, Mahmoud Z. 2008. "Effect of information and communication technologies (ICT) on non-industrial countries-digital divide model". *Journal of Computer Science* 4 (4): 315–319. Science Publications. doi:10.3844/jcssp.2008.315.319.

Ito, M., Gutierrez, K., Livingstone, S., Penuel, B., Rhodes, J., Salen, K., Schor, J., Sefton-Green, J., & Watkins, S. C. 2013 "Connected learning: an agenda for research and design, technical report", Digital Media and Learning Research Hub , Irvine, CA.

Katz, James E., Rice, Ronald E., & Aspden, Philip. 2001. "The internet, 1995–2000". *American Behavioral Scientist* 45 (3): 405–419. doi:10.1177/0002764201045003004.

Kenniston K. 2003. "The four digital divides". In Bridging the Digital Divide: Lessons from India, Kenniston K., Das D. K. (eds). New Delhi, Sage Publications, pp. 14–35.

Ladias, C. 2020. "Educator Reflections: How Did You Respond to the Sudden Shift Online?" Available via app. academic.hbsp.harvard.edu. http://app.academic.hbsp.harvard.edu /e/es?s=1578928263&e=116488&elq=c13ab58d162d4673a2c02b83af2bdd20. Accessed date: 21 September 2020.

Mak, K. K., Lai, C. M., Watanabe, H., Kim, D. I., Bahar, N., Ramos, M., Young, K. S., Ho, R. C., Aum, N. R., & Cheng, C., 2014. "Epidemiology of internet behaviors and addiction among adolescents in six Asian countries". *Cyberpsychol. Behav. Soc. Netw.* 17 (11), 720–728. https://doi.org/10.1089/cyber.2014.0139.

Mathew, Anju Ann. 2020. Yourstory. https://Yourstory /socialstory /2020/07/support-students-old-laptops-bengaluru-online- class.

Mishra, Lokanath, Gupta, Tushar & Shree, Abha. 2020. "Online teaching-learning in higher education during lockdown period of COVID-19 pandemic". *International Journal of Educational Research Open* 1: 100012. Elsevier BV. doi:10.1016/j.ijedro.2020.100012.

Nath, S. 2019. Effortsforgood. Available via https:// effortsforgood.org /innovations/affordable-laptop. Accessed date 21 September 2020.

Pal Singh Balhara, Yatan et al. 2019. "Correlates of problematic internet use among college and university students in eight countries: an international cross-sectional study". *Asian Journal of Psychiatry* 45: 113–120. doi:10.1016/j.ajp.2019.09.004.

Parker, Edwin B. 2000. "Closing the digital divide in rural America". *Telecommunications Policy* 24 (4): 281–290. doi:10.1016/s0308-5961(00)00018-5.

Reich, R. 1991. The Work of Nations: A Blueprint for the Future. London, Simon & Schuster.

Resta, Paul & Laferrière, Thérèse. 2015. "Digital equity and intercultural education". *Education and Information Technologies* 20 (4): 743–756. doi:10.1007/s10639-015-9419-z.

Ruiu, Maria Laura & Ragnedda, Massimo. 2020. "Digital capital and online activities: an empirical analysis of the second level of digital divide". First Monday. *University of Illinois Libraries*. doi:10.5210/fm.v25i7.10855.

Saenz de Miera, Oscar. 2016. "Efecto del Zero Rating sobre la penetraciin de la Banda Ancha MMvil en MMxico (Effect of zero-rating on the penetration of mobile broadband in Mexico)". *SSRN Electronic Journal*. doi:10.2139/ssrn.2861992.

Selwyn, N. 2002. "Defining the digital divide: developing a theoretical understanding of inequalities in the information age". Occasional Paper 49. *School of Social Sciences, Cardiff University*. www.cf.ac.uk/socsi/ict/definingdigitaldivide.pdf. Accessed date: 6 October 2006.

Sen, Amartya.1992. Inequality Re-Examined. Oxford, Oxford University Press.

Srinivas, G. & Salil, S. 2020. "Online learning: debate, design and digital equity". *University News*, July 27–August 02, 2020.

Straubhaar, J. (ed.). 2012. Inequity in the Technopolis: Race, Class, Gender, and the Digital Divide in Austin. Austin, University of Texas Press.

Van Dijk, J., 1999. The Network Society: Social Aspects of New Media. Thousand Oaks, CA, Sage Publications.

Van Dijk, Jan & Hacker, Kenneth. 2003. "The digital divide as a complex and dynamic phenomenon". *The Information Society* 19 (4): 315–326. doi:10.1080/01972240309487.

West, D. M. 2015. Digital Divide: Improving Internet Access in the Developing World Through Affordable Services and Diverse Content. Brookings Institution.

Williamson, Kirsty, Balnaves, Mark & Caputi, Peter. 1992. "Information, communication and telecommunications: a pilot study of the behaviour of citizens". *Prometheus* 10 (2): 311–322. doi:10.1080/08109029208629115.

Wilson, E. J. 2004. "The information revolution and developing countries." Cambridge, MA, MIT Press.

Wise, J. 1997. Exploring Technology and Social Space. London, Sage.

World Bank. 2020. "How countries are using edtech (including online learning, radio, television, texting) to support access to remote learning during the COVID-19 pandemic". www.worldbank.org/en/topic/edutech/brief/how-countries-are-using-edtech-to-support-remote-learning-during-the-covid-19-pandemic. Accessed date: 21 September 2020.

Wresch, W. 1996. Disconnected: Haves and Have-Nots in the Information Age. New Brunswick, Rutgers University Press.

Yuen, A. H., Park, J., Chen, L., & Cheng, M. 2018. "The significance of cultural capital and parental mediation for digital inequity". *New Media & Society*, 20 (2), 599–617.

Section B

Innovations and Applications of Digitalization of Higher Education: A Cloud Perspective

8

Technology: Perception of Higher Education

Rajan Gupta

Centre for Information Technologies & Applied Mathematics, University of Nova Gorica, Nova Gorica, Slovenia

Saibal Kumar Pal

Defense Research & Development Organization, Delhi, India

8.1 Introduction

COVID-19, or more popularly known as novel coronavirus, is associated with the respiratory disorder in humans which was declared a global pandemic in the first quarter of

DOI: 10.1201/9781003203070-10

2020 by the World Health Organization (World Health Organization 2020). According to data from Johns Hopkins University (2020) and other tracking websites, at the time of writing, there are currently more than 20 million people infected by the novel coronavirus all around the world, and close to 700 thousand deaths. The top 10 countries with the maximum number of infected cases are the USA, Brazil, India, Russia, South Africa, Mexico, Peru, Colombia, Chile and Spain. The top countries with the maximum number of reported deaths are the USA, Brazil, Mexico, the UK, India, Italy, France, Spain, Peru, and Iran. For the recovered patients' list, the USA is at the top of the list, followed by Brazil, Russia, and India. India (www.mohfw.gov.in/) was placed comfortably low down on the list of infected nations by considerable margins in the early days (January–May 2020) (Sarkodie & Owusu 2020). Still, certain events led to its rise into the top 3 positions, a point of concern. The mortality rate is controlled at less than 2% right now, which is better than the 3.5% mortality rate of the world, but the model of spread has moved towards an exponential trend (Meo et al. 2020), which can lead to a massive loss of lives and infrastructure (www.mygov.in/covid-19/).

Many nations look to India as a world leader. Even the World Health Organization acknowledged that the world is looking towards Indian strategies to contain this epidemic's outbreak (Sharma 2020). India accounts for almost one-fifth of the world's population and is the second highest country in terms of the number of people in the world. India contributes heavily to the world's GDP and is among the most prominent developing countries with reasonably stable economic growth percentages (Myers 2020). India's good camaraderie with most nations World and its practical nature makes it a perfect ally for other countries. Therefore, analysis of the COVID-19 outbreak in the Indian region, and the strategies adopted in multiple sectors, is closely watched and monitored by the rest of the world. There is a need for comprehensive analytical studies based on different approaches taken by Indian administrators from time to time. India followed a nationwide lockdown from 22 March 2020, a one-day lockdown, followed by a 21-day lockdown after two days (Pulla 2020). Every activity in India has happened with permission from various administration units (Chaurasiya et al. 2020). All domestic and international travel has either been banned or is monitored closely (Sarkar et al. 2020; Mishra et al. 2020). India is yet to get into the third phase of the COVID-19 outbreak fully, that is, the community outbreak seen by various countries around the world, but cases have been rising continuously.

During this time, the Indian Prime Minister has been trying to connect with Indian citizens through innovative strategies and various engagement activities that impact the whole nation. Many sectors are still under the lockdown phase. The education sector has faced a complete transition since the lockdown was announced (Jena 2020; Bokde et al. 2020). With so much happening in India right now, it becomes imperative that we study the current situation and impact of various such events in the Indian education sector through perceptions and surveys and come up with different plans for the future, which can help the Indian administrators and educational professionals.

The current study explores various aspects associated with the education sector during the COVID-19 outbreak in India. The specific research questions (RQ) in this study are as follows.

- RQ1: What are the major problems faced by students, teachers, administrators, and parents of a higher educational university like the University of Delhi?
- RQ2: What are the various strengths and weaknesses of the University of Delhi, which helped manage the online teaching-learning process?

- RQ3: Did the image and perception of the University of Delhi change due to the COVID-19 outbreak and lockdown in India?
- RQ4: How has the University of Delhi been able to gain competitive advantage due to COVID-19 difficulties?

The current study consists of five sections. The first presents the study's current context, followed by a literature review in the second section. The third section presents the methodology and research variables of the study. The fourth section presents the study results and findings, along with a discussion of the achievements of the various research questions explored in this study. And finally, the fifth section concludes this study and presents limitations and future directions for this research work.

8.2 Literature Review

8.2.1 Higher Education in India

The education industry is one of India's rapidly growing industries in recent times (Verger et al. 2017). With a large percentage of the population being young and in need of quality higher education, this industry continuously aims for growth and reinvention. As per the World Bank Report in conjunction with the Ministry of Human Resource Development, it is estimated that around 75 million students would be available immediately after 2020 for secondary education, giving rise to a vast number of students for higher education in the next decade (Zapp 2017). With a requirement of INR 20,000 crore and more in this sector, numerous management, technical, and medical institutions are in demand. Existing ones are not sufficient to cater to the present and future needs of the present generation.

There are two types of institutes or universities currently operating in India – public/government and private (Singh 2018). Public universities/institutions are funded by the Government of India, while the private ones are self-funded. The public institutions of higher learning come directly under the Ministry of Education and their councils. In contrast, the private ones are governed independently with prior affiliations and a set of rules and regulations specified by the government. In India, the central universities, state universities, deemed universities, private universities and institutes, open universities, national institutes, and agricultural universities are available for higher education, as dictated by the University Grant Commission of India (Tandi 2020).

In the engineering/technical education areas, the Indian Institutes of Technology (IITs) are the first choice of students. However, due to very tough competition for selection, only a fraction of aspirants gets a chance each year. Several Indian Institutes of Management (IIMs), a few central universities, and a few private institutions were placed in the top ten engineering/technical institutes this year. In the management education area, the top priority is for the IIMs, where again only a small percentage of students get through the entrance exams each year. There are many private institutions of high repute where students pursue their graduate, post-graduate, and doctoral studies in general and specialized management areas. This year many IIMs, national institutes, and private institutes of management studies appeared in the top 10 management institutes in the country.

The IITs and IIMs follow world-class standards in teaching and other academic activities (Chauhan 2020). Due to the professional environment, outstanding faculty, and excellent educational infrastructure and facilities, students develop expertise, confidence, and energetic personalities while studying in these institutes. Whether the students are in India or abroad, they are offered the best jobs by companies, public sector undertakings, R&D institutes, and academia. On the negative side, many aspirants cannot afford the fees required for studying in these institutes. Many others cannot keep pace with the rigorous academic schedule and commitment demanded by these institutes. Hence, they opt for regular courses in reputed universities like the University of Delhi.

8.2.2 Role of Technology in Education Sector

The education industry has played a significant role in adopting the latest technology to keep on a par with modern educational standards (Budhwar 2017). The campus infrastructures are being built up with facilities of digital and virtual classrooms and wi-fi-enabled campuses. Students can access the internet any time from any place inside the campus. Similarly, internal portals are being designed for students where their exam schedule, results, and other necessary information are being updated. The notice boards' role is reducing inside the campus, and online portals are being provided for 24-7 information dissemination. Online lectures via video conferencing are being conducted by experts, which a large number of students can attend. These online lectures have the advantage of being delivered by renowned experts from different parts of the world and can also be recorded and digitally stored for future access. Video cameras are installed on the campus to monitor visitors and maintain discipline on the campus premises. Instead of traditional libraries, digital libraries are being offered, which are easy to access and support. Online books and journals are made available to students and teachers, which are much handier and quicker to access. Assignments are posted on common portal groups saving resources and time (Toto 2018).

A few universities/institutes have started conducting online examinations for students. Even one of the highest levels of management entrance exams in the country, the Common Admission Test, is conducted online, making technology an inevitable part of the admissions process. Even in promotional schemes, technology is widely used. For information dissemination, websites are carefully designed, and important facts are updated regularly. The admissions procedure is streamlined using an online filling of forms and facilitating payments online. The use of Web 2.0 by educational institutes is increasing, making it easier for students to interact with authorities, experts, and friends and get admission-related and other details quickly. Technology has made life easier for students, teachers, and the administrative staff of the institutes.

8.2.3 University of Delhi

University of Delhi (Kaur 2020) was established in 1922 (www.du.ac.in/). It had only 3 colleges affiliated to it at the beginning, with approximately 700–800 students being enrolled. But now, it is one of the largest and most highly reputed educational centers in the public sector education of India. It is a government-funded central university. The Visitor of University of Delhi is the honorable President of India, while India's Honorable Vice-President occupies the Chancellor's position. In fact, University of Delhi's Pro-Chancellor position is being held by the coveted Chief Justice of the Supreme Court of India. The university rankings are consistently amongst the world's best 500 universities; however, its generous size beats most of its competitors.

University of Delhi sits in the capital city of India, Delhi. The University is affiliated with the University Grant Commission (UGC) India, National Assessment and Accreditation Council (NAAC), and Association of Indian Universities (AIU). Famous celebrities and eminent personalities are the alumni of the University of Delhi. Some of them are British Prime Minister Gordon Brown, Ms. Shiela Dikshit (late Chief Minister of Delhi), Bollywood personality Amitabh Bachchan, cartoonist R. K. Laxman, and cardiologist Dr. Jayantibhai Patel. Many prominent fields like science, sports, journalism, entertainment, politics, movies, administration, and corporates have the presence of alumni from University of Delhi.

The whole of India awaits the cut-off lists of the University of Delhi for various programs. Every year the student admissions process gains a lot of media attention. With a high percentage in 12th class, some of the brightest of the students take admission in the various University of Delhi colleges. Every year students plan to visit the campus for admission purposes and dream of becoming part of the vibrant youth culture in Delhi.

However, during India's lockdown, the University of Delhi faced a tough time transitioning from traditional classroom teaching to the online teaching-learning process. Numerous teachers faced difficulties in conducting online classes and taking online assessments. Even the administrative work was held up for weeks due to the absence of robust technological support. Open book examinations were a significant nightmare for final-year students, while first-year and second-year students were promoted to the next year without the conduct of final exams. Glitches in the online examination system, failure of mock tests, absence of a standardized portal for managing the teaching-learning process, and delays in information dissemination made it difficult for various stakeholders like students, teachers, administrators, and parents to adjust to the situation. It did tarnish the reputation of the university, but some members were still in favor of it. Even after sharp criticism by media houses, the University of Delhi is going strong. This is where this study has been designed – to check the problems of various stakeholders and see whether the issues arising due to COVID-19 impacted the lives of stakeholders or not.

8.2.4 Image Perception and Competitive Advantage

Mats Urde (1994) and Frans Meline introduced 'brand orientation' in the 1990s when many companies were unaware of it. It helped in creating a strategic advantage for the products and services offered by the organization. It also helped in better customer attraction. The marketing department identified target customers easily and introduced activities related to the branding amongst them. Market orientation and the role of brands influences the concept of brand orientation, which helps create the brand identity. Branding has the power to dominate the product features as it conveys the emotional and symbolic value of the product to the customer as well as the consumer. Different definitions were given around brand orientation, which involved building brand, brand equity creation, and brand management for various products amongst multiple stakeholders. In the most straightforward of terms, the degree of association of an organization with the brand may be classified as brand orientation. It may also be the extent to which an organization aims to reinforce distinctiveness from other organizations (Gromark & Melin 2013).

In today's competitive business environment, merely providing products and services is insufficient to build a brand identity. A company needs to be innovative with its products to attract new customers and retain existing customers. Apart from superior products and services, companies also need to look into the marketing tools used. Innovation in marketing tools should also be explored to improve customer relationships. Traditional marketing included strategies that were used to attract and retain customers with the help of conventional marketing tools like telephone, newspapers, magazines, radio, and TV broadcasts. But marketing tactics and strategies have changed (Stanislaw 2014). The media has also emerged in a new form. Businesses have evolved with innovative marketing tools in recent years. Digital marketing and web marketing are so much in vogue these days. The majority of companies use innovative marketing tools to attract customers (Hirt & Willmott 2014). But not all new marketing techniques are useful for all types of businesses. Traditional business owners still use traditional marketing tools for advertising their products. In the past, most individuals used to read newspapers and magazines in their daily lives. Again, a large number of people now prefer online news and social media to gain information about products. In this world of changing technology, business owners are shifting from traditional to innovative marketing tools, as creative marketing opens up many opportunities for business owners (Forbes 2013).

The same is happening with educational institutions and universities. They have to go with the flow of online education and the learning process. If they get stuck in the traditional form of teaching, their value may go down. And thus, the branding may get impacted, leading to a loss of competitive advantage (Rana et al. 2020; Crawford et al. 2020). Like the University of Delhi, renowned universities are struggling to gain a foothold in the modern world and hence may be on the path to losing their competitive edge.

8.3 Methodology

8.3.1 Research Design and Approach

This research presents the impact of lockdown due to COVID-19 on higher educational institutions in India through the University of Delhi. It studies this in the context of India. This emerging economy has witnessed rapid growth in the number of students and universities over the years. The study follows a deductive approach of research, which is generally quantitative in nature and therefore requires numeric data analysis. It involves searching for patterns from observations in the data and the development of explanations from those patterns. It aims to generate insights from the data to identify the relationship between the variables in consideration (Antwi & Hamza 2015).

The research analyses the relationship between the stakeholders, institutions, and their impact on the perception of the university due to an awkward transition to the online system during the COVID-19 pandemic period as shown in Figure 8.1.

8.3.2 Research Validity and Reliability

The validity of research determines the extent to which the concepts in a quantitative study are measured accurately. In other words, validity ensures that the scores represent the variable that they intend to (Heale and Twycross 2015). For instance, if research measures

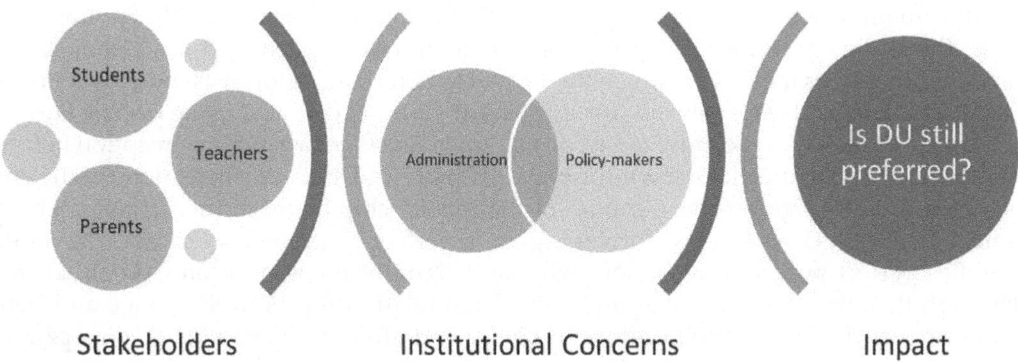

FIGURE 8.1
Research variable and stakeholders of the proposed method.

the person's assignment score to measure their intelligence, it may not be a valid measure to quantify intelligence variables. Therefore, a validity score shows the appropriateness of the measure. On the other hand, reliability conveys the consistency to which the measure gives similar results when the experiment is repeated similarly (Charalambous 2018). For instance, automated devices such as water flow sensors in a smart home environment might provide an alarm every time the water leaks, which makes them reliable. Still, since they ring the signal at the wrong time when the water tank has already leaked, they are not valid. This study considered only reliable and accurate responses, checked through the Cronbach alpha value. The overall responses had an alpha value of more than 0.7, which is a good score for considering the data's further analysis.

8.3.3 Data Collection

The research analyzes the primary data, which is the data that the researcher has collected during the conduct of the study. It can be managed through sources like the internet and is flexible for analyses (Johnston 2017). A total of 273 students and 94 parents/guardians of these students participated in the survey from 15 different colleges and 3 faculties under the University of Delhi. Similarly, a total of 122 faculty members and 21 administrative members contributed in the data collection. A simple questionnaire was designed based on the common issues arising during the lockdown phase and was distributed to the prospective participants through email, WhatsApp Groups, and Telegram Groups. Data collection was done during July 2020 when some stability entered the University of Delhi system regarding a new academic calendar and conduction of exams for the final-year students. The data has then been analyzed to assess the relationship between the variables through appropriate exploratory statistical methods. Data has been transformed using necessary mathematical transformation to reduce the skewness and get the variable measure on the same scale. Missing values in the datasets were treated with the mean or mode responses from other respondents for a particular question, depending upon the variable's nature.

8.3.4 Data Analysis

The research has implemented an exploratory data analysis technique that involves discovering, exploring, and detecting patterns in the data. It is concerned with 'exploring' the data to understand if there is a phenomenon behind it (Jebb et al. 2017). For this purpose, the study has analyzed the response frequencies and identified the respondents' mood for the issues they face, along with the perception changes towards the University of Delhi. The data has been analyzed using SPSS software and collected using Google Forms.

Further, the study has conducted a correlation analysis between the perception before the lockdown and after lockdown for the University of Delhi. A correlation coefficient is a measure that signifies the strength of the relationship between the variable, which ranges between –1 and 1; the former signifies perfect negative correlation, the latter signifies perfect positive correlation, while a 0 signifies no association (Akoglu 2018). Through this, the researcher can understand the relationship between image and perception towards the University of Delhi before and after the lockdown. Also, a paired sample t-test was used to check whether the opinions differed before and after the lockdown in the University of Delhi.

8.3.5 Research Ethics

The study has been researched in accordance with all the ethics that form an essential part of research (Makhoul et al. 2018). It has collected the data only from the people associated with the University of Delhi. Those who were ready to contribute to the study were only given the main questionnaire. The respondents' identities have been kept anonymous and will not be shared with anyone without their permission. The study considers the reliability and trustworthiness of the quantitative analysis data as an essential component of this research.

8.4 Findings

8.4.1 Students' Issues

Several issues emerged for students pursuing graduate and post-graduate studies at the University of Delhi. Figures 8.2–8.5 show the percentage of responses towards various categories of problem.

Shifting from the traditional paradigm of teaching to a visual model is a new experience in itself. While some students have adopted this new technique easily, others are still suffering. There are specific pros and cons to online teaching. Online classes have given a practical implementation of topics and contents that will benefit students in the future. Students are working hard to increase their responsiveness and concentration to gather notes and listen to their teacher simultaneously. There has been a lot of chaos and confusion as students and teachers are not well versed in using applications like Zoom and Google Meet. As we all know, the environment for teaching and studying plays a crucial role. Teachers and students are distracted by household chores at home. Considering the scale of poverty in India, there have been many problems in gathering the equipment required for online classes. Students miss essential points while the network is weak, which leads to sparse quality notes being made. People who have left for villages are not able to join in due to network issues.

Some students do not have a laptop or smartphone for attending classes. Some might borrow from other family members, who also might be busy doing some online work. Therefore, the lack of resources is a primary concern here. Students willing to study suffer

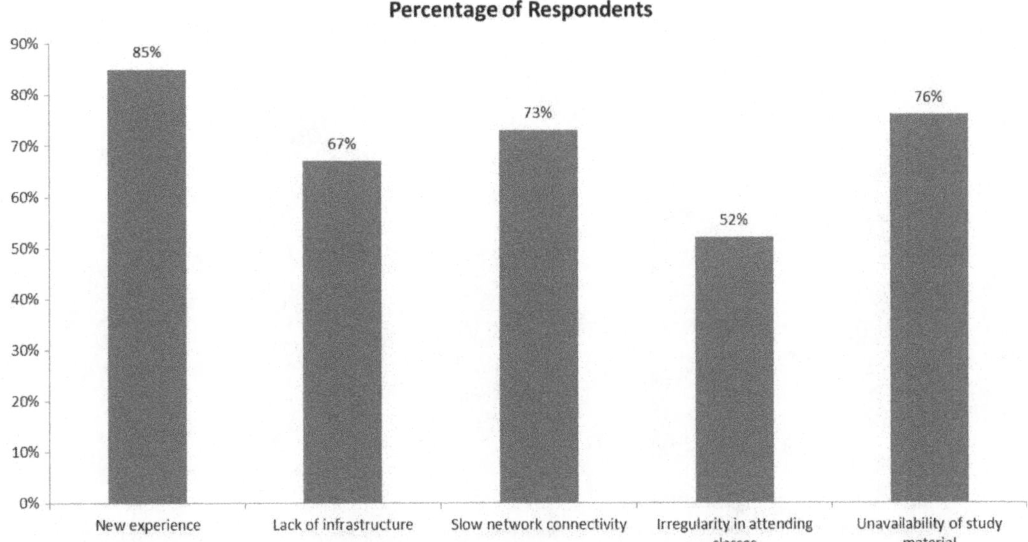

FIGURE 8.2
Percentage of student respondents for infrastructure and experience.

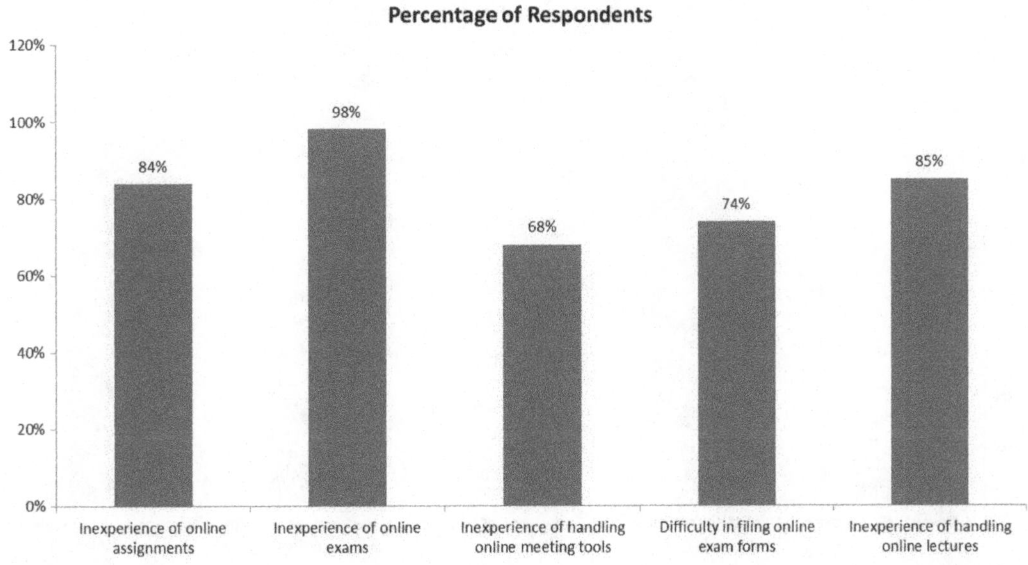

FIGURE 8.3
Percentage of student respondents for online classes and assessments.

a lot in this case. People at home can become lazy and spend their time watching television or sleeping. This lackadaisical attitude could result in the irregularity of online classes. Students practice procrastination, which leads to incompletion of homework and a reason not to attend courses further. Also, students have been following the traditional method of completing assignments. Writing in notebooks and attempting tasks on sheets is a pattern

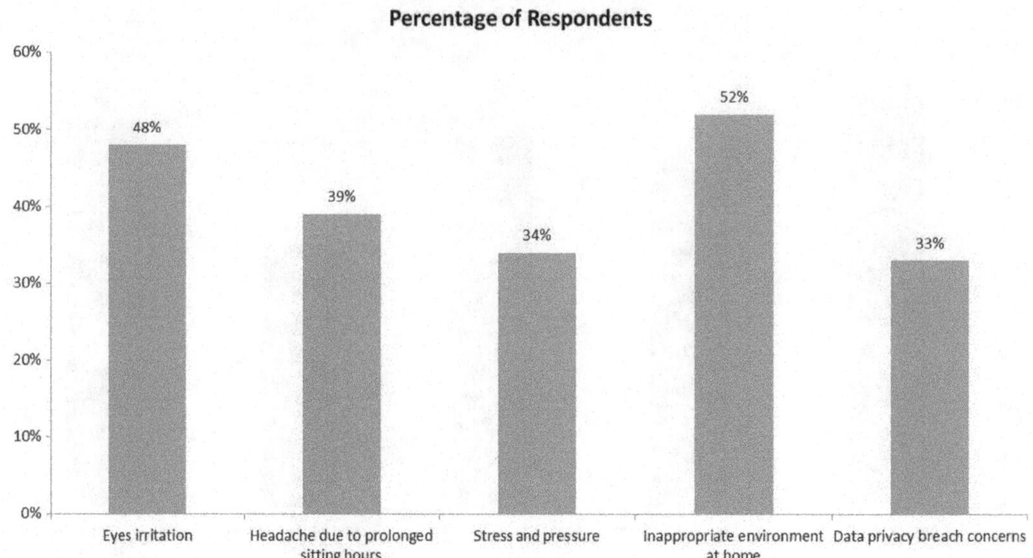

FIGURE 8.4
Percentage of student respondents for physical and mental issues.

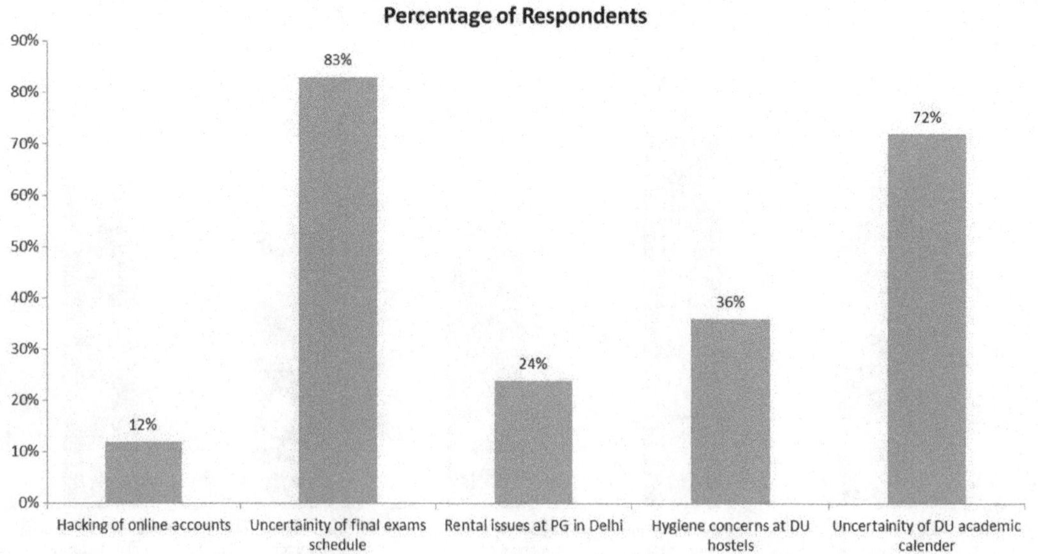

FIGURE 8.5
Percentage of student respondents for security, uncertainty and hygienic issues.

that has been followed since the world of education began. Adapting to the new tools and technology has been very difficult for students. Errors in uploading and scanning of documents arose when submitting projects and work on online platforms. Most of the students have smartphones of their own or their parents but not laptops. Smartphones could be sufficient for attending classes but not in attempting long assignments and homework.

Online examination has generated a feeling of relaxation among the students. Students in colleges and universities feel online examinations are like open-book tests as they feel no urge to study. They try to copy answers from Google and other secondary resources available to them. Students are not taking online exams as seriously as they take offline examinations. With family members around, there is an inappropriate environment to appear for exams. This has also made the seriousness, enthusiasm, and concentration disappear. Therefore, ignorance of exam writing has increased on a massive scale among the students in various universities and colleges.

Unavailability of e-books and reference material has also been an issue. Several professors said that it took a significant amount of time to collect and assemble e-books and articles. This meant students' crucial time was not effectively utilized in learning. Some teachers said that a large amount of time was wasted in making a proper schedule and online drive for the syllabus, and the students had to wait for this to be done. Portals such as the National Library and Information Services Infrastructure for Scholarly Content, which provide peer-reviewed journals, e-books, and other research material for college and university teachers, are inaccessible. Simultaneously, a lot of e-journals are also unavailable because the university has not paid for them for a long time. The other portals that the university has suggested, like SWAYAM, have very little information for teachers at the college level. A member of the faculty at a College of South Campus said: 'Of all the things that the university has suggested, N-List is the only portal which has quality journals, and they are all inaccessible to us.'

Students at several colleges have complained that online exam filing services are not entirely working. Some of the online portals are not compatible with specific networks and also have incomplete detail filling forms. Some of them lack clarity in terms of dates and duration of examinations. Disrupted online exam filing services is a significant disadvantage for students and should be amended.

Apart from the disrupted services, security concerns also loom over online classes. During the coronavirus pandemic, students and teachers face a new challenge during their online courses. Hackers are targeting e-learning classes and are posting obscene content. According to a report in the *Times of India*, new hacking cases have emerged from Mumbai, Maharashtra. A class 10 student reportedly logged into a class 9 online class and posted obscene content. In another case, an unidentified person hacked into an e-class and shared obscene messages. Later, the school stopped online courses for a few days after the incident. A student's parent said that teachers have now started taking attendance once the class begins and don't allow students to join when they know all are in. Two Twitter users pointed out the severe data privacy breach problems arising in the admit card 2020 download portal of the University of Delhi, which is part of their official website. Anyone with the 'gateway password' could download all students' admit cards in any University of Delhi college.

Other than security issues, physical health concerns are also emerging for the students. Sore eyes, headache, back pain, and high stress levels are severe problems faced by both students and children for spending a lot of time on computer screens. Teachers have complained that they had throbbing headaches and dizziness when they get up from work after class. Sitting for more than eight hours can lead to postural problems like disc damage, strained neck, and swayback issues in the long run.

Homes are also not the best place to conduct classes. There has been a lack of concentration and responsiveness in students with the presence of family members and household chores. Background noise can disturb teachers while explaining topics. Several students asking queries at the same time causes chaos and confusion. And even staying in hostels is not a feasible option for the students. Students are facing hygiene issues at the university hostels. There is no proper cleaning and sanitization of rooms. Girls have regularly complained of not having enough space for living, and due to this, they have had hygiene problems.

Irregular announcements by the university regarding exams are also a big headache for students. Eleven days after the Centre asked the University Grants Commission to review its guidelines, there was still no clarity for many anxious students across the country. At least seven states canceled their college and university exams – Punjab, Haryana, Rajasthan, Odisha, Maharashtra, Madhya Pradesh, and West Bengal without waiting for the UGC's new guidelines. However, some private universities continued to conduct online exams in these states. And the University of Delhi decided to do online exams for the final-year students while canceling exams for first-year and second-year students.

8.4.2 Parents' Issues

Parents also registered their issues with respect to the shifting from traditional setup to the online structure with their children attending classes from home. The majority of the parents said that sharing laptops or other devices amongst various kids at home is a problem for them. No personal equipment is available for each child at home, making it difficult to make necessary arrangements for their children to attend online classes. Also, some working parents need a laptop for their office work too. This makes it an awkward situation at home.

Apart from this, many parents complained that sharing of the internet happens when simultaneous video classes take place for the children, which lowers the speed and slows down the whole network. This causes frequent disruption and connectivity issues.

Parents also said that their children suffered from headaches, eye irritation, and increased stress levels due to prolonged hours on laptops or devices for attending online classes. They said that the lectures need to be attended online in the first place; then, the assignments need to be submitted along with the lab work, and then their children are also spending time on entertainment on phones, TVs, and laptops. Since children cannot go out to play, the constant exposure to digital devices has harmed the students physically. On top of all this, the parents were not happy with the erratic scheduling of classes and uncertainty over the college and the university's examinations.

8.4.3 Teachers' Issues

Like the student issues, the teachers face many problems in transitioning from the traditional classroom teaching system to the online teaching-learning system. There are individual colleges where teachers face problems with the online platforms as they complain of no training being held for the same. Both government and non-government organizations and ed-tech companies are making efforts to support the system to make a smooth transition to the virtual world, however. Teachers also have the new experience of conducting online classes. Many teachers, who are in the second half of their careers, are finding it very difficult to speak in front of their screens without looking at the students.

Like the students, teachers also lack adequate infrastructure at their homes. Due to lockdown, they could not even arrange the laptops and desktops from the college/university for online teaching. They are facing low network connectivity issues as internet speed is not the best during these times.

Unavailability of e-books and reference material, low student attendance, low interactivity within the online class, noise and video disturbances in online courses, and repetition of concepts due to frequent network issues with some participants, are some of the leading problems cited by teachers taking online classes. In fact, due to all these problems, teachers are also experiencing high-stress levels, headaches, backache, and eye irritation, as a consequence of regularly sitting in front of screens for lecture preparation and delivery.

The teachers also had problems related to conducting online assignments and exams as it had never happened in the university before, and there were no concrete guidelines available. They also felt that an irregular schedule of classes and exams is a big headache for them. The policy for COVID-19 by the administrative department is not supportive during these times. The majority of the teachers agreed that residential places are not appropriate to conduct classes due to noisy backgrounds. They felt that the workplace and home should not be mixed in the case of teaching.

8.4.4 Administrative Issues

The University of Delhi and allied colleges' administrative department is also under severe pressure to ensure the online teaching-learning system's smooth functioning. The respondents overwhelmingly shared similar concerns with respect to lockdown in the University. They said that it has become difficult to function in the system due to the uncertainty of the pandemic. They have a dependence on paper-based processes and environment, which is challenging to transform during the current situation.

The administrative staff is involved in non-teaching activities, maintenance, accounts, general office work, and allied services. They confirmed the difficulty in coordination with staff, students, and teachers for various purposes. Many people are not even available on emails for responding to some urgent queries posed by the office staff, like exam form filing for the students or submitting the evaluation mark sheets by the teachers. This has interrupted the administrative work of the university.

Also, they faced difficulties in setting up an online platform quickly for immediate transitioning. They did not have any training support for operating online meeting software or functioning through various new software that was being used for makeshift purposes. They also expressed concerns as there was no coherence found in the think-tank of the University of Delhi and other universities regarding scrapping of the exams. That is why they had to deal regularly with students' fears of online exams and assignments.

8.4.5 Perception of University of Delhi

The perception of University of Delhi was measured through some of the literature measures (Rauschnabel et al. 2016) on a 5-point scale, where 1 denotes least likely and 5 denotes most likely situation. The results are shown in Table 8.1.

The image and perception were measured through the love for 'DU' tag in the educational programs and how much they refer it to others through word-of-mouth. It was found that, except for parents, who saw a brief downfall in the image and perception of the university, all other stakeholders were fairly stable on the perception due to the COVID-19 lockdown. There was no significant change observed in the image and perception towards the University of Delhi before and after lockdown. Even after facing so many problems, students, teachers, and administrators were quite convinced about the positive image of

TABLE 8.1
Image and Perception Results towards the University of Delhi Constituting Response Mean and Significance Value Obtained from Paired t-Test for before and after Lockdown

Measures	Before Lockdown	After Lockdown	Significance Value
Students			
Love for 'DU' tag	4.1	4.0	0.072
Word of Mouth Promotion	3.9	3.8	0.121
Teachers			
Love for 'DU' tag	4.5	4.2	0.030
Word of Mouth Promotion	4.3	4.3	0.541
Parents			
Love for 'DU' tag	4.4	3.9	0.003
Word of Mouth Promotion	4.5	3.8	0.002
Administrators			
Love for 'DU' tag	4.2	4.1	0.063
Word of Mouth Promotion	3.9	3.9	0.512

the university and were ready to be a part of it with its shortcomings as well. And that is why the correlation value was found to be 0.92 in the perception before and after lockdown. However, the University of Delhi also showed transitioning from the traditional system to an online system through several steps, as discussed in the next sub-section.

8.4.6 Advantages at the University of Delhi

The University of Delhi saw a significant transition from classroom teaching to online teaching. Being a central university, it was not an easy task to move things towards the online mode, yet the administrative and teaching staff made it a comfortable process, as much as possible. The university ordered the colleges and faculties to use platforms like Google Meet, Google Classrooms, Microsoft Teams, and Zoom for online teaching and conducting internal meetings. For this purpose, the various colleges' computer centers and respective ICT centers helped in issuing email IDs to every staff member and student in the university domain. GSuite accounts were purchased instantly for teachers and students to conduct online classes smoothly. E-library access was brought to operation in rapid time, and many resources were made available to the teachers and students. For administrative purposes, a video-conferencing facility was made possible in all the prominent offices which were operating with appropriate social distancing guidelines, under the Ministry of Home Affairs, and limited staff members. Sanitization of the campuses was carried out regularly, and sanitizer machines were installed in the majority of the colleges and faculties.

During studies and exam preparation, a helpline number for mental health-related queries was established, and students were counseled regularly. Similarly, a helpline email and number were developed for any online exam-related questions for the students. Dedicated teams and committees were also formed for looking after the process of online classes and assessments. Regular updates on the website were posted regarding any announcements and changes to the academic calendar and examination process. For this purpose, dynamic scheduling of the calendar was done frequently in order to adjust to the needs of the COVID-19 situation. And when it became unfeasible to conduct the exams, the University of Delhi decided to promote the first-year and second-year students without conducting the final theory exams.

8.5 Discussion and Conclusion

8.5.1 Discussion

The current study discovered many issues and their impact on the University of Delhi in terms of its image and perception. The first research question was: What are the major problems faced by students, teachers, administrators, and parents of a higher educational university like the University of Delhi? This study considered different types of issues faced by various groups of people. The problems ranged from new experiences to unavailability of the infrastructure. They also included aspects like security, physical health, mental health, and uncertainty for exams/classes.

The second research question was: What are the various strengths and weaknesses of the University of Delhi, which helped manage the online teaching-learning process? There were a variety of options exercised by the University of Delhi for managing the teaching-learning process during the lockdown phase. A variety of online tools are used, and dedicated teams take care of students' health issues and conduction of exams. Continuous evolvement of the academic calendar is being done in order to help the students and teachers.

The third research question was: Did the image and perception of the University of Delhi change due to the COVID-19 outbreak and lockdown in India? It was answered through two measures of the love for 'DU' tag and word-of-mouth promotion, and it was found that, except for parents, all other stakeholders perceived the image of the University of Delhi in a similar manner as before the lockdown. No significant impact of lockdown was seen on the perception and image of the University of Delhi.

The fourth research question was: How has the University of Delhi been able to gain competitive advantage due to COVID-19 difficulties? This has been studied through various secondary sources like media articles and website announcements, in addition to the analysis carried out in this study. Proper communication, quick decision-making, flexibility in adapting to the situation, and using the best available resources, were the significant pillars in getting a competitive advantage for this central university.

8.5.2 Conclusion

The University of Delhi is not a private university that can quickly consider privatization of the processes and system without the consent of all the stakeholders, including the Government of India via UGC. The university has to follow all the norms and regulations along with the smooth conduct of online classes, salary processing for staff members, examinations and assessments, and other processes related to the education sector. And with the limited resources and difficult conditions, the university has been able to manage the operations well. All this work is significant in creating a positive and healthy image of the university. The other state and central universities can also learn the art of image building from the University of Delhi, due to which every year it attracts students from different parts of India and across the world. This study will be useful for administrators, teachers, and researchers from public and private institutions. It will help find solutions to significant problems through online technologies, innovative policies, and world-level practices.

8.5.3 Limitations

The current study faces some limitations as follows.

- The study has been conducted only on the University of Delhi's stakeholders, and other universities could not be targeted due to data collection constraints during the pandemic times.
- The study's sample size was limited, which could have positively impacted the study's accuracy.
- The study did not explore the reasoning in-depth behind the emerging concepts from the respondents.

8.5.4 Future Scope

Other researchers can emulate this study in different regions and other universities in order to validate and compare results with the current research. This will provide a holistic view of the situation of higher education and the usage of technology in this sector. Also, researchers can try to collect a higher sample size for their findings and try to relate the reasoning behind the various results. This will help in better policy-making and implementation of higher education to the benefit of multiple stakeholders.

References

Akoglu, Haldun. 2018. "User's guide to correlation coefficients." *Turkish Journal of Emergency Medicine* 18(3): 91–93.

Antwi, Stephen Kwadwo, and Kasim Hamza. 2015. "Qualitative and quantitative research paradigms in business research: A philosophical reflection." *European Journal of Business and Management* 7(3): 217–225.

Bokde, Vaishali, H. L. Kharbikar, M. L. Roy, Pratibha Joshi, and Atheequlla Ga. 2020. "Possible impacts of COVID-19 pandemic and lockdown on education sector in India." *Food Scientific Reports* 1(1): 1–7.

Budhwar, Kanika. 2017. "The role of technology in education." *International Journal of Engineering Applied Sciences and Technology* 2(8): 55–57.

Charalambous, Charalambos, Agoritsa Koulori, Aristidis Vasilopoulos, and Zoe Roupa. 2018. "Evaluation of the validity and reliability of the Waterlow pressure ulcer risk assessment scale." *Medical Archives* 72(2): 141–144.

Chauhan, Jigeshkumar D. 2020. "Higher Education in India – Issues, Challenges and Suggestions." *Research Review Journals* 5(1): 33–36.

Chaurasiya, Prem, Pragati Pandey, Upendra Rajak, Krishnakant Dhakar, Manoj Verma, and Tikendranath Verma. 2020. "Epidemic and challenges of coronavirus disease – 2019 (COVID-19): India response." https://papers.ssrn.com/sol3/papers.cfm?abstract_id=3569665. Accessed on 15 January 2021.

Crawford, Joseph, Kerryn Butler-Henderson, Jürgen Rudolph, Bashar Malkawi, Matt Glowatz, Rob Burton, Paulo Magni, and Sophia Lam. 2020. "COVID-19: 20 countries' higher education intra-period digital pedagogy responses." *Journal of Applied Learning & Teaching* 3(1): 1–20.

Forbes. 2013. *Is traditional marketing still alive?* www.forbes.com/sites/davelavinsky/2013/03/08/is-traditional-marketing-still-alive/. Accessed on 15 January 2021.

Gromark, Johan, and Frans Melin. 2013. "From market orientation to brand orientation in the public sector." *Journal of Marketing Management* 29(9–10): 1099–1123.

Heale, Roberta, and Alison Twycross. 2015. "Validity and reliability in quantitative studies." *Evidence-Based Nursing* 18(3): 66–67.

Hirt, M. and Willmott, P., 2014. "Strategic principles for competing in the digital age." *McKinsey Quarterly*, 5(1): 1–13.

Jebb, Andrew T., Scott Parrigon, and Sang Eun Woo. 2017. "Exploratory data analysis as a foundation of inductive research." *Human Resource Management Review* 27(2): 265–276.
Jena, Pravat Kumar. 2020. "Impact of Covid-19 on higher education in India." *International Journal of Advanced Education and Research (IJAER)* 5(3): 77–81.
Johns Hopkins University 2020. *Novel Coronavirus (COVID-19) Cases, provided by JHU CSSE.*
Johnston, Melissa P.2017. "Secondary data analysis: A method of which the time has come." *Qualitative and Quantitative Methods in Libraries* 3(3): 619–626.
Kaur, Parminder. 2020. "Transformative agenda of teacher education: A case of Delhi University." *Voices of Teachers and Teacher Educators*: 27. https://ncert.nic.in/pdf/publication/journalsand periodicals/vtte/vtte_July2020.pdf. Accessed on 15 January 2021.
Meo, Sultan Ayoub, Thamir Al-Khlaiwi, Adnan Mahmood Usmani, Anusha Sultan Meo, David C. Klonoff, and Thanh D. Hoang. 2020. "Biological and epidemiological trends in the prevalence and mortality due to outbreaks of novel coronavirus COVID-19." *Journal of King Saud University-Science* 32(4): 2495–2499.
Mishra, Swasti Vardhan, Amiya Gayen, and Sk Mafizul Haque. 2020. "COVID-19 and urban vulnerability in India." *Habitat International* 103: 102230.
Pulla, Priyanka. 2020. Covid-19: India imposes lockdown for 21 days and cases rise. *BMJ* 2020: 368. www.bmj.com/content/368/bmj.m1251. Accessed on 15 January 2021.
Rana, Sudhir, Arpan Anand, Sanjeev Prashar, and Moon Moon Haque. 2020. "A perspective on the positioning of Indian business schools post COVID-19 pandemic." *International Journal of Emerging Markets* https://doi.org/10.1108/IJOEM-04-2020-0415. Accessed on 15 January 2021
Rauschnabel, Philipp A., Nina Krey, Barry J. Babin, and Bjoern S. Ivens. 2016. "Brand management in higher education: The university brand personality scale." *Journal of Business Research* 69(8): 3077–3086.
Sarkar, Kankan, Subhas Khajanchi, and Juan J. Nieto. 2020. "Modeling and forecasting the COVID-19 pandemic in India." *Chaos, Solitons & Fractals* 139(1): 110049.
Sarkodie, Samuel Asumadu, and Phebe Asantewaa Owusu. 2020. "Impact of meteorological factors on COVID-19 pandemic: Evidence from top 20 countries with confirmed cases." *Environmental Research* 191(1): 110101.
Sharma, Niharika. 2020. *India's swiftness in dealing with Covid-19 will decide the world's future, says WHO, Quartz India.* https://qz.com/india/1824041/who-says-indias-action-on-coronavirus-critical-for-the-world/. Accessed on 15 January 2021.
Singh, Surinder. 2018. *Higher education in India* (Doctoral dissertation, India).
Stanislaw, Brewster. 2014. *Traditional advertising is dying (and that's just fine), Digiday.* http://digiday.com/agencies/traditional-advertising-dying-thats-just-fine/. Accessed on 15 January 2021.
Tandi, Subal. 2020. *Historicity and status of higher education* in India https://papers.ssrn.com/sol3/papers.cfm?abstract_id=3675757. Accessed on 15 January 2021.
Toto, Giusi. 2018. "From educational contexts to addictions: The role of technology in teaching methodologies and in prevention as an educational function." *Journal of e-Learning and Knowledge Society* 14(2): 203–212.
Urde, Mats. 1994. "Brand orientation – a strategy for survival." *Journal of Consumer Marketing* 11(3): 18–32.
Verger, Antoni, Gita Steiner-Khamsi, and Christopher Lubienski. 2017 "The emerging global education industry: Analysing market-making in education through market sociology." *Globalisation, Societies and Education* 15(3): 325–340.
Zapp, Mike. 2017 "The World Bank and education: Governing (through) knowledge." *International Journal of Educational Development* 53: 1–11.

9

Creating a Sustainable Future with Digitalization using Cloud Computing in Online Education

Muralidhar Kurni

Assistant Professor, Department of Computer Science, School of Science, GITAM (Deemed to be University), Hyderabad, India

Srinivasa K. G.

Professor, Department of CSE, National Institute of Technical Teachers Training and Research, Chandigarh, India

9.1 Online Learning Growth during the COVID-19 Pandemic

The COVID-19 pandemic has transformed education for ever (Li and Lalani 2020b). That is how it is.

DOI: 10.1201/9781003203070-11

- The COVID-19 pandemic resulted in the worldwide shutdown of schools. Worldwide over 1.2 billion children are missing their classroom.
- Consequently, education has changed efficaciously, and e-learning has increased significantly, with teaching being initiated remotely and on digital platforms.
- Research intimates an increase in information retention through online learning. The changes caused in online education by coronavirus will remain for a long time.

Infection rates mean that school closures have occurred in 186 countries (Unicef 2020). In Denmark, after initially closing on 12 March 2020, children up to 11 may return to nurseries and schools (BBC 2020). Professors call their students online in South Korea (Bicker L 2020).

In many parts of the world, with this sudden shift away from school, people question whether online learning will progress after the pandemic and how it affects the world education market (Teräs et al. 2020).

Before COVID-19, education technology was growing, with global investment in ed-tech rising to US$18.66 billion in 2019 and the market of online education globally estimated to reach US$350 billion by 2025. Following COVID-19, there is a significant increase in use, whether online learning software, language apps, video-conferencing tools, or virtual tutoring (AI TechPark 2020).

9.1.1 What Is the Response of the Education Sector to COVID-19?

Various online educational platforms provide free access to their services, including the Bangalore-based education technology company BYJU'S, which is now the most valued e-technology company globally (Gokulnath 2020). After the announcement of free live classes in the Think and Learn App, the company's CEO, Mrinal Mohit, saw BYJU'S value rise 200% due to the new students using their product (Li and Lalani 2020a).

Since mid-February 2020, a quarter of a billion full-time students have requested that the Chinese Government restart their online education; the Tencent Classroom became commonly used. The most significant online movement in education history was the Tencent K-12 Online School in Wuhan, with about 730,000 or 81 percent of K-12 students (Pandey 2020).

Other companies are strengthening the ability to offer teachers and students a one-stop-shop. For instance, Lark, a collaborative suite initially developed in Singapore with ByteDance as an internal tool, to meet its own exponential growth, started offering unlimited video conferencing, the ability to self-train, real-time project work co-editing, and smart calendar planning (Huang 2020). Lark has increased its engineering capabilities and global server infrastructure to assure reliable connectivity to do so quickly and in crisis times.

DingTalk, the remote learning solution for Alibaba, had been preparing for a similar influx: "To support large-scale remote work, the platform tapped Alibaba Cloud to deploy more than 100,000 new cloud servers in just two hours last month – setting a new record for rapid capacity expansion," said DingTalk CEO Chen Hang (British Lyceum 2020).

There are exciting collaborations with some school districts, such as The Los Angeles Unified School District and PBS So Cal/KCET, to help local educational broadcasts and offer various multimedia options. Media outlets like the BBC are promoting interactive learning, with Bitesize Daily, supported by celebrities like footballer Sergio Aguero teaching some content, launched on 20 April, providing 14 weeks on children's education across the whole of the UK (PBS SOCAL 2020).

9.1.2 What Is the Implication for Learning's Future?

Some believe that an unplanned and hasty transition to online education, without sufficient training and preparation and with insufficient bandwidth, will lead to poor user practice that does not support sustained growth. Others consider that a new hybrid education model with significant advantages will emerge. "I believe that the integration of information technology in education will be further accelerated and that online education will eventually become an integral component of school education," says Wang Tao, Tencent Cloud vice president and Tencent Education vice president (Li and Lalani 2020b).

Many universities have already made successful transitions. For example, the University of Zhejiang has succeeded in just two weeks in getting over 5,000 courses online using the "DingTalk ZJU," a course launched in 2020 by Imperial College London (Li and Lalani 2020a).

Many have already seen the advantages: Dr. Amjad, a university professor who used Lark to teach his students, says,

> The teaching has changed. It enables me to reach my students more effectively and efficiently, particularly during this pandemic, through chat groups, videos, voting, and document sharing. It is also easier for my students to communicate on Lark. Even after the Coronavirus, I will stick to Lark and believe that traditional offline learning and e-learning can go hand in hand. (Li and Lalani 2020b)

9.1.3 A Changing Education Imperative

This pandemic has entirely disrupted the education system that has already lost significance to numerous claims. This chapter outlines India's readiness for online education in the current coronavirus crisis and beyond.

9.2 An Overview of India's Higher Education System

The overall enrolment in higher education in 2018–19 was 37.4 million, 19.2 million men, and 18.2 million women. In overall enrolment, females account for 48.6%. There are 993 universities, 39,931 colleges, and 10,725 private education institutions. The gross enrolment ratio (GER) rate is 26.3 percent in India's higher education, estimated in the 18–23 age group. GER is 26.3% for the male population and 26.4% for the female population. In universities and colleges, the Pupil-Teacher Ratio (PTR) at the time of yearly enrolment is 29, while PTR for universities and their constituent units is 18 for annual registration (MHRD 2019; Tatsuoka 2014).

India has one of the world's biggest and largely private-sector higher education networks. While governed by the University Grants Commission, the three-tier structure of higher education in India covers universities, colleges, and courses (Cheney et al. 2005). Specific educational courses are regulated by various regulatory bodies, including the Indian Medical Council, the All India Technical Education Council, and the Indian Bar Council (Hiranandani 2020).

9.3 An Overview of the Indian Environment for Online Education

In the online education environment, internet providers play a crucial role (Khaitan 2017). The platform was initially used to allow prospective students to be linked to service providers. Network providers have increasingly taken on the role of content providers and curators recently.

Online education is only available in India with the cooperation of committed online and offline members. C2C business models have also evolved, with the network bringing future students and teachers together. B2B transactions are prevalent in higher education, where institutions market graduation/diploma courses for students through aggregators or platforms.

The corporate tie-up enables industry-certified content partnerships, which increase overall acceptance within the target online learning user base (Khaitan 2017). The growth of online education in India has been accelerated by growing internet connectivity and digital payment solutions.

9.4 Is India Ready for Online Education in the Current Coronavirus Crisis and Beyond?

Unforeseen events may often, although unintentionally, unleash unimaginable circumstances. Today under the influence of coronavirus, businesses, markets, nations, and human lives are reeling. The education of 1.2 billion students has been interrupted globally. Reports of school and educational shutdowns occur almost every hour (UNESCO 2020).

However, this awful trend has a flip side: Online educational firms announce a worldwide rise, and carbon emissions have fallen significantly as people work from home, and businesses have free online training courses for employees. In coronavirus time, it is new age prep! Every year nearly 600,000 students fly abroad for higher education. The likelihood of this happening any time soon with COVID-19 is low. At this crucial period, when the coronavirus ravages the planet, online education is their savior.

Many vital issues cannot be resolved in online education without stakeholders' committed participation – academics, state and central governments, businesses, students, and faculty (Mittal et al. 2020). Some of the most important advancements are: providing secure online access to students and teachers through live stream platforms, app collaboration, outsourcing, and the use of in-house technology to facilitate online learning. Additional considerations include adapting classes to online mode with appropriate modifications and inventiveness, enabling lesson playbacks, using live feedback, and a simple and effective communication technique for teachers and students.

Is India ready to deal with those? Yes, because it has immense experience in technology and a political will to succeed. In addition to the Digital India initiative, the government's recent move to help more foreign direct investment in education, provide Rs 3,000 crore for skill-building (Press Trust of India 2020), and accept international online degrees for Indian students is a clear indication of this.

Let us look at Indian online education. This are is expected to jump from $247 million in 2016 to around $1.96 billion by 2021 (Khaitan 2017). This is an annual growth rate of 52%. By the end of 2021, participating users will rise from 1.6 million in 2016 to around

9.6 million in various online learning courses. Indians are the second-largest consumers of free massive open online courses (MOOCs) like Coursera. Government initiatives such as E-Basta, SWAYAM, E-Pathshaala, and Rashtriya Madhyamik Shiksha Abhiyaan (RMSA), etc., facilitate online education (Opel 2016).

The online education movement has been brewing in India for some time, with brisk global technological advancements in the background. It has been held back by conservatism, academic leadership, outdated rules, and lack of understanding. Unfortunately, it took a crisis such as the one we are facing now to bring this concern to the forefront. Universities and organizations are struggling in the current situation to find answers to their own created problems. In comparison, many of the world's leading colleges have moved smoothly to online learning. Most students have returned to their homes without any interruption and are studying online. The institutions have also suggested that assessments and examinations should be carried out online. That demonstrates progressive thought.

Progressive institutions of education face the challenge head on and set compelling examples of compassionate leadership. Pearl Academy, the country's leading design school, and Dehradun-based Petroleum and Energy Sciences University (UPES), plus a few other Indian institutions, are succeeding in integrating online learning. What made the difference for these institutions? They understood the need well ahead of most and made sure they made the best investments in technology, faculty training, and students. Myths surrounding online learning have been eliminated, high-quality content has been developed, and collaborations have been formed with global players such as Coursera to ensure a top-notch student practice. UPES and Pearl students have access to nearly 3,600 courses from top universities worldwide, such as Brown, Duke, Michigan, Insead, NYU. Both institutions have invested in Blackboard, which is the gold standard of online learning, rather than going for free off-the-shelf learning systems. Such efforts have paid off, and these two organizations operate smoothly while many today fail.

With government funding, this learning can be repeated in many institutions in India. This involves defining essential criteria in online learning such as strategic planning, outlining student and faculty goals, maintaining digital equilibrium, developing regular flexible schedules for students and staff, preparing and delivering classes, assignments, and assessments. Everything India can do!

9.5 Barriers to Online Education in India

The obstacles facing people in online education in India are numerous. Some of those issues that need to be overcome are (Pal and Chahal 2020):

1. **Resistance to change**: People are generally resistant to change, even though things are superior to what they had before. They may not believe that an online education would be as successful as engaging with a teacher face-to-face. It is a fact that online learning will generate massive change within the educational system, and some resistance can be expected.
2. **Learners' motivation**: Classes running in seminar form and discussions have the benefit of transparency and overview. That is one of online learning's biggest challenges. Additionally, students may dislike using their own time to do the

coursework instead of enjoying the "vacation." To achieve these goals, how do we keep our students motivated, and how can we make our students enjoy their learning experience?

3. **Teachers'/learners' technological skills**: Teachers' and students' lack of familiarity with technology is one of the significant challenges of online learning, as most of the Indian population live in villages and rural areas. The implementation of online learning will rely on the computer literacy of the people who use it. Learners' willingness to access and engage with the course content defines the value they can get out of the program.
4. **Lack of adequate training**: Lack of qualified teachers, specifically trained in the production of content tailored to online education, is a significant impediment to the development of online educational content in India. Research studies have identified many barriers and obstacles faced by teachers in developing content for online learning. These include lack of access to services, insufficient training opportunities, lack of trust, lack of time, technological challenges, weak administrative support, restricted institutional and educational priorities in this area, failure to project and finance online learning costs adequately.
5. **Language barriers**: A significant proportion of world market-developed educational software is in English. The bulk of material available online is in English. India is a multi-lingual nation, and rural areas make up a vast majority of the population. Consequently, some students who are unable to speak English are struggling with the language content available. Therefore, it is the responsibility of programming professionals, educators, administrators, language content developers, and content disseminators to sit together and offer learners who only know Indian languages a viable platform and standard solution.
6. **Resource-related problems and broadband**: High-speed internet and reliable power supply are the biggest problems in India's rural areas. Most students are not able to pay high internet fees, even though the internet is available, and slow or intermittent access undermines the very nature and effect of learning online.
7. **Motivation**: Some students need an incentive to enter college. Students can procrastinate in the case of self-paced online programs. In online education, the dropout rate could be very high. Self-discipline is needed if the assignments are to be completed and submitted on time. Students who have difficulties working independently in an online program can struggle to complete assignments and meet deadlines.

India has several barriers to address before providing access to emerging technology like online learning to its entire population. Significant parts of the population live in poverty, and many are incapable of coping with technology. Service provision around the world only helps those who can afford it. However, that is no excuse for the country to give up on online learning. The future looks bright for online learning in India despite all the obstacles. The private sector and the public sector are working hard to establish content standards for the education industry, including higher education, universities, vocational education, professional training, and lifelong learning. Online learning can deliver education to a vast population if it is used effectively.

9.6 Online Education Is Becoming Necessary – Why?

The following will have a considerable effect in the future on making online education accessible (Opel 2016).

- India has around 3.5 million students in higher education, and 900 universities meet their needs. In 2030, we will have about 14 million students, a 4-fold increase. Since we need to train four times the number of colleges, universities, and teachers – are we ready? Would we be able to without playing a part in online learning?
- Millennial learners behave differently in the way they absorb and understand. They are technology-friendly. Let us admit that, let them learn by the method they want and not push our teaching methods.
- India has the potential to face a likely shortage of 250 million industry-wide specialists (FICCI/EY 2018) by 2022.
- Convergence in the e-learning needs of higher education and corporates: a growing number of businesses accept MOOC at the cost of proprietary content for internal learning.

9.7 Factors Pushing India's Online Education

Today, India is among the top educational destinations in the world. It is known for its innovation and high quality, with some of the finest colleges and universities. Such state-of-the-art technologies are being used to grow this sector further while at the same time attracting the interest of entrepreneurs, governments, corporates, and venture capitalists. Here are the factors enabling online education to grow (Ratrey 2017).

1. **Personalized and adaptive learning**: Together, learning tools, apps, and digital devices build endless distinct ways to transform education. In this form, every student's academic strengths, abilities, aptitude, shortcomings, and learning speed are reviewed. Specific mobile and secure apps are developed to educate students, support them in practicing their learning, take up assignments, and handle schedules. Schools are also providing their students with digital tools such as desktops, laptops, and tablets. These tools help teachers teach while also allowing them to understand how students learn and develop their learning process.
2. **Two-way conversations in e-learning**: Students cannot get the personalized attention they need due to time constraints in the conventional classroom setting. The one-on-one learning history in digital media, on the other hand, is simply video learning and talking to an expert. The New LMS (Learning Management System) will extend the trend of two-way student-professional interaction. Most importantly, it will allow students to monitor their progress in course work, identify areas for enhancement, and suggest ways to optimize them. With the support of 'Big Data,' experts in the provided information will collect feedback from students. With this alone, they'll be able to improvise and enhance their offerings in new ways to further benefit students.

3. **Mobile-based learning**: People have taken up mobile learning over the past few years, and slowly assimilated it into their lives. This allows students to easily access educational content through various digital platforms such as tablets, smartphones, desktops, and laptops. India's user base of smartphones is expected to grow in both rural and urban areas. Throughout subsequent years, users will gain significant access to most of their educative content by internet-enabled smartphones. Most educational content will be wholly targeted to mobile devices, including online courses.
4. **Video-based learning**: Video learning always attracts students as it resembles the conventional teaching style of the classroom. Students usually watch video lectures as a method of homework and discuss them in the next session. This trend has had a significant improvement in results over the years, with grade increases. Video lectures enable students to research the subject syllabus at their own pace and contribute time to engage with classmates. This will continue to be a trend for students to access relevant and engaging content in the future, which is useful both for formal training and for better success. Mobile video-based learning has increased internet traffic in recent times.
5. **Open educational services**: Free digital education platforms are commonly used in distance learning courses. They comprise material that is freely available for research, study, and teaching objectives. Teachers are allowed to review and disseminate material freely amongst students, which helps them gain access to complete study material that would be otherwise be limited. It also encourages a flexible environment where teachers can customize instructional material for classes to an individual or in the classroom. The aforementioned refers to traditional curricular subjects, such as math, science, fine arts, language, and business.
6. **Use of VR and AR for learning**: In the technology world, augmented reality and virtual reality are now buzzwords. The e-learning methodology has an enormous effect on the quality with which it accommodates learners and evaluates success. VR helps learners to communicate directly with study material using e-learning tools on mobile devices. That keeps their commitment level high and motivates them to learn more and for longer. AR facilitates trainers and teachers in performing tasks they previously have not, or could not, in a safe environment.

9.8 Cloud Computing Enabling Online Learning

Cloud computing technology is making the delivery of education services to students easier. Alongside nearly anyone's ability to use education through laptops and internet connections, online education can flourish internationally through learning technology interoperability.

Cloud learning has streamlined and enabled education-as-a-service in many ways. The web is easily accessible via e-learning and distance learning content, and rarely requires the installation of any customer-side software. Easily consumable online learning services are available at low costs, subscription fees are paid, and e-learning platforms for state schools generally give millions of students free access.

Cloud computing technology offers a variety of key benefits to the student. Scalability and accessibility are two significant advantages. A student's online application that integrates video streams provided by instructors, including downloadable learning materials and whiteboards, is relatively simple to develop. However, when you add scale, designing such a solution becomes more complicated.

Millions of institutions have already started their students' cloud education, and the technology is available to cloud services providers to do so. Due to the many concurrent links between student devices and the learning content, network traffic and server load's influx can significantly strain the e-learning infrastructure.

The scalability, applications, and server workloads can be extended and expanded when appropriate if cloud technology handles this risk. Almost unlimited CPU cycles and memory can be available, and the network layer can spread heavy workloads to different endpoints, usually a cloud load balancer.

In practical terms, this ensures that tens of thousands of students can stream content, and discuss and submit work seamlessly. Accessibility is essential since every student has access from a different point of view to the learning platform. The relation must be stable, protected, and encrypted in transit in many cases. The huge cloud infrastructure can absorb this intensive workload on-demand.

The cloud tackles many other technical problems that online learning introduces. One of these challenges is to ensure the security, privacy, and confidentiality of the students registered. Several cloud service providers carry out a significant audit and certification of data safeguards. In overloading the infrastructure, cloud computing provides high availability, error tolerance, and instant recovery.

9.9 Success Stories

The following are the various teaching and learning practices adopted by institutions in India during COVID-19.

1. **VIT Online Learning (VITOL) Institute – asynchronous courses:** A total of 20,202 students from all VIT campuses with over 43,000 registrations offered VITOL 22 asynchronous mode courses via vitol.ac. on the Open Edx platform. Intro-to-Bio-Inspired Design and 21 other student courses were included. Students receive additional courses to continue productive participation during the pandemic and to add value to their degree. The platform included provisions for online programming workshops with MCQs and assignments for students. The courses were offered in asynchronous mode, so students could easily learn.
2. **Strategies for online learning at University of Agricultural Sciences, Raichur:** A team of teachers engaged in the workshop on 31 March 2020, when the Association of Indian Universities revealed the online workshop on "Faculty learning: How to know and plan for the successful transformation of your curriculum." All the teachers attending this workshop met with the university's officials on 3 April 2020 and developed strategies to conduct online classes, participate, and evaluate online learning. A committee was formed on 4 April 2020 to pursue online study courses at the university level. It has teaching nodals from all four universities and is led by a senior faculty. The priority of the committee is:
   - Online lesson preparation and distribution
   - Student engagement online through apps like Zoom and WhatsApp (wherever connectivity problems are there)

- Online learning tools, such as laptops and smartphones
- Weekly online learning review across campuses
- Teaching faculty and students grappling with online class delivery

Students were told to download the Zoom software on laptops and smartphones, and by the evening of 4 April 2020, over 90 percent of students were able to access the courses online. The teachers started taking online courses as per the daily classes' timetable.

3. **Shreemati Nathibai Damodar Thackersey Women's University, Mumbai:** Teachers have taken online training courses to complete the curriculum, clarify issues, address conflicts, engage in the practice, and perform internal projects/ tasks. For such communications, WhatsApp and emails are commonly used. To address forum events, submissions, and online questionnaires, faculty used LMSs such as Moodle, Edmodo, Google Classrooms, and Canvas. Zoom, Skype, WizIQ, BigBluebutton, Google Hangout, and DuoPair were used for synchronous sessions. Screencasts and podcasts were conducted related by faculty. Teachers have used Google forms, Socrative quizzes, and simulation resources like Buble.us, ezTalk, Kutuki, Open Matlab, and Online Octave LTspice. Services like SWAYAM, NMEICT, and ePG-Pathashal were also used.
4. **Sharda University, Greater Noida:** This university has successfully ensured the timely completion of the curriculum without interruption, offering 150 programs for over 12,000 students from India and abroad across its 14 schools. Faculty has duly completed the courses scheduled from 20 March 2020 (lockdown start) to 2 April 2020. Students also received digital lectures/studies. Quizzes and assignments involving the students were also carried out frequently and in tandem with online classes. The students were well engaged in online mentorship of slow/advanced students by their respective instructors. They also had access to old question banks in preparation for examinations. The University Grants Commission directions also provided links to the Swayam Prabha platform for students with their topic resources. The university provided free tele-counseling services through competent and professional psychologists/counselors to ensure students' mental well-being (and that of staff and parents).

   The teaching-learning process with PeopleSoft, V-Attendance, TED Monitoring Platform, LMS, and a smart ERP system started by Sharda Tech was made easier through a robust Information and Communication Technology (ICT) research environment. iCloud Examination Management System, online timetable, attendance, assignments, lecture materials, and so on, were successful with its high-end software. At this time of crisis, online e-resources of the university with platforms such as J-STOR and renowned journals were indiscriminately needed to ensure unimpeded study work for students and the faculty. Also, students were advised to download the COVID-19 knowledge AarogyaSetu App.
5. **O. P. Jindal Global University, Sonepat:** Within one week of the official announcement of a national emergency lockdown in India, JGU switched to online classrooms. In close cooperation with Microsoft India, the IT department at JGU used MS Teams as an online classroom platform. Since then, JGU has delivered more than 400 courses, with over 5,000 JGU students in attendance. A customer relationship management and an IT task force offered sufficient support for groups' continuity. Further facilities provided residential faculty members with additional bandwidth and continuous power supplies for critical devices. About 8,500 online classes took part in this program. JGU was first to receive the "E-Learning Excellence

for Academic Digitisation (E-LEAD) Certificate" of the prestigious QS IGAUGE e-learning excellence following the full audit of Quacquarelli Symonds (QS).

6. **Jagan Nath University, Jhajjar:** The university has implemented a multi-pronged approach to minimize coronavirus's impact on educational delivery, including online courses, student webinars, interactive academic tools, student assignments, online evaluation assessments, student feedback systems, and online end-of-term exams. Open applications such as Zoom, Google Meet, Goggle Classroom, Microsoft Teams, and so on, were used in the faculty and regularly in classes according to the timetable. Since the semester has been extended, some professors have also conducted revision lessons to ensure student preparation is adequate. Each department of the university arranged an external participant, at least one webinar on emerging discipline issues. Each teacher shared the material in conjunction with the curriculum. The students have submitted online assignments and participated in internal assessment exercises. Feedback on the delivery of content and general online training experiences were collected at the end of the semester. Though students gave positive feedback on curricula coverage, they also shared experiences accessing digital infrastructure and technology.

   The use of online technology and transitioning to online lessons highlighted some of the issues facing the majority of institutions during COVID-19. These issues include internet connectivity, internet speed and connections, and the lack of online learning equipment. Many teachers present psychological reluctance, and not all staff have been trained to work online. Institutions must improve digital technologies, train staff in online education, and have sufficient learning content to solve all of these problems. Student digital support systems must also be improved. Jagan Nath University has taken steps to promote successful teaching processes.

7. **IMS Unison University, Dehradun:** IMS Unison University continuously invests in technology and services to ensure students can access high-quality education. In these testing pandemic times, online learning has become a savior. Due to impromptu closing, these online learning platforms are a blessing in disguise. During the lockdown, the university made considerable efforts to effectively conduct online classes via G-Suite. Online semester and trimester end-of-term assessments for all programs were performed by Artificial Intelligence-based Proctored Software.

   Most faculty members were unsure how to run online courses during the initial lockdown days in March 2020. Online learning was still unclear to students. Such obstacles, however, can offer hidden opportunities. Faculty members unfamiliar with online delivery have since developed in-house training programs and developed their online teaching skills. The key to successful education is nothing more than good instruction. The university implemented two campus training programs with the university's lockdown on 25 March 2020 for all members on Google G-suite and, later, on Microsoft Teams. All students were provided with similar services online.

   Furthermore, for each of the programs, three to five mock tests were done to reduce student anxiety over online proctor testing. A weekly assessment, case analyses, and assignments were carried out to ensure full participation and study attendance. In Excel, a comprehensive Management Information System (MIS) was also created and regularly reported to faculty members, and corrections were made based on MIS from time to time. Individual students were approached and thus informed.

   Online courses offered full monitoring of student education and freedom of learning during COVID-19 at their own pace. The critical development ensured that COVID anxiety did not leave any room for idle ruminations by the initial class schedule and concentrated on the learning process. Parents were also helped, without breaking lockdown, by seeing academic delivery directly. Teachers found that not all courses are appropriate to deliver online. For different subjects, different efforts and approaches are needed.

The classes took place through an online platform using Google Classroom and Google Meet. The remaining classes after lockdown have taken place on Microsoft Teams. It made teaching without disruption easier for faculty members. Google Classroom, Google Meet, and MS Teams later became viable platforms for both students and instructors to learn online.

Students from different regions, including remote villages and hilly regions, were faced with bandwidth challenges in the early days. By harmonizing technological facilities, the university made every attempt to enhance student lives. As part of the courses' ongoing assessment process, students received weekly online graded tasks and quizzes.

This "forced" online learning has its problems behind the proactive decisions! While learning continues, it cannot replicate the teacher–student relation and peer-to-peer learning in a face-to-face classroom. There are technological solutions, but the implied physical classroom instruction cannot be supplanted. Students having old technology will have difficulty maintaining their education. For many of the students scattered across the country, this is not easy. Online learning is a challenge for students unfamiliar with it or students with low revenues, housing problems and food poverty, lack of internet and wi-fi access, and lack of access to laptops/desktops.

8. **ICFAI University, Jharkhand, Ranchi:** The Vice-Chancellor had a brainstorming session with the instructors' team on issues facing the university when the lockdown was declared and how to continue with students throughout the middle of the semester. The Digital LMS was uniformly implemented in management, engineering, IT, and law after exploring various options. In the space of ten days after lockdown, the university started the "Swaadhyay," digital learning platform, to allow students to continue their studies while at home. The university quickly trained its faculty members and encouraged them to upload various digital research materials into Swaadhyay, such as videos, video lectures, PowerPoint presentations, quizzes, assignments, case studies, and so on. Students were pleased to obtain the material for all the course programs at their convenience.

   In a student survey, it was noted that 56 percent of students accessed it via smartphones and the rest via laptops and desktop computers. Survey results showed that 83 percent of students studied using Swaadhyay for 2–3 hours a day, and 73 percent thought it was easy to use. Although 53 percent of students liked PPTs, 33 percent liked teachers' videos and video lectures. When asked about the benefits of Swaadhyay, 35 percent listed ease, while 27 percent liked the facility to go through the study material repeatedly; students also liked the features of self-testing and additional study material such as e-books and articles. The biggest challenge facing 66 percent of students was internet latency. In short, the ease of use and the advantages motivated the students to adopt the new learning platform, Swaadhyay.

9. **Indian Institute of Teacher Education, Gandhinagar:** The Indian Institute of Teacher Education (IITE) has an outline, role, and objectives that support its place in academia and society, exclusively devoted to teacher education and training. During the COVID-19 outbreak, the university approach was to seek and identify the best possible opportunities for advancement to retain normality for routine

teaching and evaluation of work, to find new ways to keep students and society in general in contact, and to maintain social distance and take all other appropriate precautions, as suggested by the guidelines of the Central and State Government.

Though COVID-19 emerged as a danger at its early diagnosis in India, a local BISAG facility based in Gandhinagar reported lectures for over seven different subjects. Curriculum transaction has been ensured via television channels Vande-Gujarat-I and Jio TV. The remaining teaching was successfully conducted via online platforms, including Zoom, Google Classroom, and other convenient facilities for students and parents.

Five separate IITE centers have made a successful effort, through webinars, seminars, workshops, and creative events, to achieve a versatile dialogue in different disciplines. As an institute dedicated to teacher education, the university ensured its position to deliver through the new normal transaction process. Society members, student societies, and academic fraternities, in general, were invited to these attempts. IITE's meticulous scholarly discussions have been endorsed and agreed as healthy and promoting practices by senior researchers, prominent academics, and even the State Department of Education.

10. **Anantha Lakshmi Institute of Technology & Sciences, Ananthapuram:** As per the registrar's directions, JNTUA dated 19 March 2020, the physical classwork has been suspended; the classwork was resumed using online mode using Zoom for all the B.Tech, MBA, and M.Tech students. Awareness programs on coronavirus were conducted, and quiz competitions on COVID-19 were also held to raise awareness for students and parents and take preventive measures duly following the bulletin updates from the respective Government of India organizations.

    Revision of the syllabus was also carried out, and the faculty conducted assignments and tests to prepare students for the semester exams. Theory and laboratory classes were conducted using virtual labs; YouTube videos, and other online modes. Five periods daily were engaged as per the guidelines from JNTUA, and attendance was monitored using Google form and uploaded to the JNTUA Examination Management System portal. Students were encouraged to do online courses and participate in various online webinars held during the COVID-19 pandemic. Department-wise online seminars/workshops/webinars were conducted on subject-related topics and recent advancements in technology. The faculty also encouraged participating in online workshops on subject-related topics and National Assessment and Accreditation Council (NAAC); National Board of Accreditation (NBA) processes held by various institutes and organizations. Each department has conducted faculty development programs duly inviting subject experts as resource persons and associations with organizations like IITB spoken tutorial. Final B.Tech and MBA project work and viva voce exams were conducted using the online mode as per the JNTUA instructions and end-of-term semester exams were conducted duly following COVID-19 guidelines during September 2020.

9.10 Key Practices for Successful Online Learning

The International Society for Technology in Education (ISTE) professional learning network members were hard at work, defining key activities during outbreaks for effective online learning (Snelling and Fingal 2020). Most of them are listed here.

1. **Ensure digital equity**: The first and prominent challenge in online learning is to ensure digital equity-capital. Suppose your institution does not have devices for everybody to take home, ask teachers and families in advance to find out who would need devices and bandwidth. Institutions need to ascertain how to rent or buy wi-fi hotspots for teachers or students without wi-fi at home and then plan to distribute the devices and hotspots. If you have been warned of an impending closure, universities will give home devices and hotspots to students until closing. If a cessation occurs abruptly, a pickup location and time has to be planned, and for those who cannot pick up, arrange for distribution.
2. **Practice**: Institutions are already providing day-to-day remote learning and operating through home access and computer issues. Take this as an opportunity, though, if your business has not laid the groundwork. Teachers who previously did not use standard LMSs need to focus now so that after a sudden shutdown, there would be no interruptions. In the event of a closure, teaches should educate themselves and their students on the technologies and resources they may need to use for growth. Train in the classroom, and then send students to practice using the equipment from home.
3. **Providing clear expectations for staff and parents**: Contact among administrators, employees, students, and parents is also more critical during a closure. In an online environment, everyone's anxiety is high, and channels of communication need to be frequent, reliable, and succinct. Prepare a large-picture correspondence FAQ outlining all the details of how the school will function so that during the closing, all workers and parents are on the same page. In addition to publishing and circulating FAQs, organizations can set up community-wide texting to connect quickly and then tell people to send follow-up emails or website updates wherever they are. First, build a step-by-step guide to accessing and using tools and curricula for online learning. Make sure to present this information in different formats such as text and video and, include screenshots and screencasting tutorials. Suggest families ensure that students are aware of their mobile sign-in and passwords. Provide extra technical resources and ensure that parents and teachers know how to seek assistance.
4. **Take time to schedule**: If the team can teach online before a shutdown happens, spend some time, maybe a day or two, planning before arranging students' online learning. In the long run, the short delay at the beginning will pay off for online lessons. Especially if a closure is unexpected and allows little time for planning until institutions are closed, it is prudent to plan before the online lessons begin.
5. **Ensure you have access to everything**: Ensure you have access from home to anything you need if you cannot go back to the institution and consider transferring your files into the cloud.
6. **Set up regular schedules**: It should be clear when creating daily schedules when teachers and students signed on. If not, make changes and be flexible. To maintain a daily schedule, you can do the following.
   - Take breaks periodically.
   - Make time for exercise.
   - Ensure a daily sleep routine.
   - Restrict distractions where possible (for example, turning off social media notifications).
   - Allow room for socialization.
   - Set daily and weekly goals.

7. **Provide robust learning**: The key concepts suggested by ISTE:
   - Split the learning into small parts.
   - Be transparent on expectations of online participation.
   - Implement instant and regular feedback through online knowledge assessments, commenting on collaborative documents, and conversing to keep students engaged and moving on.
   - Provide virtual meetings, video tutorials, and live chats for maintaining a link between people.
8. **Plan independent learning**: It is essential to plan learning that does not entail much help from parents who may be overwhelmed beforehand. It is also important to advise parents about how they should support their children in an online learning environment.
9. **Addressing the emotional cost**: It is just as essential to check in on anxiety levels as it is to check on academic progress. Consult with students and colleagues, especially those who are less familiar with digital services, to see if they need help or to talk to someone. Employ the same dress code that is used for school attendance.
10. **Select and stick to the correct tools**: A wide variety of development resources are available for support, many of them free. Seek not to use them all, with so much out there. Instead, restrict the number of tools, devices, and websites so as not to overwhelm students and their parents. Consider creating images rather than text for instructions. Try to keep short, quick, and straightforward instructions online. Online learning is also an excellent way of updating digital etiquette and incorporating digital citizenship into shared online activities.

9.11 Conclusion

Now is the time to read online. Coronavirus has created a rare ability to force deeply impactful changes. Educational institutions that still oppose this transition are less likely to expand. A radical change in attitude, policy, and conviction is required. In every area of our life, we have embraced technology, and it has had a profound impact. Our digital inhabitants are also able to immerse themselves in the conflict of online learning. It is time for online education to shift beliefs and misconceptions. The government will take note and advance in making an online education policy that promotes entry, concentrates on efficiency, and enables the country to hit a GER in the high seventies that will transform the country permanently. Coronavirus may remain the catalyst, but it does not end the openness to online learning and teaching. To make a difference, the discussion must start with concrete action at the bottom. An educated society is a free society, and it is time we gave India wings, "Wings of technical transition."

9.12 Implications of the Study

The pandemic COVID-19 shows how vital online learning resources are for teachers, students, and parents. Few expected that the closed schools and colleges all over the world would result in chaos. Cloud technology has brought a considerable change to many students' lives, providing an on-demand education platform for everyone.

9.13 Limitations and Directions for Future Research

Considering online education from the perspective of only one country, i.e., India, is the major limitation of this study. Further studies are planned to cover more geographic regions.

References

Agrawal, P. 2015. "Massive Open Online Courses: EdX.org, Coursera.com and NPTEL, A Comparative Study Based on Usage Statistics and Features with Special Reference to India." *10th International CABLIBER* 390–402.

AI TechPark. 2020. "The rise of AI-powered E-learning in 2020: How the education sector is responding to COVID-19? How E-learning will evolve." https://ai-techpark.com/the-rise-of-ai-powered-e-learning-in-2020. Accessed 30 October 2020.

BBC. 2020. "Coronavirus: Denmark lets young children return to school." *BBC*. www.bbc.com/news/amp/world-europe-52291326. Accessed 20 April 2020.

Bicker L. 2020. "Coronavirus: How South Korea is teaching empty classrooms." *BBC News*. www.bbc.com/news/world-asia-52230371. Accessed 20 April 2020.

British Lyceum. 2020. "Teach from home – change lives." https://britishlyceum.com/problem/defination/covid/education. Accessed 18 June 2020.

Cheney, G., Ruzzi, B., and Muralidharan, K. 2005. "A profile of the Indian education system." *National Centre on Education and the Economy* 29. www.teindia.nic.in/files/articles/indian_education_sysytem_by_karthik_murlidharan.pdf. Accessed 30 April 2020.

FICCI. (2018). Future of jobs in India. In *FICCI: Vol. I.* www.ey.com/Publication/vwLUAssets/ey-future-of-jobs-in-india/$FILE/ey-future-of-jobs-in-india.pdf. Accessed 8 September 2020.

Gokulnath, D. 2020. "BYJU'S: World's most highly valued ed-tech and digital learning company." www.orfonline.org/expert-speak/byju-world-most-highly-valued-ed-tech-digital-learning-company. Accessed 15 November 2020.

Hiranandani, N. 2020. "Role of regulating authorities for higher education institutions." *BW Education*. http://bweducation.businessworld.in/article/Role-Of-Regulating-Authorities-For-Higher-Education-Institutions/16-11-2020-343150. Accessed 20 November 2020.

Huang, Z. 2020. "ByteDance to launch Google-like work tools during outbreak." *Bloombedrg*. www.bloombergquint.com/business/bytedance-plans-google-like-office-tools-as-virus-spikes-demand. Accessed 20 March 2020.

Khaitan, A. 2017. "A study by KPMG in India and Google." May.

Li, C., and Lalani, F. 2020a. "Students retain more in online classrooms, shows data." https://theprint.in/india/education/students-retain-more-in-online-classrooms-shows-data/412669. Accessed 10 May 2020.

Li, C., and Lalani, F. 2020b. "The COVID-19 pandemic has changed education forever. This is how." *World Economic Forum*. www.weforum.org/agenda/2020/04/coronavirus-education-global-covid19-online-digital-learning. Accessed 10 May 2020.

McIntyre, C. 2018. "MOOC platform league table | MoocLab – connecting people to online learning." 1–2. www.mooclab.club/pages/mooc_league_table. Accessed 10 May 2020.

MHRD. 2019. "All India Survey on Higher Education." 58 (1): 73–96.

Mittal, P., Pani, S. R. D., and Thakur, Y. 2020. "Protecting academic interest of students during COVID-19 pandemic sharing best practices." https://en.unesco.org/news/290-million-students-out-school-due-covid-19-unesco-releases-first-global-numbers-and-mobilizes. Accessed 5 May 2020.

Opel, A. 2016. "Online education in time of corona and beyond." *The Pioneer*. www.dailypioneer.com/2020/state-editions/online-education-in-time-of-corona-and-beyond.html. Accessed 7 June 2020.

Pal, B., and Chahal, S. 2020. "Challenges and opportunities for online education in India".

Pandey, D. 2020. "Covid-19 lockdown: an opportunity to explore new frontiers for Online-training." *Electronic Journal of Social & Strategic Studies* 01 (01): 53–66. https://doi.org/10.47362/ejsss.2020.1104. Accessed 1 October 2020.

PBS SOCAL. 2020. "Los Angeles Unified announces school closures as partnership with PBS SoCal and KCET plans to provide educational content to students." www.pbssocal.org/press/los-angeles-unified-partnership-pbs-socal-kcet-plans-provide-educational-content-students. Accessed 12 July 2020.

Press Trust of India. 2020. "Budget 2020: Online degree courses to students from weaker sections." https://yourstory.com/2020/02/budget-2020-online-degree-courses-weaker-sections. Accessed 10 February 2020.

Ratrey, R. 2017. "6 technology trends that pushing up digital education in India." *India Today Web Desk*. www.indiatoday.in/education-today/featurephilia/story/digital-education-1027965-2017-08-08. Accesses 10 August 2020.

Snelling, J., and Fingal, D. 2020. "10 Strategies for online learning during a coronavirus outbreak." *Deas, Content and Resources for Leading-Edge Educators*. www.iste.org/explore/10-strategies-online-learning-during-coronavirus-outbreak. Accessed 20 March 2020.

Staff, R. co. 2020. "Introduction to Massive Online Open Courses." January Issue: 7–9.

Tatsuoka, M. M. 2014. "Educational statistics." *Wiley StatsRef: Statistics Reference Online*. https://doi.org/10.1002/9781118445112.stat00043. Accessed 13 April 2020.

Teräs, M., Suoranta, J., Teräs, H., and Curcher, M. 2020. "Post-covid-19 education and education technology 'solutionism': a seller's market." *Postdigital Science and Education* 2 (3): 863–878. https://doi.org/10.1007/s42438-020-00164-x. Accessed 17 July 2020.

UNESCO. 2020. "290 million students out of school due to COVID-19: UNESCO releases first global numbers and mobilizes response." https://en.unesco.org/news/290-million-students-out-school-due-covid-19-unesco-releases-first-global-numbers-and-mobilizes. Accessed 5 May 2020.

Unicef. 2020. "COVID-19 and children." *Unicef Data*. https://doi.org/10.18093/0869-0189-2020-30-5-609-628. Accessed 5 August 2020.

Annexure-A: Notable MOOCs Comparisons

Some of the notable MOOCs providers that offer courses in the English language are compared in Table 9.1 on five parameters (McIntyre 2018; Staff 2020; Agrawal 2015).

- **The openness of content**: Whether the MOOC provides access to content on a free or payment basis.
- **Course diversity**: Whether the MOOC offers courses that belong to multiple domains or only to limited domains.
- **Course type**: Whether the MOOC offers courses on a predefined schedule or on-demand basis.
- **Type of certificate**: Whether the MOOC offers verified/non-verified certificates on a free or payment basis.
- **Institution credits**: Whether there is the opportunity to transfer the learners' credits into their organization/institution.

A seven-column table (Table 9.1) provides a comparison between notable MOOCs.

TABLE 9.1
Notable MOOCs Comparisons

S. No.	Platform/ Provider	Openness of Content (Free/Paid)	Course Diversity (Varied/ Limited)	Course Type (Scheduled/ On-Demand)	Type of Certificate (Verified/Non-Verified)	Institution Credits (Yes/No)
1	Open2Study	Free	Varied	Scheduled	Non-Verified (Free)	No
2	OpenLearning	Free	Varied	Both	Verified (Free & Paid)	CPD
3	CNMOOC	Free	Varied	Both	Verified (Free)	Yes
4	FUN-MOOC	Free	Varied	Scheduled	Non-Verified (Free) & Verified (Paid)	ECTS
5	OpenClassrooms	Both	Limited	On-Demand	Non-Verified (Paid)	CPD
6	Iversity	Both	Varied	Both	Verified (Paid)	ECTS
7	OpenHPI	Free	Limited	Both	Non-Verified (Free)	No
8	OpenSAP	Free	Limited	Both	Non-Verified (Free)	No
9	Open Course World	Free	Limited	On-Demand	Verified (Paid)	No
10	NPTEL	Free	Varied	Both	Certification Exam (paid)	Yes
11	SWAYAM	Free	Varied	Both	Certification Exam (paid)	Yes
12	Polimi OPEN KNOWLEDGE	Both	Varied	Scheduled	Non-Verified (Free)	No
13	OpenLearning	Free	Varied	Scheduled	Non-Verified (Free)	No
14	K-MOOC	Free	Varied	Scheduled	Verified (Free)	Yes

15	Futurelearn	Both	Varied	Scheduled	Non-Verified & Verified (Paid)	Yes
16	Canvas Network	Free	Varied	Both	Non-Verified (Free)	No
17	Cognitive Class	Free	Limited	On-Demand	Non-Verified & Verified Badges (Free)	No
18	Coursera	Both	Varied	On-Demand	Verified (Paid)	Yes
19	EdX	Both	Varied	Both	Verified (Paid)	Yes
20	Janux	Both	Varied	Both	No	Yes
21	Saylor Academy	Free	Varied	On-Demand	Non-Verified (Free)	Yes
22	Stanford Lagunita	Free	Varied	Both	Non-Verified (Free)	No
23	Udacity	Both	Limited	On-Demand	Verified (Paid)	No
24	MongoDB University	Free	Limited	Scheduled	Non-Verified (Free)	No

Annexure-B: Protecting Academic Interest of Students During COVID-19 Pandemic – Best Practices

The recent coronavirus pandemic swept through the international higher education system. Millions of students were isolated, having to remain in their homes for their own protection. Universities and their students were forced to go online for their education. However, everybody knew that COVID-19 was expected to become a watershed for higher education, leading to new higher education delivery models. We are going to change to a new university model. In India, educational institutions are closed until further notice. Many universities have already set their year plans.

Global economic paralysis is felt in almost all facets of existence. Those hardest hit by the virus are students and workers confined to their homes, and the educational transaction among them is technology-dependent. It is a matter of "division and complexity" for different higher education institutions to adopt and adapt technology. Some organizations do not have enough bandwidth access, computers, and so on, for online education. Universities have online systems, but they tend to fail under the weight of demands, causing instability and unpredictability. India's higher education system is filled with many types of diversities and extremes – geographical, economic, and social. Although universities in India try their best to tackle the situation very carefully, they are still too slow.

Life provides opportunities to discover deeper forces within ourselves. Disturbances can be terrible in the beginning but later turn out to be beneficial. We saw that many disruptors could change history. This is because we must shape the future by drawing lessons from the benefits and drawbacks of disruption. Institutions need to act as virtual institutions that enroll, teach, review, and publish outcomes online. We can also have ICT sports. Many possibilities exist and should be explored with caution.

So a seven-pronged strategy is proposed to address students' interests during the COVID-19 pandemic and to secure their academic interests. A healthy relationship should also be maintained with students and society. Here are the measures involved (Mittal et al. 2020).

1. **Strengthening infrastructure:** This requires:
   - **Information technology (IT) equipment:** The revolution introduced by COVID-19 may set many new standards and trends worldwide. Virtual education can become a modern form of teaching. To make a smooth, simple, and comfortable e-governance, management, assessment, and evaluation process, it is essential to build an IT environment with enough bandwidth, wi-fi, and connectivity to make online learning easy and comfortable.
   - **Physical infrastructure:** Following social distancing, which is an essential protective step that both students and universities must take once campuses are physically accessible, a new look may be needed in several areas. Changes in physical distance may be required in classroom architecture in colleges, universities, and schools. New desks, new chairs might need to be installed. Extra spaces and furniture must be created to enable students' physical distance – particularly in familiar places such as classrooms, hostels, libraries, mess, recreational activities, toilets – including sanitization facilities, distribution of masks, and maintenance of hygiene.
   - **Digital infrastructure:** To complete the whole syllabus, online education will not be appropriate. A blended learning approach or flipped classroom model integrating Open Education Tools (OERs), MOOCs, and so on, with online content would be involved in such a scenario. To help them begin the new academic session without hiccups, universities need to pre-identify OERs and provide connections to students in advance.
2. **Capacity building of teachers:** There is highly professional and scientific online instruction. It is not the same as face-to-face training in the classroom. Using technology and platforms needs various teaching skills and orientation. Teachers need detailed theory and knowledge of online teaching. The number of teachers who are qualified to teach online is almost negligible in India. It is unprofessional and unethical to force all teachers to teach online without

training. Therefore, before permanently accepting online education, institutions need to provide teacher training. Many institutions provide advanced training for teachers to teach online and build online tools for students.

3. **Review various online platforms available:** There is now a wide range of online teaching-learning sites, evaluation and assessments, and numerous other activities available. Therefore, each university should determine the available platforms' suitability for their functions and choose the most suitable and cost-effective ones. This process needs to be carried out well in advance so that both teachers and students are aware of open university platforms when the academic session starts.
4. **Assessment and evaluation:** The assessment and evaluation or examination system is the center of university education. In their academic and executive councils, the alternative methods of continually monitoring and reviewing students during the semester can be discussed by the university, including assignments, tasks, activities, quizzes, face-to-face interviews, discussion boards, and so on. The method being used should be mentioned beforehand, including the online proctored examination facility accessible on different platforms.
5. **Internships and placements:** University success depends on the employability of graduates from universities. Each university should ensure that students get internships online, along with online placement opportunities. Universities need to recognize online platforms available for student internships and placements and guide students to use these platforms efficiently.
6. **Collaborations:** One of the threats detected by the lockdown of COVID-19 was its impact on partnerships and relationships, especially internationally. However, it is increasingly thought that it is now possible to achieve national and international collaborations cost-effectively through virtual means. Universities may invite foreign/Indian professors at almost negligible cost from reputable online teaching and research institutions. Collaborative forms should be discussed successfully.
7. **Student counselling:** During the COVID-19 pandemic, students are in compulsory isolation. They are forced to sit at home, making them miss campus life. The university can ensure student campus life by coordinating online cultural and other services linked to the youth. For many students, this situation is very distressing due to its instability. In this case, it is the university's responsibility to guide and train students for new norms and complexities. It must provide students with mental, social, academic, and professional therapy and cultivate personal qualities such as breadth of mind, bravery, self-reliance, versatility, adaptability, and resilience to understand the complexities, cope with them, and healthily react to them. That is the universities' most critical job.

Annexure-C: Google Tools for Online Education (Figure 9.1)

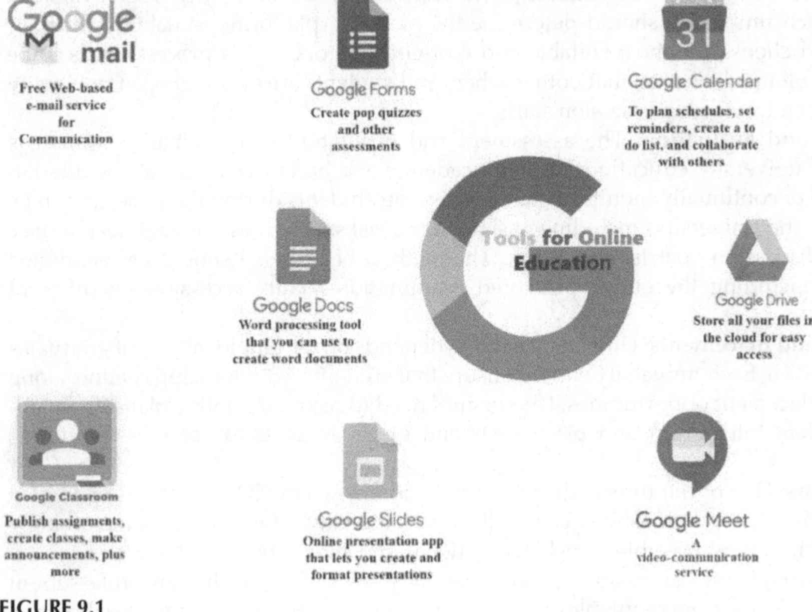

FIGURE 9.1
Google Tools for Online Education.
Source: Google.

10

Importance of MOOCs in Cloud-Enabled Digitalization of Higher Education

Deepika Jhamb and Pawan Kumar Chand

Chitkara Business School, Chitkara University, Punjab, India

10.1 Introduction

Methods of knowledge acquisition are an ever-evolving phenomenon, especially in an accelerated, connected world. Today, the one-fit-for-all knowledge delivery and assimilation model is being challenged every single moment with the growing expectation to perform better. This has brought the need to introduce a platform for continuous learning with domain experts being able to coach through collaboration. A plethora of choices and options are available for students to improve their knowledge on a subject and further enhance their skill level. Massive Open Online Courses, popularly referred to as MOOCs, attract a large population of young students, who have already attained a secondary level of education, aspire to grow in their career and are quick to utilise the strength of a learning community (Dillahunt et al. 2014; Guerrero et al. 2021). Seen as a disruptor,

DOI: 10.1201/9781003203070-12

MOOCs are being considered as a knowledge improvement tool for students as well as working professionals (Meister 2013; Bates 2014). This is supported by rapid growth in information sharing through the internet and the availability of communication devices to build the skills of tomorrow (McAuley et al. 2010; Van Deursen and Mossberger 2018; Bordoloi et al. 2020).

For traditional universities yet to figure out a structured way for an inclusive education platform across age brackets, MOOCs is undeniably a platform which can benefit the masses, especially learners who have attained a level of formal education but seek to acquire higher knowledge levels which can be practically utilized in their work area and enhance their career advancements (Raffaghelli et al. 2015). MOOCs bring an immense degree of innovation connecting technology and consumable-content, which enables students to invest in learning to keep their talent and skill index high (Literat, 2015). This has led to the creation of content and making the best use of it as per the learner's choice of subject and learning capacity. There are no barriers to learning through MOOCs as the information is readily available and accessible to everyone, everywhere and at any time with just a click of a button on the internet.

This remarkable digital revolution in education and learning has made a positive impact on students with a quest to learn and perform better in their endeavours (Daniel 2013). The Indian Government is also training the youth through the MOOCs model to tap employment opportunities in the IT sector, including business process services yielding a progressive ecosystem impacting the entire value chain (Kumar and Mishra 2015). Today's IT industry professionals and many companies bet heavily on MOOCs to identify, recruit and train talent in an engaging method. A decent percentage of MOOCs subscribers come from the IT industry itself (Glass et al. 2016) and private MOOC providers like UpGrad are targeting this segment which is well-versed with technology and keen to acquire cutting-edge modern technology skills like data analytics. The stupendous opportunity and supportive government policies are generating profound interest among the learner community in India, resulting in a higher degree of MOOC adoption by students as well as other groups (Park et al. 2015). Richard Levin, CEO of Coursera mentioned in an article published in (*Economic Times* 2014) that "India is the second-largest user base already with 800,000 students registered. It is also one of the top five countries in terms of revenue generated for Coursera."

The reliability of MOOCs has further increased because students and higher educational institutions are looking at the MOOC format with renewed interest, as COVID-19 has forced an unparalleled change to online teaching at universities around the world (Young 2020). The pandemic is refocusing attention on the prospects for MOOCs to "democratize" higher education by providing everyone in the world with cheap or free access (Impey 2020). Looking at the remarkable importance of MOOCs, this chapter highlights their role in reshaping higher education in India. The research also opens the door to further study the learning behaviour of millennials who are joining as the new-age workforce. The present research is an effort to find out the answer to research questions such as: How is MOOC is perceived by Indian learners? What are the factors which make MOOC effective for the Indian higher education system? What are the critical issues that the Indian education system must look into for the proper implementations of the MOOC system in academic institutions? Can the MOOC system be summarized as a quality moderator in the Indian education system now?

10.2 Literature Review

10.2.1 Evolution of MOOCs

The evolution of MOOCs can be linked over 150 years with the introduction of distance learning programmes in Great Britain (Leber 2013). The courses designed during that time were intended to promote a specialized skill for the learner who could not gain this through formal education due to various reasons like geographical distance, cost burden, or even class division in society (Oliver 1999). The popularity of the distance learning model caught the attention of a few higher education institutes in the USA like Cornell University, but didn't take off (Hansen and Reich 2015), unlike in Great Britain where, in 1860, the University of London established a successful distance learning model worldwide. This led to the formation of pedagogy revisions for learners and faculty operating outside of their geographical proximity.

Initially, information and knowledge distribution was confined between the sender and the receiver with minimal interaction (Knoedler 2015). The next phase of advancement involved computerization, where the sender and receiver started quality interaction with each other and two-way communication redefined the learning process, with geographical barriers being diminished by online learning (Liu et al. 2014). The adoption of online learning led to the next phase of a web-enabled and self-computing system (Liu et al. 2015). The collaborative learning model is transformative, and telecommunication makes it digitized to an extent as many educational institutions deployed a learning management system to support their pedagogy (Byerly 2012; Falloon 2020).

Online learning further led to the creation of networks of individuals and information on the intranet or internet, paving the way for MOOCs, highlighting the true essence of "open" and "online" learning culture (Wiley 2015). In the beginning, MOOCs as a concept evolved in the year, 2008 (Longstaff 2014), which described a course experiment that utilized connectivism. There is a continuous discussion about whether connectivism is a complete learning concept or mainly just another learning model (Taylor 1995), but in the recent past, ongoing trials in distributed learning mention connectivism, irrespective of the situation, as a vital tool in modern learning (Pérez-Sanagustín et al. 2016).

10.2.2 MOOCs in Higher Education

Forbes mentions MOOCs as the "next big profitable thing" providing a one-trillion dollar business opportunity challenging the current education model (Allen and Seaman 2013). This opens the growth window for MOOC providers as well as the new learning environment for learners. Investment in human capital is key to an organization's growth and to achieving improved employee competency to retain its competitive strength. Corporates today are more aware and knowledgeable of the benefits of MOOCs than ever before. The element of professional learning and development can be customized to the best interest of employee and employer (Littlejohn and Milligan 2015).

Another view is that MOOCs are satisfying the need of effectively contributing towards an organization's growth and in its absence, there is a logical question as to MOOCs' necessity. MOOCs are becoming popular but corporates may consider their seriousness only when they bring non-tangible and tangible benefits and not just novelty (Dodson et al. 2015). MOOCs should also help bridge the performance gap among employees, and the content creation should be aimed towards a particular audience type rather than a generic feel-good factor of learning (Swink 2014). MOOCs can be sustainable for professional development if measured correctly for meeting the learning objective and its effectiveness. Corporations like Sony, Apple, Toshiba, CISCO, and many IT companies are leading the way in MOOCs adoption for their employee learning needs. MOOCs are seen as a game-changer and offer a learning opportunity to many (Lewin 2012). For successful MOOCs, one has to tackle three key barriers: time, technology skills and language. Leading technology companies are developing MOOCs for training their employees (Bogdan et al. 2017).

Multiple studies recognize MOOCs as a popular platform for self-learning, paving the way for self-learning through internet-based collaborative experiences (Wu and Chen 2017). MOOCs are credited with the democratization of education since they provide free access to learning content and require just a basic internet connection (Wulf et al. 2014). While anyone anywhere can access MOOCs, studies show a higher number of employed people taking advantage of this learning model more (Dillahunt et al. 2014) with the motive of enhancing their professional development and upskilling for better job prospects (Pappano 2012). The proliferation and success of MOOCs have forced higher educational institutions to change their traditional methods of teaching and incorporate MOOCs into their curriculum to cope with the changing industry requirements (Zakharova and Tanasenk 2019; Koutsakas et al. 2020).

10.3 Theoretical Framework

Knowledge can be derived from a well-networked environment that inspires building a theory termed "connectivism." Triggered by the proliferation and adoption of technology, connectivism describes changes within the learning ecosystem. In 2008, Siemens and Downes partnered to build a new online learning format that is available to any individual interested in learning. This class is recognized as the first connectivist MOOC or cMOOC with the course named "Connectivism and Connective Knowledge / 2008" or CCK08 (Downes 2008). cMOOCs, by design, promote a connected learning environment where individuals can participate in the learning process. This model not only provides a cost advantage but also offers scale to accommodate a large number of individuals collaborating among themselves, to commence meaningful discussions, and share their knowledge to assist others and add to the subject content. It also helps groups to exploit social networks to their learning advantage (Joseph and Nash 2013). MOOCs are considered an educational innovation (Cepeda et al. 2009). They offer a combination of different learning models like self-paced, synchronous, and asynchronous. Different MOOCs providers are accredited for this behaviour such as Udacity, a for-profit MOOCs provider, which provides self-paced and asynchronous learning as the course can be taken months and even years after the instructor publishing the course modules, rather than within a defined period. Conversely, MOOCs providers like Coursera and edX offer a synchronous model as the learners have to complete the course modules within defined timelines. MOOCs also replicate the traditional model of online learning by providing videos and features of online conferences to a given group of learners. This is a synchronous learning model and interestingly, both Coursera and edX offer asynchronous learning as learners do not have to meet up or assemble at a given time during the learning process (Poon 2014). Considering the fast growth in MOOCs adoption for learning (Porter 2015), research into factors influencing learners to continue MOOCs and assess their effectiveness may reveal practical insights into their sustainability (Muñoz-Merino et al. 2015).The theoretical framework is formed based on the availability of classical theories and literature connecting MOOCs and their usage in enhancing higher education. The emphasis is on the overall global MOOCs scenario followed by MOOCs coverage in the Indian context by describing their role as well as their effectiveness for higher education.

10.3.1 Theory of Constructivism and Online Learning

Constructivism as a theory of learning has a deep standing in psychology and philosophy. The underlying characteristic is to have learners based on their experiences actively and enthusiastically construct knowledgeable information and concepts on their own (Campbell 2008). Constructivism is based on the principle of learners being active participants who take charge of their learning. This theory outlines knowledge being received based on an individual's perception and senses which build knowledge. The learner is centre stage while the instructor takes on the role of facilitator. Instead of an instruction-based learning environment, the learner begins to learn by themselves (Cunningham and Duffy 1996). Constructivism is widely seen as a contextual and online method of learning that promotes MOOCs well. Learning undergoes change from traditional instructor-led to constructing and finding knowledge (Cunningham and Duffy 1996).

This has changed information and knowledge delivery to a process rather than knowledge being seen as a product. Learning is inclusive of social negotiation. The self-belief system, thoughts, perceptions, and current knowledge should be challenged by the learner through collaboration with others (Annabi et al. 2016). The primary reason for computer-internet-based online learning is the flexibility offered to the learner, not being restricted to content and course timing alone (Wahid and Sani 2015). A study conducted by Waite et al. 2013, while exploring learners' experience of participation, states that constructivism recognizes the diversity of participants in MOOCs and aligns with the emphasis on knowledge creation and interpretation within MOOCs.

10.3.2 Theory of Adoption and Diffusion

The theory of adoption assesses the individual's decision on either accepting or rejecting a select innovation. It is not just limited in accepting an innovation but also to the level of its usage. This theory provides a micro-perspective on the element of change that builds up the perspective on the whole. Conversely, the theory of diffusion refers to a macro-perspective on the increase of innovation over a period.

There isn't a single model to figure a process on an individual's engagement before adopting an innovation. Traditionally, adoption refers to a degree of change in an individual's behaviour. Common opinion on the adoption of new technology is not seen as a one-time event but can be seen as such if an individual takes a decision (yes or no) to adopt the innovation. Over time, decisions can be influenced by a variety of reasons like attitude, self-discipline, and belief, to name but a few (Straub 2009). Al-Rahmi et al. (2019) indicated that a theory of innovation and diffusion is used for the adoption of MOOCs to enhance the standard of learning by students, which can enable decision-makers in higher education, universities, and colleges to prepare, assess and enforce the use of systems (MOOCs).

10.3.3 Theory of Technology Acceptance Model (TAM)

Unlike the above theories, which deal with a precise adoption environment, this theory deals with a particular innovation. Technology changes at a rapid pace, hence organizations have to develop a broad program to promote the use of information technology (Ehrmann 1995). TAM has been employed in quite a few educational scenarios, explaining the acceptance phenomenon in online learning (Bandura 2001). TAM is based on two observed characteristics that define the outcome of innovation. Firstly, the convenient hassle-free use of technology is linked to self-efficacy. Second is the possible use of technology to the extent of enhancing an individual's performance at work (Davis et al. 1989). In many types of research, a perceived benefit is seen consistently influencing an individual's future adoption and use of technology. The technology's usefulness is also associated with an individual's innovativeness (Straub 2009).

Limited work has been done on the technology acceptance model concerning acceptance or use of MOOCs. (Wu and Chen 2017) studied the features of MOOCs and social motivational factors for using MOOCs among learners. TAM considers the short-term beliefs and attitudes of learners before and posts MOOCs acceptance (Wu and Chen 2017). TAM was applied to examine the relationship between perceived usefulness, ease of use, behavioural attitude, and intentions for the continuance of MOOCs. The findings of the study indicate that TAM is valid for MOOCs analysis as a significant relationship was established between the variables of MOOCs and TAM (Wu and Chen 2017).

10.4 Research Methods

The present study relies on secondary as well as primary data. The secondary data was collected from scholarly research papers, articles, and government reports. The secondary data plays an important role in the current study because MOOCs have led to a transformation in the Indian education system and the government is making significant efforts in promoting them (Kampani and Jhamb 2020). For the primary data, the study has followed the qualitative research design using a non-probability purposive sampling technique. Thirty-six in-depth interviews of experts in the MOOCs area were conducted as these experts were frequently involved in promoting the MOOCs programme in Indian and multi-national organizations. They also had prior experience in designing the course curriculum for the MOOCs programme in the Indian higher education system and foreign universities. Such efforts were considered necessary to fill the gap between industry and academia and to get prompt insight into the MOOCs programme. The personal contribution on MOOCs by such experts was given much significance. The experts' profiles were thoroughly referred to and studied before approaching them, and it is also worth mentioning that most of them had written articles and books, presented research papers in national/international conferences and published research papers with reputed international journals on MOOCs programmes. The present research study included 18 senior professors of Indian universities and 18 Vice Presidents of IT organizations in India. Of the total 36 experts, 10 were female and 26 male, with a length of service more than 17 years of experience. All the respondents in the study were subjected to in-depth interviews which included open-ended unstructured questions on the factors referred from critical literature review affecting MOOCs such as social motivation, innovation, outcomes, connective knowledge, sustainability, accommodation, and the timeline. How are MOOCs perceived by Indian learners? Is the MOOCs system summarized as a quality moderator in the Indian education system now? It took approximately thirty minutes for the respondents in the in-depth interviews to answer such questions. All the experts were highly educated and highly knowledgeable and had shown a keen interest in answering the questions asked.

10.5 Results and Discussion

As the current study has taken a mixed approach to data collection, the results and discussion section is also divided into two sections, namely secondary data analysis and primary data analysis.

10.5.1 Secondary Data Analysis

10.5.1.1 MOOCs Journey

The learning models have to undergo substantial evolution, from an instructor-based, classroom teaching method, to distance education with the distribution of course material changing from print to multi-media for self-study and part-time classes, to online courses, blended learning, and then the MOOCs (Longstaff 2017). The key differences between MOOCs and older online methods of learning is the scale, structure and design, which permit higher levels of learner collaboration through meaningful engagement (Sumedrea 2015). MOOCs can reach this scale and continue to grow because some elite academic institutions and organizations with profit motives have come together (Gaebel 2014).

10.5.1.2 The MOOCs Scenario

To build a better understanding of the MOOCs scenario, the literature has been reviewed to significantly highlight the demographic and psychographic indicators, relevance and adoption of MOOCs in higher education, MOOCs proliferation in India, the overall motivational factors of MOOCs, and their effectiveness for learners.

MOOCs have been viewed as one of the best alternatives to enhance skills for professional development and attract potentially high-paying career choices (Pappano 2012). They helps in offering flexible learning for individuals' interest in the subject (Yuan et al. 2013). MOOCs fulfil professionals' desire to incorporate an opportunity for skill development (Czerniewicz et al. 2014). Figure 10.1 and Table 10.1 reveal the meteoric growth of MOOCs.

Table 10.1 provides a view of the world's top five MOOCs providers: interestingly they all established themselves between 2012 and 2013 and have captured a sizeable market globally with several courses to meet the demands of learners. These providers also have strong ties with leading universities and corporates (Thompson 2013). As of 2016, the rapid increase in the number of courses by the top MOOCs providers indicates the growing demand for MOOCs, especially for working professionals (Reich 2017).

MOOCs have contributed greatly towards the democratization of education (Gamage et al. 2015) and are seen as a disruptor based on technology adoption (Lucas 2014), which

TABLE 10.1
Country-wide Top MOOCs Enrollments

Continent	Country	Registrations	Registrations (%)
North America	USA	242,279	42.29
Asia	India	54,230	9.47
North America	Canada	21,853	3.81
Australia	Australia	12,474	2.18
Africa	Nigeria	12,067	2.11
South America	Brazil	11,243	1.96
Europe	Spain	10,582	1.85
Asia	Philippines	10,099	1.76
Asia	Pakistan	9,505	1.66
Europe	UK	8,066	1.41

enables lower cost implications, offers scale beyond geographies, and widens the scope for innovation in learning (Sharma and Jhamb 2017). The digital mode of learning has been the most popular way to upgrade skills and increase knowledge levels, especially for students, as well as working professionals. The opportunities provided by the online learning platform are being extended to more people, are gaining immense popularity (Bragg 2014) and are seen as an alternative to traditional education programmes. The online learning platform has registered a 10-fold increase in growth compared to other education models. Thus, it is imperative to understand the role of MOOCs, which have witnessed exponential growth and expansion in the last few years (Macleod et al. 2016). MOOCs are comprehended as a massive initiative which is related to hundreds of thousands of people; it is open, which means free of charge and provided to all, across different age brackets and online which means the courses are presented through the internet (Wulf et al. 2014; Macleod et al. 2015). MOOCs hold an important place in educating individuals and are attributed as an alternative, non-formal, continuing, and open education system (Bates 2014). It is imperative to focus on the areas below to make MOOCs successful (Joseph and Naith 2013).

Research done on MOOCs reveals that they have a global reach and scale that bring diversity in demographics. MOOCs participants come from 194 different countries, dominated by male registration count (Breslow et al. 2013). Below is a HarvardX MOOCs study highlighting registrations for MOOCs by country with the US, India and Canada being the top three, where English is widely spoken, and the trend continues (Nesterko et al. 2013). The study also revealed that male MOOCs registrations represent a vast majority, with an estimated 63.4% of registrations from 206 countries for HarvardX courses. The study also factored in the certifications completed by learners who registered for the course. However, the course completion or certification rate doesn't describe learning advantages with MOOCs well (Jordan 2014).

The United States Bureau of Labor Statistics data shows that slightly over half (51.1%) of the 2013 workforce lacked the skills needed for a job, thus creating a gap between higher education and workplace expectations. MOOCs might help in filling that gap (Swink, 2014). The focal point of the learning process is teaching a skill that is in demand by employers. Such courses foster a social mode of learning and trigger effective knowledge sharing in the network (Chin et al. 2000). The courses are conducted by experts or professionals, and hence become relevant for learners as experience is better utilized through this platform than just the theoretical concepts. MOOCs are interactive and engaging by offering quizzes, games, video presentations, analogies and more. Companies like edX, Coursera and NovoEd are working with universities to design hybrid courses that include the power of social collaboration, experiential learning and online learning (Castellano 2014).

While 2012 was mentioned as "The year of MOOCs" (Pappano 2012), 2014 is being referred to as "The year of corporate MOOCs" (Bogdan et al. 2017). MOOCs have also been positioned by many researchers as the "future of education" (Swink 2014). The initial research focused more on the relevance of MOOCs in the higher education landscape but from 2013 onwards there is a high degree of focus on the role which MOOCs play specifically to bridge the gap in the corporate environment (Bogdan et al. 2017). MOOCs eliminate the high cost of implementing a learning management system and procuring software licenses to conduct student training. They are successful for learners who are self-directed, disciplined, own the learning process, and remain motivated to complete the course (De Coutere 2014).

MOOCs have had a notable influence on adult learning. Their usage is fuelled by a variety of factors where technology, demography, pedagogy and the role of economics combine in their success (Thompson 2013; Jordan 2014). In the modern business environment, where unimagined technological changes are impacting the lives of everyone, there is an urgency to rapidly scale up the workforce, which is important for any organization's survival. A recent study by (Alhzanni 2020) has also confirmed that the MOOCs online courses affect higher education institutions and assist in improving the three dimensions, namely, improving educational outcomes, developing students' learning skills, and deploying effective communications with instructors, as depicted in Figure 10.1.

10.5.2 Primary Data Analysis

After consulting industry experts and experts from academia, and reviewing the literature, a model has been proposed in Figure 10.1. The figure shows the ovals and rectangle which represent the factors social motivation, innovation, outcomes, connective knowledge, sustainability, accommodation, the timeline, and their relationship with MOOCs effectiveness. Linking arrows in the figure explain the probable relationship among the factors. The proposed research model in Figure 10.1 further shows that there must be a positive significant relationship among the factors affecting MOOCs, which needs to be further validated in future research work. The proposed model states that social motivation is required to encourage learners to participate in the MOOCs programme, which

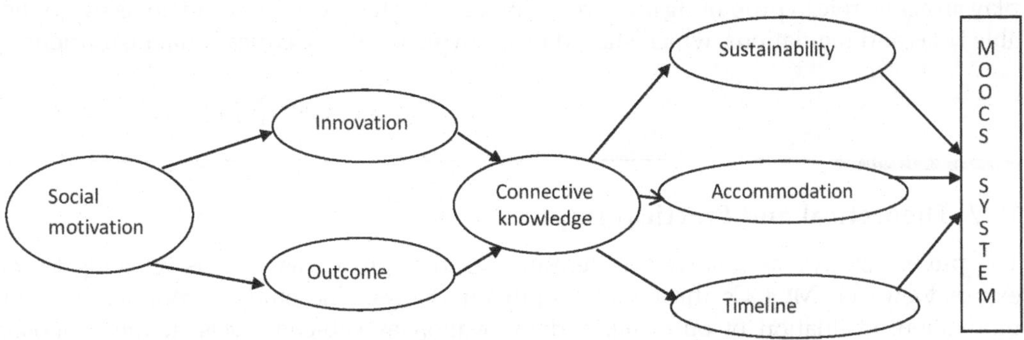

FIGURE 10.1
The MOOCs model.

results in the innovation (new techniques and practices adopted) and also the outcomes (learning behaviour and the reaction of the learner). Learners show their interest if the content meets the expectation, standard of quality and is well connected to the subject. The connective knowledge can be a proposed significant mediator to establish further relationships in the learning process of MOOC: timelines, sustainability and accommodating the members in the group, which will be a matter of high priority. The proposed model further recommends that future researchers examine the constructs such as social motivation, innovation, outcomes, connective knowledge, sustainability, accommodation and timeline for establishing the inter-relationship to recognize the MOOCs effectiveness in the Indian higher education system.

10.6 Conclusion and Future Scope

This section discusses the scenario of MOOCs and the way they impact the learning aspirations of students to achieve their motives. MOOCs have been identified as creating disruption and a revolutionary trend impacting the higher education industry (Lucas 2014). The significant disruption factor is the huge number of participants who can avail themselves of the knowledge passed on by any professional expert or a teacher (Bragg 2014). The teacher acquires the position of a facilitator or is completely absent from the process of learning through this model of education (Savino 2014). Here MOOCs are visibly seen as adopting higher open education practices to meet the learning objectives of individuals (Glennie et al. 2012). They eliminate the worry of taking a sabbatical, travel and accommodation costs, course fees of on-campus programmes, and the necessity of physical presence in the classroom (Chang et al. 2016). Indian education institutions are considering MOOCs as a skill-building platform to bridge knowledge gaps, enhance career progression, remain competitive in the workplace, and to utilize the flexibility offered by MOOCs. Students using MOOCs find them effective as they provide a high degree of learning satisfaction, especially through a collaborative learning community. The Government of India is also promoting MOOCs under the "digital India" initiative SWAYAM, which encompasses higher education and skill sector courses but there is an absence of a standard policy for educational institutions on proactive learning initiatives introducing MOOCs. India also lacks the basic infrastructure to fully implement online learning platforms like MOOCs. To strengthen their effectiveness, the government should come up with a formal policy and play an active role in promoting and providing MOOCs for the masses and devising applicable rules and regulations, which should be followed by all the educational institutions.

10.7 Theoretical and Practical Implications

The present study has followed a literature-based approach as well as referring to the expert views on MOOCs through in-depth interviews. The study recommends social motivation, evaluation of outcome, and innovation as sub-constructs in the proposed model, thus reinforcing the technology acceptance model (Wu and Chen 2017). The study emphasized the significant need for active learning by students, thus reinforcing the constructivism theory (Cunningham and Duffy 1996). The study discussed basic infrastructure as an important basic necessity for the Indian higher education system, and this finding will be of importance to academia while framing the new policy programme for MOOCs implementation. The study also highlighted the active learning environment and social motivation in India. This finding will provide an insight to the parents and people of Indian society to promote the MOOCs excellence learning environment for their wards because MOOCs are recommended as a significant moderator in the future teaching and learning process in the Indian higher education system. Furthermore, the measures taken by educational institutions towards the acceptability of online education during the COVID-19 pandemic have triggered the growth of MOOCs. Although this pandemic had a devastating impact on the economy in general, it has been a blessing in disguise for online education and MOOCs providers.

References

Alhazzani, Noura. 2020. "MOOC's impact on higher education." *Social Sciences & Humanities Open* 2 (1): 100030. https://doi.org/10.1016/j.ssaho.2020.100030.

Allen, I. Elaine, and Seaman, Jeff. 2013. *Changing course: Ten years of tracking online education in the United States*. Sloan Consortium.

Al-Rahmi, Waleed Mugahed, Yahaya, Noraffandy, Alamri, Mahdi M., Youssef Alyoussef, Ibrahim, Al-Rahmi, Ali Mugahed, and Bin Kamin, Yusri. 2019. "Integrating innovation diffusion theory with technology acceptance model: Supporting students' attitude towards using a massive open online courses (MOOCs) systems." *Interactive Learning Environments*: 1–13. doi.org/10.1080/10494820.2019.1629599.

Annabi, Carrie Amani, and Wilkins, Stephen. 2016. "The use of MOOCs in transnational higher education for accreditation of prior learning, programme delivery, and professional development." *International Journal of Educational Management* 30 (6): 959-975. doi.org/10.1108/IJEM-05-2015-0057.

Bandura, A. 2001. "Social cognitive theory: An agentic perspective." *Asian Journal of Social Psychology* 22 (1): 1–26. doi.org/10.1146/annurev.psych.52.1.1.

Bates, T. 2014. "A balanced research report on the hopes and realities of MOOCs." Online *Learning* and *Distance Education Resources*. Retrieved May 15, 2014, from www.tonybates.ca/2014/05/15/abalanced-research-report-on-the-hopes-and-realities-of-moocs/.

Bogdan, R., Holotescu, C., Andone, D., and Grosseck, G. 2017. "How MOOCs are being used for corporate training." *eLearning & Software for Education* 2: 254–261.

Bordoloi, R., Das, P., and Das, K. 2020. "Lifelong learning opportunities through MOOCs in India." *Asian Association of Open Universities Journal* 15 (1): 83–95. doi.org/10.1108/AAOUJ-09-2019-0042.

Bragg, A. B. 2014. "MOOCs: Where to from here?" *Training & Development* 41 (1): 20–21.

Breslow, L., Pritchard, D. E., DeBoer, J., Stump, G. S., Ho, A. D., and Seaton, D. T. 2013. "Studying learning in the worldwide classroom: Research into edX's first MOOC." *Research & Practice in Assessment* 8: 13–25. ERIC Number: EJ1062850.

Byerly, A. 2012. "Before you jump on the bandwagon." *The Chronicle of Higher Education* 59 (2).

Campbell, D. E. 2008. "Voice in the classroom: How an open classroom climate fosters political engagement among adolescents." *Political Behavior* 30 (4):437–454. doi.org/10.1007/s11109-008-9063-z

Castellano, S. 2014. "E-learning in higher education." *Talent Development*, 68 (11): 64–66.

Cepeda, N. J., Coburn, N., Rohrer, D., Wixted, J. T., Mozer, M. C., and Pashler, H. 2009. "Optimizing distributed practice: Theoretical analysis and practical implications." *Experimental psychology* 56 (4):236–246. doi.org/10.1027/1618-3169.56.4.236.

Chang, Ya-Chih, Shire, Stephanie Y., Shih, Wendy, Gelfand, Carolyn, and Kasari, Connie. 2016. "Preschool deployment of evidence-based social communication intervention: JASPER in the classroom." *Journal of Autism and Developmental Disorders* 46 (6): 2211–2223. doi.org/10.1007/s10803-016-2752-2.

Chin, C., and Brown, D. E. 2000. "Learning in science: A comparison of deep and surface approaches." *Journal of Research in Science Teaching* 37 (2): 109–138. doi.org/10.1002/(SICI)1098-2736(200002)37

Cunningham, D., and Duffy, T. 1996. "Constructivism: Implications for the design and delivery of instruction." *Handbook of Research for Educational Communications and Technology* 51:170–198. doi.org/10.1.1.138.2455.

Czerniewicz, Laura, Deacon, Andrew, Small, Janet, and Walji, Sukaina. 2014. "Developing world MOOCs: A curriculum view of the MOOC landscape." *Journal of Global Literacies, Technologies, and Emerging Pedagogies* 2 (3): 122–139.

Daniel, J. 2013. "Making sense of MOOCs: Musings in a maze of myth, paradox and possibility." *Open Education Research:* 3–6. doi.org/10.5334/2012-18

Davis, F. D., Bagozzi, R. P., and Warshaw, P. R. 1989. "User acceptance of computer technology: A comparison of two theoretical models." *Management Science* 35 (8): 982–1003. doi.org/10.1287/mnsc.35.8.982.

De Coutere, B. 2014. "To MOOC, or not to MOOC." *Training Journal* 1 (4): 18–22.

Department of Business, Innovation and Skills. 2013. "The Maturing of the MOOC: Literature Review of Massive Open Online Courses and other forms of Online Distance Learning." https://assets.publishing.service.gov.uk/government/uploads/system/uploads/attachment_data/file/240193/13-1173-maturing-of-the-mooc.pdf.

Dillahunt, T. R., Wang, B. Z., and Teasley, S. 2014. "Democratizing higher education: Exploring MOOC use among those who cannot afford a formal education." *The International Review of Research in Open and Distributed Learning* 15 (5): 177–196. doi.org/10.19173/irrodl.v15i5.

Dodson, Michele Nicole, Kitburi, Karat, and Berge, Zane L. 2015. "Possibilities for MOOCs in corporate training and development." *Performance Improvement* 54 (10): 14–21. doi.org/10.1002/pfi.21532.

Downes, Stephen.2008. "Places to go: Connectivism & connective knowledge." *Innovate: Journal of Online Education* 5 (1): 6. https://nsuworks.nova.edu/innovate/vol5/iss1/6.

Economic Times. 2014. "India among top 5 revenue generators for US: Coursera." https://economictimes.indiatimes.com/industry/services/education/india-among-top-5-revenue-generators-for-us-coursera/articleshow/45166154.cms?from=mdr.

Ehrmann, S. C. 1995. "Asking the right questions: What does research tell us about technology and higher learning?" *Change: The Magazine of Higher Learning* 27 (2): 20–27. doi.org/10.1080/00091383.1995.9937734.

Falloon, G. 2020. "From digital literacy to digital competence: The teacher digital competency (TDC) framework." *Educational Technology Research and Development* 68 (5): 2449–2472. doi.org/10.1007/s11423-020-09767-4.

Gaebel, M. 2014. *MOOCs: Massive open online courses*. EUA Occasional Papers.

Gamage, Dilrukshi, Fernando, Shantha, and Perera, Indika. 2015. "Quality of MOOCs: A review of literature on effectiveness and quality aspects." In *2015 8th International Conference on Ubi-Media Computing (UMEDIA)*: 224–229, IEEE.

Glass, C. R., Shiokawa-Baklan, M. S., and Saltarelli, A. J. 2016. "Who takes MOOCs?" *New Directions for Institutional Research* 2015 (167): 41–55. doi.org/10.1002/ir.20153.

Glennie, Jenny, Harley, Ken, Butcher, Neil, and van Wyk, Trudi. 2012. "Open educational resources and change in higher education: Reflections from practice." *Commonwealth of Learning*. http://hdl.handle.net/11599/80.

Guerrero, M., Heaton, S., and Urbano, D. 2021. "Building universities' intrapreneurial capabilities in the digital era: The role and impacts of Massive Open Online Courses (MOOCs)." *Technovation* 99: 102–139. doi.org/10.1016/j.technovation.2020.102139.

Hansen, J. D., and Reich, J. 2015. "Democratizing education? Examining access and usage patterns in massive open online courses." *Science* 350 (6265): 1245–1248. doi.org/10.1126/science.aab3782.

Impey. 2020. "Massive online open courses see exponential growth during COVID-19 pandemic." www.thejakartapost.com/life/2020/08/12/massive-online-open-courses-see-exponential-growth-during-covid-19-pandemic.html.

Jordan, K. 2014. "Initial trends in enrolment and completion of massive open online courses." *The International Review of Research in Open and Distributed Learning* 15 (1): 133–60. doi.org/10.19173/irrodl.v15i1.1651.

Joseph, A. M., and Nath, B. A. 2013. "Integration of massive open online education (MOOC) system with in-classroom interaction and assessment and accreditation: An extensive report from a pilot study." In *Proceedings of the international conference on e-learning, e-business, enterprise information systems, and e-Government* 105 (1).

Kampani, N., and Jhamb, D. 2020. "Analyzing the role of E-CRM in managing customer relations: A critical review of the literature." *Journal of Critical Review* 7 (4): 221–226. doi.org/10.31838/jcr.07.04.41

Knoedler, J. T. 2015. "Going to college on My iPhone." *Journal of Economic Issues* 49 (2): 329–354. doi.org/10.1080/00213624.2015.1042729.

Koutsakas, P., Chorozidis, G., Karamatsouki, A., and Karagiannidis, C. 2020. "Research trends in K–12 MOOCs: A review of the published literature." *International Review of Research in Open and Distributed Learning* 21 (3): 285–303. doi.org/10.19173/irrodl.v21i3.4650.

Kumar, S., and Mishra, A. K. 2015. "MOOCs: a new pedagogy of online digital learning." *Int. J. Sci. Innov. Res. Stud* 3 (4):8–15.

Leber, J. 2013. "The technology of massive open online courses." *Technology Review* 116 (1): 63–64.

Lewin, T. A. M. A. R. 2012. "Free online course will rely on multiple sites." *New York Times*.

Literat, I. 2015. "Implications of massive open online courses for higher education: mitigating or reifying educational inequities?" *Higher Education Research & Development* 34 (6): 1164–1177. doi.org/10.1080/07294360.2015.1024624.

Littlejohn, A., and Milligan, C. 2015. "Designing MOOCs for professional learners: Tools and patterns to encourage self-regulated learning." *eLearning Papers* 42.

Liu, M., Kang, J., Cao, M., Lim, M., Ko, Y., Myers, R., and Schmitz Weiss, A. 2014. "Understanding MOOCs as an emerging online learning tool: Perspectives from the students." *American Journal of Distance Education* 28 (3): 147–159. doi.org/10.1080/08923647.2014.926145.

Liu, M., Kang, J., and McKelroy, E. 2015. "Examining learners' perspective of taking a MOOC: Reasons, excitement, and perception of usefulness." *Educational Media International* 52 (2): 129–146. doi.org/10.1080/09523987.2015.1053289.

Longstaff, E. 2014. "The prehistory of MOOCs: Inclusive and exclusive access in the cyclical evolution of higher education." *Journal of Organisational Transformation & Social Change* 11 (3): 164–184. doi.org/10.1179/1477963314Z.00000000028.

Longstaff, E. 2017. "How MOOCs can empower learners: A comparison of provider goals and user experiences." *Journal of Further and Higher Education* 41 (3): 314–327. doi.org/10.1080/0309877X.2015.1100715.

Lucas, Henry. 2014. "Disrupting and transforming the university." *Communications of the ACM* 57 (10): 32–35. doi.org/10.1145/2661055.

Macleod, H., Haywood, J., Woodgate, A., and Alkhatnai, M. 2015. "Emerging patterns in MOOCs: Learners, course designs and directions." *TechTrends* 59 (1): 56–63.

Macleod, H., Sinclair, C., Haywood, J., and Woodgate, A. 2016. "Massive open online courses: Designing for the unknown learner." *Teaching in Higher Education* 21 (1): 13–24. doi.org/10.1080/13562517.2015.1101680.

McAuley, A., Stewart, B., Siemens, G., and Cormier, D. 2010. "The MOOC model for digital practice." 1 (1): 1–63.

Meister, J. 2013. "How MOOCs will revolutionize corporate learning and development." Retrieved August 7, 2014 from www.forbes.com/sites/jeannemeister/2013/08/13/how-moocs-will-revolutionizecorporate-learning-development/.

Muñoz-Merino, P. J., Ruipérez-Valiente, J. A., Alario-Hoyos, C., Pérez-Sanagustín, M., and Kloos, C. D. 2015. "Precise effectiveness strategy for analyzing the effectiveness of students with educational resources and activities in MOOCs." Computers in Human Behavior 47: 108–118. doi.org/10.1016/j.chb.2014.10.003.

Nesterko, S. O., Dotsenko, S., Han, Q., Seaton, D., Reich, J., Chuang, I., and Ho, A. D. 2013. "Evaluating the geographic data in MOOCs." Neural Information Processing Systems 1 (1): 1–7.

Oliver, R. 1999. "Exploring strategies for online teaching and learning." *Distance Education* 20 (2): 240–254. doi.org/10.1080/0158791990200205.

Pappano, L. 2012. "The Year of the MOOC." *New York Times* 2 (12): 2012.

Park, Y., Jung, I., and Reeves, T. C. 2015. "Learning from MOOCs: A qualitative case study from the learners' perspectives." *Educational Media International* 52 (2): 72–87. doi/abs/10.1080/09523987.2015.1053286.

Pérez-Sanagustín, M., Hernández-Correa, J., Gelmi, C., Hilliger, I., and Rodriguez, M. F. 2016. "Does taking a MOOC as a complement for remedial courses have an effect on my learning outcomes? A pilot study on calculus." In *European Conference on Technology Enhanced Learning*: 221–233. Springer, Cham.

Poon, J. 2014. "A cross-country comparison on the use of blended learning in property education." *Property Management* 32 (2): 154–175. doi.org/10.1108/PM-04-2013-0026

Porter, S. 2015. "The economics of MOOCs: A sustainable future?" *The Bottom Line* 28 (1/2): 52–62. doi.org/10.1108/BL-12-2014-0035.

Raffaghelli, J. E., Cucchiara, S., and Persico, D. 2015. "Methodological approaches in MOOC research: Retracing the myth of Proteus." *British Journal of Educational Technology* 46 (3): 488–509. doi.org/10.1111/bjet.12279.

Reich, J. 2017. "Are MOOC forums echo chambers or bridging spaces?" *Education Week.*

Savino, David M. 2014. "The impact of MOOCs on human resource training and development." *Journal of Higher Education Theory and Practice* 14 (3): 59–64.

Sharma, A., and Jhamb, D. 2017. "MOOCs users in India – A study of demographic and psychographic profile of working professionals." *International Journal of Research in Management, Economics and Commerce* 7 (10): 148–154.

Straub, E. T. 2009. "Understanding technology adoption: Theory and future directions for informal learning." *Review of Educational Research* 79 (2): 625–649. doi.org/10.3102/0034654308325896

Sumedrea, S. 2015. "Knowledge sharing between the economic environment and universities using innovative entrepreneurial learning techniques." *Bulletin of the Transilvania University of Brasov. Economic Sciences, Series V* 8 (2): 233–242.

Swink, S. 2014. "Is now the time to move on MOOCs?" *Chief Learning Officer Magazine*, 1 (8): 6–7.

Taylor, J. C. 1995. "Distance education technologies: The fourth generation." *Australasian Journal of Educational Technology* 11 (2). doi.org/10.14742/ajet.2072

Thompson, G. 2013. "MOOCs for PD: Will massive open online courses revolutionize professional development?" *The Journal (Technological Horizons in Education)* 40 (11): 8–14.

Van Deursen, A. J., and Mossberger, K. 2018. "Any thing for anyone? A new digital divide in internet-of-things skills." *Policy & Internet* 10 (2): 122–140. doi.org/10.1002/poi3.171

Wahid, R., and Sani, M. A. M. 2015. "MOOCs and youth employment strategy." *The Social Sciences* 10 (7):1726–1731.

Waite, M., Mackness, J., Roberts, G., and Lovegrove, E. 2013. "Liminal participants and skilled orienteers: Learner participation in a MOOC for new lecturers." *Journal of Online Learning and Teaching* 9 (2): 200–215.

Wiley, D. 2015. "The MOOC misstep and the open education infrastructure." In Curtis J. Bonk, Mimi L. Lee, Thomas C. Reeves, and Thomas H. Reynolds (eds), *MOOCs and open education around the world*: 3–11. Routledge: London.

Wu, B., and Chen, X. 2017. "Continuance intention to use MOOCs: Integrating the technology acceptance model (TAM) and task technology fit (TTF) model." *Computers in Human Behavior* 67: 221–232. doi.org/10.1016/j.chb.2016.10.028.

Wulf, J., Blohm, I., Leimeister, J. M., and Brenner, W. 2014. "Massive open online courses." *Business & Information Systems Engineering* 6 (2): 111–114. doi.org/10.1007/s12599-014-0313-9

Young, J. R. "Will COVOD-19 Lead to Another MOOC Moment?" 2020. www.edsurge.com/news/2020-03-25-will-covid-19-lead-to-another-mooc-moment.

Yuan, L., Powell, S., and CETIS, J. 2013. "MOOCs and Open Education: Implications for Higher Education." www.cetis.org.uk/.

Zakharova, U., and Tanasenko, K. 2019. "MOOCs in higher education: Advantages and pitfalls for instructors." *Вопросыобразования* 3 (eng).

11

Bridging the Digital Divide in the Indian Education Sector: A Multi-Stakeholder Perspective

Subhendu Kumar Mishra

Centurion University of Technology and Management, R. Sitapur, Odisha 761211, India

DOI: 10.1201/9781003203070-13

11.1 Introduction

The proliferation of digital learning platforms and tools has created enormous potential, especially for the education sector, as learning is no longer limited within the boundaries of physical institutions. However, in a country like India, access to digital technology is still exclusive and leaves a sizable portion without it, known as the digital divide. This is a crucial dimension and its effect on the education sector cannot be ignored. Particularly in India, with its education system consisting of more than 1.5 million schools and 50,000 higher education institutions with close to 300 million students enrolled, the impact can be significant. The recent COVID-19 pandemic revealed the most glaring examples of the digital divide. While it forced educational institutions to adopt a digital route to impart education, and many private institutions were among the fastest to take a lead, there is a majority mostly located in rural areas that lagged. Hence, it raised many questions for evaluation such as lack of last-mile digital infrastructure in remote areas, frequent power failures and the unaffordability of computers or smart phones, posing challenges for the learner located in those areas and raising the issue of equal access to the digital mode of education for those excluded. Secondly, although India stood second after China in terms of internet penetration, still more than 900 million are living without it. As per the National Statistical Organisation's Household Social Consumption on Education survey, the availability of computers in rural households is just 4% in comparison to 23 percent of urban households. These figures not only corroborate the presence of a digital divide in the education sector but also raise some pertinent questions. First, what will the future of education be and will online education persist after the post-COVID-19 scenario? Second, how will government, the private sector and academic institutions deal with such a scenario? Third, what steps need to be taken to ensure that the divide is bridged?

In this chapter, the author explores the realm of the digital divide in the education sector in particular and presents an integration of the efforts and solutions from multiple stakeholders to bridge the gap by providing access, affordability and opportunity.

11.1.1 Digital Divide: An Evolution of the Concept

Donohue, Tichenor and Olien (1975) were among the first to mention the challenge of the digital divide by proposing the knowledge gap hypothesis. It is believed that Larry Irving, an advisor to the Clinton administration, popularized the term in the 1990s. Subsequently, the National Telecommunication and Information of the US government in its published report titled "Falling through the Net" in 1995 mentioned the digital divide as applying to households with no telephone, computer or modem connectivity and internet access in rural and urban America. The body also suggested two significant elements driving the digital divide: education and income, later on adding disability as another dimension. In the year 1998, the United Nations, realizing the unequal access to resources and opportunities in information and communication technologies (ICT), declared a new form of poverty called "information poverty". The Organization for Economic Cooperation and Development in 2001 defined the digital divide as "the gap between individuals, households, businesses and geographic areas at the different socio-economic levels with regard to their opportunities to access ICTs and their use of Internet. It reflects differences among and within countries". At the World Summit on the Information Society, digital divide was described as "a gap with those who have a greater accessibility to digital technologies versus those without it".

11.2 Literature Review

In a knowledge society, the access and utilization of knowledge are considered to contribute significantly to the economy. The role of ICT, and specifically the internet, has been regarded as crucial as it can open multiple avenues for people from various sectors to improve their lives through the development of human capital, and accessing better job opportunities and information regarding healthcare. However, the negative side, associated with a varying level of internet accessibility and usage, can widen the gap between those privileged to have it and those who do not.

The digital divide started to gain attention in both political and scholarly discussions as it has presented the challenge of the digital inequality in society. Hence, from the beginning of the new millennium, there have been several academic, technical and policy conferences organized to deliberate upon the subject. van Dijk (2006) in his review paper on digital divide research spanning five years from 2000 to 2005, emphasized three basic assumptions: first, the type of inequality addressed by the digital divide; second, the uniqueness of access to digital technologies in comparison to other resources in society; and third, the new type of inequality that exists in the information society. While departing from the access point of view, some studies emphasized the usage, and distinguish it at three levels: a difference among the developed and less developed nations, referred to as global divide; a difference among the population within a nation, referred to as social divide; and a divide among the population of those who could not use digital technologies for participation in public life, referred to as democratic divide (Norris 2001). Chandra et al. (2020) explained three critical reasons by reviewing the states in the USA, suggesting that affordability in terms of infrastructure, and challenges in terms of accessibility are crucial in terms of the adoption of digital technologies in K12 education.

Riggins and Dewan (2005) conducted a review of the studies concerned with digital divide at both the individual and global level and suggested that greater collaboration is required from a policy level, businesses (for-profit and non-profit) and academia to bridge the divide.

Srinuan and Bohlin (2011) reviewed the literature on the subject of digital divide for 10 years and argued that it is a multifaceted phenomenon, hence it is not sufficient to look at it from a technological viewpoint; rather, studies have explained the phenomenon through sociological, physiological, political and institutional lenses.

According to the Global Information Technology Report, 2014 (Bilbao-Osorio et al.), published by the World Economic Forum, the Northern European economies and Western economics lead, along with some Asian Tigers, in the networked readiness index rank, while in the South American economies and Africa the index falls way behind.

Pick and Sarkar (2016) compared four critical theories that helped to explain the phenomenon of digital divide, including the adoption-diffusion theory, digital technology access model, unified theory of acceptance and use of technology, and the spatially aware technology utilization model.

Li and Lalani (2020) presented anecdotal evidence of how the pandemic has changed the education sector specifically and the challenges encountered in the adoption of digital routes for teaching and learning in various parts of the world.

11.2.1 Reasons for Digital Divide

The reasons for a digital divide can be many and include multiple levels, starting from regional to global. The most prominent among the models suggesting a digital divide is the access gaps model (van Dijk 2005).

11.2.1.1 The Motivational Access

Motivation becomes a major problem for individuals who have a computer but never use it. Some reasons for the refusal of using computers or the internet are: no significant usage opportunity, no time, less likability, or a perceived rejection of the media. The factors can be social or psychological. A social explanation could be that digital technologies or the internet have less appeal among those on low-incomes or who are less educated. For psychological factors, a major attribute can be due to fear or stress felt while using computers, which is termed computer anxiety.

11.2.1.2 Material Access

A vast portion of research on the digital divide focuses on the material or physical accessibility of computers and the internet, considering the demographics, age, gender, education, income and ethnicity. The three most important characteristics of the material access divide can be classified as income, education and occupation. In the case of India, there is a significant trend in the rise in the percentage of internet penetration in both urban and rural India (see Figure 11.1).

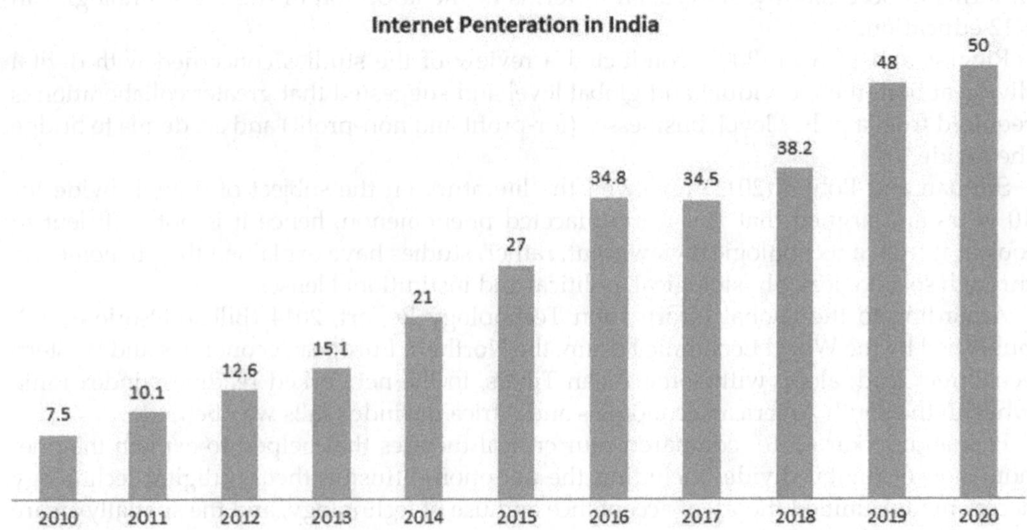

FIGURE 11.1
Internet penetration in India.

11.2.1.3 Skills Access

Lack of skills can become a major obstacle despite one having the desired motivation and physical access to technology. Hence, the concept of digital skill is introduced (Steyaert 2000; van Dijk 1999, 2005). The skill requires proficiency to work with the hardware and software, known as operational skills. The proficiency to search for and process information using a computer is termed information skills, and the ability to process information for the desired purpose is known as strategic skills (Ghobadi and Ghobadi 2015).

Specifically referring to the education context, where technology integration can dramatically change both access and quality of the learning outcome, the digital skill possessed by teachers and students can be of great importance and needs to be examined from all three dimensions.

11.2.1.4 Usage Access

Actual usage of digital technologies is vital among all four types of access mentioned. van Dijk (2005) noted that there are four determinants of assessing the usage: usage time, usage application and diversity, quality of internet/broadband or narrowband availability, the frequency and quality of use. Studies have found a significant difference among usage, varying according to different social class, education, age and income. The usage gap hypothesis is thus proposed, which suggests the application of internet or other digital application in everyday life (Bonfadelli 2002; Cho et al. 2003).

Apart from the four, physical disability can be another impediment to accessing computers and the internet. All five types of access discussed above have significant relevance for investigating the digital divide in the education sector.

11.3 Digital Divide in the Indian Education Sector

Like other infrastructure, ICT infrastructure is a must for modern society. A good ICT infrastructure can help in transferring good governance practices and services to its citizens. It brings transparency and fairness to the service delivery mechanism. India, with a population of about 1.37 billion, represents a diverse social class, with 70 percent of the total population living in rural areas; with an Digital Illiteracy rate close to 30 percent and digital literacy even higher, it presents a perfect example of the digital divide.

In recent times there has been a rapid growth in terms of digital adoption, and with 560 million internet subscribers in 2018 India stood second to China. The wireless subscriber base has increased to 160 million but this only indicates the rise in number whereas usage in terms of online classes, e-governance facilities, which require a skill set for operating the devices using the internet, is far behind, and there is a stark difference in the urban and rural setups. Still, we have a population of about 700 million who can not access or afford computers or internet, due to which they are excluded from the advantages that could have come their way.

The most significant impact of the digital divide has been on the education sector. Despite India receiving credit for one of the largest ever schooling systems in the world, and more youth aspiring for higher education in every consecutive year, quality education is the need of the hour. The prospect of leveraging the ICT to address perennial issues such as alternate modes of education, teacher competency development, and learning management systems for schools and colleges is huge. However, till now, many schools and colleges in the country do not have the basic infrastructure for access to computers or the internet. Teachers are not competent enough in digital skills. The recent COVID-19 pandemic has forced schools and colleges to shut down classes and opt for an online mode of operation. This has revealed the fault lines in the education sector where discrimination is visible between students from poorer sections of society or those living in areas with low internet availability as well as lack of electricity or frequent power failure. The forced closure of schools and lack of alternate arrangements forced many children enrolled in pre-primary and primary education to leave their education. There have been several efforts from various stakeholders to bridge the digital divide and the next section discusses the role and initiatives undertaken by multiple stakeholders including the government, for-profit and non-profit organizations and academic institutions.

11.4 Bridging the Digital Divide in Education: Role of Multiple Stakeholders

Riggins and Dewan (2006) have suggested that a greater collaborative effort is required from multiple stakeholders to bridge the digital divide. In particular for the education sector in India we have the following stakeholders: the government, private corporate sector, NGOs and other non-profit organizations. To promote digital learning and also assist learners in remote locations, several schemes have been launched by the government. Some of the schemes are discussed below.

11.4.1 National Policy on ICT in Schools

There was a need felt at policy level to include computer literacy in the school curriculum as early as 1986 with the launch of the Computer Literacy and Study in Schools (CLASS) project. The national policy on education 1986, revised in 1992, emphasized implementing digital technologies to improve the quality of education, and with the launch of the policy of ICT in schools in 2004, the objective was to use IT tools for the development of e-content in digitally aided learning activities for students.

11.4.2 National Broadband Mission

The National Broadband Mission, launched in 2019, envisages connecting 6 lakh villages across the country by laying optical fibre to 50 lakh kilometres from the current 22 lakh kilometres with an internet speed of up to 50Mbps. Under the Bharat the net initiative has been taken as a mission of national importance and aims to connect all 250000 Gram Panchayats with an optical fibre network.

11.4.3 Pradhan Mantri Gramin Digital Saksharta Abhiyan (PMGDISHA)

The Pradhan Mantri Gramin Digital Saksharta Abhiyan (PMGDISHA) under the digital India initiative aims to reach out to 6 crore households in the age group of 14–60 years to make them digitally literate.

11.4.4 Digital Infrastructure for Knowledge Sharing (DIKSHA)

Launched in 2017, with the initiative of the National Council of Education, Research and Training (NCERT) and Ministry of Human Resource Development, The Digital Infrastructure for Knowledge Sharing (DIKSHA) takes the credit as a national level platform for school education. It was developed based on the core principles of open architecture, open access, open licensing diversity, choice and autonomy. The DIKSHA platform is built upon using Massachusetts Institute of Technology open source licensing software, "Sunbird". It offers end-to-end solutions for learning across multiple locations and during the COVID-19 pandemic was beneficial for learners in remote locations.

11.4.5 SWAYAM

The program was launched to bridge the digital divide in education through access, equity and quality. The program is offered from class 9 to post-graduate and can be accessed by anyone, anywhere, anytime. The courses are offered free of charge and delivered by some of the finest teachers in the country. Nine specialized institutes are appointed as nodal coordinators. The courses available in SWAYAM consist of video lectures, reading materials, self-assessment quizzes and an online discussion forum for peer-level discussion.

11.4.6 PM e Vidya

To ensure that learning is not affected by the COVID-19 pandemic, PM e Vidya was launched. The top 100 institutes and universities under the National Institution Ranking Framework are allowed to offer multimode access to digital education. It hosts 12 direct-to-home channels to support learners from the K-12 group who do not have access to online classes. The initiative will integrate other platforms such as Swayam and DIKSHA for ensuring that the digital divide is bridged.

11.4.7 Swayam Prabha

Swayam Prabha is another initiative to reach out to learners through a direct-to-home platform. Using the GSAT-15, Swayamprabha is a group of 34 direct-to-home channels for telecasting educational programs for learners without internet or access to online classes. The contents are created by Institutions like IITs, IGNOU, UGC, NCERT, NPTEL and NIOS.

11.4.8 National Digital Library (NDL)

The NDL project developed a virtual repository of learning resources with a single-window search facility. It has a vast deposit of more than three crore digital resources available. The contents cover almost all major domains of education and all major levels of learners, including life-long learners, with 5 million learners registered.

The role of organizations (both for-profit and non-profit) is vital in terms of providing solutions to bridge the digital divide across multiple sectors. Some of the cases are discussed below.

11.4.9 e.Choupal

The e.choupal initiative has been a game-changer in the Indian agriculture system. Launched in the year 2000, the project provided information to farmers on inputs, agro practices and market prices in the local language. With 6,500 kiosks, the initiative reached out to 10 states with a beneficiary strength of about 4 million households.

11.4.10 Internet.org

Realizing that the internet played a significant role in people's lives, and to make it more accessible, Facebook and six other tech companies joined forces to form internet.org. The goal was to connect everybody through the internet. The initiative consists of features such as free basics, to provide basic internet accesses for free, and express wi-fi for affordable internet access anywhere and everywhere.

11.4.11 NIIT: Hole in the Wall Experiment

The Hole in the Wall experiment was credited to Dr. Sugata Mitra at NIIT technologies. He carved a hole in the wall that separated NIIT premises from the slum in Kalakaji, New Delhi. Dr. Mitra installed a computer in the hole for free use by the slum dwellers. It soon became a huge hit, especially among the children. Looking at the success of the Kalakaji experiment, the same idea was extended to isolated villages in Madhya Pradesh and Uttar Pradesh. Inspired by the success of the experiment, International Finance Corporation collaborated with NIIT to scale the experiment inside and outside India.

Besides the Hole in the Wall experiment, NIIT, under its computer-aided education, has signed memorandums of understanding with state governments like Maharashtra, Bihar, Rajasthan, Andhra Pradesh and Gujarat to offer computer education in schools.

11.4.12 Hindustan Lever: Project i-Shakti

The project i-Shakti has been executed by Hindustan Unilever by setting up rural information kiosks for rural households.

11.4.13 Hewlett-Packard (HP): i-Community Project

HP's i-Community initiative was launched in Kuppam, Andhra Pradesh with 3.2 lakh people in four villages, along with Mogalakwena in South Africa. Under this initiative, the i-Community team took time to understand the needs of people in rural areas and take a people-centric approach. Based on the needs articulated by the community, HP developed solutions under the domains of education, health, economic development, social empowerment and interface with the government. The model launched in 2001 has been a success and has been replicated in other parts of the world.

11.4.14 Google for India Project

The tech giant Google has been a major player in India's digital transformation story and with a list of products and services, it has been among the front runners to bridge the digital divide in India. In 2020, Google announced a 10 billion USD investment in India to strengthen the digital ecosystem and will focus on: firstly, providing affordable access and information for every Indian in their own languages; second, building new products and services that are relevant to India's unique needs; thirdly, empowering businesses as they continue or embark on their digital transformation; fourth, leveraging technology and AI for social good, in areas like health, education and agriculture.

11.4.15 Wipro Applying thought Initiative (WATIS)

The WATIS initiative launched in 2001 in Bengaluru has helped schools transitioning from moving away from the chalk and talk method of teaching. The program emphasises collaborative learning, practical teaching aids and innovative techniques. Wipro has roped in Educomp Datamatics Limited for executing this initiative in schools.

11.4.16 NASSCOM Corporate Social responsibility Foundation

The National Association of Software and Service Companies (NASSCOM) has established a corporate social responsibility fund consisting of IT and non-IT firms for taking up activities for the digital inclusion program. The foundation works closely with the government to implement the digital literacy program. As a collaborator in the National Skills Mission, the foundation created a pool of digital-savvy workers.

11.4.17 Personalised Digital Learning Platforms

The global market for education technology is projected to exceed 350 billion USD in 2025, with investments in the ed-tech sector exceeding 18 billion USD in 2019. There has been a steady growth in terms of personalised digital learning platforms in India and these organizations are changing the education landscape of the country. Some of the popular organizations operating in the space are: Khan Academy, Byjus, Toppr, Vedantu, Extramarks, Unacademy, Gradeup, Coursera and Udemy. Besides the role played by the government and businesses in terms of bridging the divide in the Indian education sector, these organizations have been working in close quarters with NGOs, civil society and academia for implementation.

11.5 Discussion and Implications

The diffusion of the internet in a country has a significant impact on the social inclusion process of the nation. Bearing in mind the increase in internet penetration and other digital technologies in several countries, a shift in focus has been recommended, from discussion of only physical access to internet technologies, suggested as the first-order digital divide (van Dijk, 2005), to have skills related to the usage of it, termed as the second-order digital divide (Hargittai 2002, 2010), or a more recently coined third-order digital divide emphasizing the outcome of the usage by various segments of the society (Van Deursen and Helsper 2015; Wei et al. 2011). However, there are arguments that the first-order divide cannot be overlooked as it has been with individuals across many developing and underdeveloped economies lacking material access, for instance, the means to access the internet (Gonzales 2016; van Deursen and van Dijik 2018). This chapter discussed the schemes and practices in bridging the digital divide in the education sector through multiple stakeholders. A large part of the debate remains within the first and second level of the digital divide and calls for attention on how to bridge the digital divide.

The implications of the chapter are threefold. First, to present the readers with a comprehensive outline of the concept of the digital divide and discuss the schemes and initiatives regarding the application of ICT technologies in the education sector, from both government and private sector. Second, for educators, the chapter offers comprehensive information on the schemes and initiatives, which they can adopt in their teaching delivery and also make the learner aware of the platforms and tools for their learning. Third, for policymakers to design accessible platforms so that learning happens seamlessly when the current and new academic sessions began.

11.6 Conclusion

Computers and the internet in today's world have become necessities. Greater access to knowledge and information has been of great importance for individuals and communities to be empowered and make use of the opportunities for a better life. Kofi Annan, the former general secretary of the United Nations, said

> People lack many things: jobs, shelter, food, health care, and drinking water. Today, being cut off from basic telecommunications services is a hardship almost as acute as these other deprivations, and may indeed reduce the chances of finding remedies to them.

Taking the Indian education sector for discussion, the chapter tried to evaluate the scenario of the digital divide that exists in the education sector. Despite the progress achieved in terms of telecommunication, broadband and internet penetration, it cannot be ignored that there is still a gap between urban and rural India in terms of their usage to get maximum advantage. The chapter also discussed the reasons that led to a digital divide and the role played by stakeholders in bridging the divide. Considering the fact that 70 percent of the Indian population lives in rural areas, the challenge for institutions is huge. At the same time, it also creates entirely new opportunities for businesses in areas like education, skills and infrastructure. There is a major thrust by the government to push the digital revolution in India through the schemes like digital India, but the success largely depends on the ability to engage the community, build their competency, provide greater access, and generate more opportunity and also greater affordability for citizens. A digital push for the education sector has been a growing need and considering the present COVID-19 scenario, it is a must-have, and every stakeholder has a significant role to play.

References

Bilbao-Osorio, Benat, Dutta, Soumitra, and Lanvin, Bruno. 2014. "Global Information Technology Report 2014. Rewards and Risks of Big Data." www3.weforum.org/docs/WEF_GlobalInformationTechnology_Report_2014.pdf. Accessed 24 July 2020.

Bonfadelli, Heinz. 2002. "The Internet and Knowledge Gaps: A Theoretical and Empirical Investigation." *European Journal of Communication*. 17(1): 65–84, doi: 10.1177/026732310201700 1607.

Chandra, Sumit, Chang, Amy, Day, Lauren, Fazlullah, Amina, Liu, Jack, McBride Lane, Mudalige, Thisal, and Weiss, Danny. 2020. "Closing the K-12 Digital Divide in the Age of Distance Learning." Boston, Mass.: Boston Consulting Group and Common Sense, 2020. www.commonsensemedia.org/sites/default/files/uploads/pdfs/common_sense_media_report_final_6_29_12-42pm_web_updated.pdf. Accessed 24 July 2020.

Donohue, George. A., Tichenor, Phillip, J., and Olien, Clarice, N. 1975. "Mass Media and the Knowledge Gap: A Hypothesis Reconsidered." *Communication*. 2 (1): 3–23, doi: 10.1177/009365027500200101.

Ghobadi, Shahla, and Ghobadi, Zahara. 2015 "How Access Gaps Interact and Shape Digital Divide: A Cognitive Investigation." *Behaviour & Information Technology*. 34 (4): 330–340, doi: 10.1080/0144929X.2013.833650.

Gonzales, Amy. 2016. "The Contemporary US Digital Divide: From Initial Access to Technology Maintenance." Information, Communication & Society. 19 (2): 234–248.

Hargittai, Eszter. 2002. "Second-Level Digital Divide: Differences in People's Online Skills." First Monday 7 (4).

Hargittai, Estzer. 2010 "Digital Na(t)ives? Variation in Internet Skills and Uses among Members of the 'Net Generation'." *Sociological Inquiry*. 80 (1): 92–113, doi: 10.1111/j.1475-682X.2009.00317.x.

Jacho, Cho, Zungia, Homero Gil de, Rojas, Hernando, and Dhavan, V. Shah. 2003. "Beyond Access: The Digital Divide and Internet Uses and Gratifications." *IT & Society*. 1 (4): 46–72.

Li, Cathy, and Lalani, Farah. 2020 "The COVID-19 pandemic Has Changed Education Forever. This is How." *World Economic Forum. Future Media, Entertainment and Culture*. www.weforum.org/agenda/2020/04/coronavirus-education-global-covid19-online-digital-learning/. Accessed 24 July 2020.

Norris. Pippa. 2001 *Digital Divide: Civic Engagement, Information Poverty and the Internet in Democratic Societies*. New York: Cambridge University Press.

NTIA. 1999. *Falling Through the Net: A Survey of the 'Have Nots' in Rural and Urban America*, National Telecommunication Information Administration, United States Department of Commerce. Washington, DC. www.ntia.doc.gov/ntiahome/fttn99/. Accessed 24 July 2020.

Pick, J., and Sarkar, Avijit. 2016. "Theories of the Digital Divide: Critical Comparison." *49th Hawaii International Conference on System Sciences (HICSS)*: 3888–3897.

Riggins, Fredrick, and Dewan, Sanjeev. 2005. "The Digital Divide: Current and Future Research Directions." *Journal of the Association for Information Systems*. 6 (12), doi: 10.17705/1jais.00074

Srinuan, Calita, and Bohlin, Erik. 2011. "Understanding the Digital Divide: A Literature Survey and Ways Forward." *22nd European Regional Conference of the International Telecommunications Society (ITS):* "Innovative ICT Applications – Emerging Regulatory, Economic and Policy Issues." Budapest, Hungary, 18th–21st September, 2011, International Telecommunications Society (ITS), Calgary.

Steyaert, Jan. 2000 "Digitale vaardigheden: Geletterdheid in de informatiesamenleving." [Digital skills: Literacy in the Information Society]. *Rathenau Institute*, The Hague, Netherlands.

van Deursen, A. J. A. M., and Helsper, E. J. 2015. "The third level digital divide: who benefits most from being online?" in L. Robinson, S. R. Cotten & J. Schulz (eds), Communication and Information Technologies Annual. Studies in Media and Communications, vol. 9, pp. 29–52.

van Deursen, A. J. A. M., and van Dijk, Jan A. G. M. 2019. "The First-Level Digital Divide Shifts from Inequalities in Physical Access to Inequalities in Material Access." New Media & Society 21 (2) 354–375.

van Dijk, Jan. 1999. *The Network Society, Social Aspects of New Media*. Thousand Oaks, CA: Sage Publications.

van Dijk, Johannes A. G. M. 2005. *The Deepening Divide Inequality in the Information Society*. CA/London/New Delhi. Sage Publications.

van Dijk, Johannes A. G. M. 2006. "Digital Divide Research, Achievements and Shortcomings." *Poetics*. 34 (4–5): 221–235, doi: 10.1016/j.poetic.2006.05.004.

Wei, K. K., Teo, H. H., Chan, H. C., & Tan, B. C. Y. (2011). "Conceptualizing and testing a social cognitive model of the digital divide." Information Systems Research, 22 (1), 170–187.

12

Computer Aided Collaborative Learning: Challenges and Opportunities

Mazhar Hussain Malik, Amjed Sid Ahmed, and Ahmad Hosseini

Department of Computing and IT, Global College of Engineering and Technology Muscat, Oman

DOI: 10.1201/9781003203070-14

12.1 Introduction

Collaborative learning is an active approach to the learning process, where a group of learners can work together to solve problems, complete a task or understand new concepts. This approach, allowing the learner to be highly engaged in the learning phase, adds active interaction to the learning process and concepts instead of the learner passively listening to lectures or just noting down facts and figures. Collaborative learning motivates learners to work on different projects and complete assigned tasks as a group while they are individually responsible for their performance and the outcomes. They defend their positions, redefine their ideas and listen to other points of view to gain complete understanding as a group instead of just as individuals.

The benefits of collaborative learning, which can be seen as organizational and individual, highlight the wide range of applicability of this approach. Every organization can benefit from having an energized and well-informed workforce, while individual workers also profit by being personally involved in the learning, and this can be achieved by embedding collaborative learning in the organization. Collaborative learning may occur in a regular classroom setting or through online delivery; however, online learning has a considerable effect on the degree of learning when done collaboratively.

Collaborative learning can also create a sense of inclusion, especially for those who may feel they are excluded in class activities or for introverted learners. Group-structured activities are helpful for early-stage learners to organize their efforts, source the needed material and references, work semi-independently without being monitored by the teacher or instructor, and most importantly, to rely on their individual potential in a positively competitive atmosphere of teamwork. It brings a sense of accountability as each learner holds a role for the teaching-learning duet to be synchronized. Collaborative learning assigns a task to a group and requires job distribution and cooperation among the team members. In the meantime, it improves the leading traits for the leader-type learners.

Collaborative learning is a comprehensive term for a vast variety of educational approaches which involve students, or students and teachers together, in the learning process. This approach is specifically productive in distance learning as it removes the barrier of non-collaboration and individualized processing of learning by creating a sense of inclusion through online methods. Federico 2000 cited Keegan 1998 by asserting that distance learning involves providing instructions through non-traditional methods, such as television, correspondence, radio and the use of satellites. This process also involves the issuance of guidelines using the internet, digital media, hardware and software. Furthermore, the instructor can communicate with many students simultaneously by electronic media. In this regard, distance learning comes in two types, namely, synchronous and asynchronous instruction.

Digital learning or computer aided learning, as a common form of distance learning, would entail developing off-campus lessons, workshops and seminars, where the teacher is not physically present. The United States recorded about 3.2 million complete online enrolments during the fall term of 2005 (Allen and Seaman 2007). This number increases with the technological advancement and rapid growth of online courses. Online learning is not only a reasonable solution for learners who would like to study at distance, or have no other option, but is also a main method for making resources accessible to a bigger audience worldwide. With the 2020 pandemic, more experts and scholars began to research for the impacts of online learning as well as its scope and benefits.

As experts need to study the impact of online classes on the academic and social well-being of children (Khalifa and Lam 2002), the scope of collaborative learning should also be included in the picture. According to (Tinto 1997), the classroom environment helps to bridge the academic and social integration of students in higher education. Moreover, the kind of relationship that occurs in online classrooms is of great importance to students. Tinto explained that the activities of teachers within the classroom environment play a significant role in enhancing their notion of scholarly belonging. Furthermore, they enhance the ability of students to persist whilst engaging in their academic pursuits. Existing evidence supports the fact that the development of an online community exerts a positive impact on the overall success of a student in the education sector (Tinto 1997).

However, questions remain about the potential provided by a fully online class to support and enhance the growth of communities with a high level of learning (Quitadamo and Brown 2001). From a general perspective, online education, relative to traditional methods, enables students to actively interact with their teachers. It also provides them with more resources and enables them to become independent in their learning journey; however, it hinders the communal features which can grow through face-to-face interaction in a regular classroom. It appears that introverts can benefit from being in an online session, particularly if they are anonymous. They can actively question their instructors without fear or stress, while at the same time enjoying the participation in group activity whenever there is a break-out session or a group project.

Computer aided learning is not limited to online learning. Offline devices and software also play a significant role in collaborative learning as they help learners review the lesson and practice multiple times while a regular class session cannot be re-performed once it ends. With the help of computers, teaching, practicing, learning and assessment can be easily conducted, and classrooms can be simulated. Online or offline teaching incorporates the learners into a virtual reality, to say the classroom, where the anxiety and stress of the actual classroom can be reduced. The assessment simulation is also a genuine way of practicing before the actual examination.

12.2 Collaborative Learning Theories

Learning theories in pedagogy have different strains depending on the target group and age range. Collaborative learning theories are divided into two groups, one related to social development and the other to cognitive development. Social development entails the sense of identity, role and purpose, whereas cognitive development involves thought, rationale and perception (Bélanger 2011). Social and cognitive development in adults and children follow different patterns and differ in collaborative learning. In this section, we discuss the theories of cognitive learning applying to children, and later we will consider the cognitive learning process which adults undertake to develop their thoughts and perceptions.

12.2.1 Vygotsky's Theory

This theory focuses on social understanding and interaction in the learning environment. According to this theory social context plays a vital role in the design and development of understanding and knowledge. The theory suggests the impossibility of perception development by an individual without implementation of social context. One of the key aspects of this theory is proximal development, which is an ability to visualize what a person can do and what they cannot (Hadwin, Sanna, and Miller 2018).

12.2.2 Piaget's Theory

Jean Piaget is the founder of "cognitive theory" development, the way infants and children understand their environment, and how they develop their understanding based on hypotheses. During this cognition process, children construct understanding about the environment based on their initial perception and how they perceive that the world changes gradually and based on the new experience. He calls this constant trend of replacing a perception with the newly and differently experienced experience the cognitive development. Hence, children construct their own individual understanding of the surrounding world, examine discrepancies between the understanding and experience, and then replace them with new perceptions. The gradual and constant growth of experience, perception, new experience, correction and new hypothesis is the core idea of cognitive theory. Children experience in order to get the correct answer and organize their mental process (Jeong, Heisawn, and Hmelo-Silver 2016). Piaget also introduced the concept of "schema", which is the unit of knowledge that allows individuals to organize and understand knowledge in efficient ways. A schema is a cohesive and repeatable sequence of actions which are intrinsically interrelated and spin around a core concept. Based on Piaget's theory there are four different stages of cognitive development which need to happen before the start of the learning. The first stage, "sensorimotor" or infancy, starts from birth to up to two years and in this stage the child develops object permanence. The second stage is "preoperational", running from the age of two to seven and is related to symbolic thinking development. The child develops the third stage, called the "concrete operational" stage, from the age of seven to eleven as a period related to logic development. Finally, the fourth stage is the "operational stage", in which the child starts developing from the age of 11 when they start to think logically and work out complex hypotheses.

12.2.3 Kegan's Theory

Both Vygotsky and Piaget consider their cognitive theories fit to children, as they believed the cognition process stops around the age of 25. However, Robert Kegan, among some other scholars, believes that cognition and learning are lifelong processes. He praises the genius of Jean Piaget but also adds new ideas to his legacy (Kegan, 1982). Based on Kegan's theory, individuals move along an attitude shift, from a subjective framework of defining themselves as "what they are" towards an objective framework of "what they have". This transformation takes place throughout life and never ceases. All the beliefs, assumptions and key behaviors can be labeled under this category in which the individual holds an up-close point of view with less possibility for self-reflection (Kegan 1994). Kegan highlights the fixed attitude one may have for a certain set of ideas without questioning them. He introduces five stages of growth and development, explaining each stage as "loss" of the previous stage. He believes the "self" develops as the person grows up. Unlike Piaget, he does not start his review of the "self" by "differentiation" with "others". However, he looks upon human beings from a more holistic point of view, which implies that human beings are born with the "self" and develop it throughout life. Therefore, in this lifelong motion, he recognizes five "selves", each one replacing the previous one throughout life, the incorporative self, impulsive self, imperial self, interpersonal self and institutional self (Kegan 1982).

12.3 Bloom's Taxonomy and Learning Domains

Educational psychologist Benjamin Bloom developed his taxonomy in 1956 intending to promote a higher form of thinking in education. These forms were: analysis and evaluation of concepts, principles, and procedures which deviated from the educational norm of rote learning. Bloom's taxonomy provides a framework that has often been used in designing academic training and learning processes. In addition, it sets three hierarchical models that categorize educational learning goals into different levels of specificity and complexity. The three models are: "cognitive", dealing with mental skills, "affective", being emotion-based, and "psychomotor", being action-based (Bloom et al. 1956).

The three-model form KSA (knowledge, skills and attitudes) is the model that instructional designers, trainers and educators use for the teaching-learning process. The "knowledge" arises from the cognitive model that denotes the aspect of recalling facts, basic concepts, answers and terms that have been taught. The "attitude" in the affective model defines how people respond emotionally, and also elaborates the ability they develop for feeling other persons' or living things' joy or pain. Attitude, thereby, arises from an affective domain that targets the growth and awareness of emotion, attitudes and feelings. Lastly, "skills" are associated with the psychomotor model that describes the ability of an individual to manipulate instruments and tools physically. The focus of the psychomotor domain is on development and change in behavior or skills.

The initial perception was that the KSA is utilized in learning behavior where learners form the goals of the learning process. That is to mean, after the learning process, the learner should have acquired the right knowledge, attitude and skills that they can use in future. The goal of education, therefore, is to elevate learners to better understanding and mental development of handling problems in life. Gaining knowledge, new attitudes and skills indicates the achievement of this goal. Later, some scholars managed to elaborate concepts on the affective and cognitive domain but failed to do so in the area of psychomotor. Conversely, other researchers have developed more than three models of psychomotor. The researchers have classified the three domains into further subdivision in a hierarchy that starts from simple to the most complex. The divisions are not outlined adequately since other rankings have been formulated, such as "Structure of Observed Learning Behavior".

12.3.1 Cognitive Domain

The cognitive domain entails the development of intellectual skills and knowledge (Bloom et al. 1956). It involves recognizing particular facts, concepts and procedural concepts incorporated in skills and intellectual abilities development. Moreover, the domain includes six categories ranked ascendingly from the simplest to the most complex as knowledge, comprehension, application, analysis, synthesis and evaluation. Each category marks the level of difficulty where the first one must be mastered before proceeding to the next category. However, some scholars, including a former student of Bloom, modified the taxonomy in the mid-1990s (Huitt 2001). The first change made by these scholars was altering the names of the six categories from noun to verb forms. The second change was rearranging the classes, and the third change was developing processes and ranks of the knowledge matrix. The newly formed taxonomy reflected an active form of thinking and was also perhaps more accurate than the previous taxonomy. The new taxonomy can be described as:

- Remembering: involves retrieving or recalling previously learned information, for example quoting prices for customers out of memory.
- Understanding: comprehending what translations, instructions and problems mean. For instance, explain in one word the steps of performing a task.
- Applying: using concepts learned in a novel situation. For example, applying statistical laws to evaluate the reliability of a written test.
- Analyzing: separating concepts or various material parts to organize it in a structure that can be understood. An example is troubleshooting pieces of equipment through logical deduction.
- Evaluating: judging the values of materials or ideas. Choosing an appropriate solution is a good example.
- Creating: developing patterns or structures from various distinct elements, for instance, writing the company operations manual.

The revised taxonomy was thereby improved in terms of usability through the use of action words and added a knowledge and cognitive matrix. Even though the previous taxonomy had the three-level of knowledge that could be processed, it failed to discuss them extensively and left the taxonomy remaining one-dimensional. The taxonomy's three dimensions were factual, involving the essential elements students must know to be acquainted with discipline and entailing conceptual interrelationships existing within essential elements, and procedural, which is a method of inquiry. In the revised version, the authors integrated these three levels with cognitive processes to form a knowledge matrix. In addition, they included another level of knowledge, which is metacognition, that is, the general knowledge of cognition, awareness and one's own cognition.

12.3.2 Affective Domain

The affective domain includes how people respond to emotional feelings such as values, enthusiasm, affection, motivation and attitude (Krathwohl 1964). The first main category of this domain is the receiving phenomenon that describes the willingness to hear, selected attention and awareness. The second category responds to phenomena which entail active participation on the part of the learner. The learner has to attend and respond to a specific phenomenon. The third category is valuing, which marks the work a person ascribes to a particular behavior, phenomenon or object. The fourth one is organization, which is prioritizing values by contrasting and resolving conflicts between them. The last category is internalized values, which have a value system that controls behavior.

12.3.3 Psychomotor Domain

The psychomotor domain integrates physical movement, coordination and the use of motor-skills (Simpson 1972). Psychomotor skills are developed through constant training practice, and are measured in terms of speed, techniques of execution, precision, distance and procedure. Therefore, psychomotor skills vary from conducting simple manual tasks to undertaking difficult, complex tasks like operating machinery. The seven main classes of this domain, from simplest to the most complex are: perception, set, guided response, mechanism, complex overt response, adaptation and origination. Perception features the ability to use sensory clues and directed motor activity, whereas set marks the readiness of a person to act. Guided response entails imitation used in early stages of learning and trial and error employed in learning complex skills. Mechanism marks the point when the response has become habitual, while complex overt response involves the skillful performance of the motor act. Lastly, adaptation is the stage when skills are well developed, and origination entails creating new movement patterns.

12.4 Collaborative Learning: Individual Benefits

12.4.1 Ignite Active Learning

When employees are involved in collaborative learning, they become actively engaged, which means that they can gain more skills and knowledge. Collaborative learning allows learners to listen and understand other points of view, which help them promote their learning abilities.

12.4.2 Boost Critical and Quick Thinking

Collaborative learning allows participants to boost their thinking power, which enables them to synthesize and adjust their responses. This enables them to acquire new information and set their point of view with the stream of new ideas. A collaborative learning environment allows learners to listen to other ideas and thoughts and provide arguments to their peers. Using this dynamic approach allows learners to gain better understanding about the domain as learners can consider all the possible angles (Nyembe and Royd Howard 2019; Ahmed et al. 2020).

12.4.3 Enhance Speaking and Listening Skills

This form of learning allows individuals to speak in front of an audience and listen to them actively. It also helps them build a framework of ideas to be executed, increasing their individual confidence and enabling them to actively interact with society.

12.4.4 Lead to Problem Solving

Collaborative learning helps to bring different teams or individuals together and present them with a problem to solve. It leads to developing new features in the product and allows team members to understand the future needs of the product. Problem solving exercises while working in a group build intellectual thinking in the employees which is useful for individuals and organizations (Nyembe and Royd Howard 2019; Ahmed et al. 2020).

12.4.5 Develop New Products

Collaborative learning plays a significant role in group work as teams can work together to identify the gaps in the existing product, coming up with different solutions and finally selecting the best possible solution to create or modify the existing product (Nyembe and Royd Howard 2019; Ahmed et al. 2020).

12.4.6 Build a Collaborative Learning Environment

Collaborative learning enables the building of a collaborative learning environment where workers can team up to solve problems, giving ample opportunities to learners and trainers to enhance their skills and expertise (Nyembe and Royd Howard 2019).

12.5 Collaborative Learning: Organisational Benefits

Collaborative learning offers many key benefits to organizations, among which we can count the following:

12.5.1 Enhance Leadership Skills

Working in a group allows individuals to achieve common organizational goals, which offers the opportunity to gain high-level skills. It also helps individuals to organize, teach, assign tasks, manage themselves and hone their leadership skills. Working in a group increases existing skills as participants are involved in teaching others and it enables them to learn new skills from other employees. Collaborative learning reduces the need for formal training and encourages employees to maximize their expertise (Nolan et al. 2019).

12.5.2 Enhance Team and Departmental Relationships

Contact building is a crucial feature while working in an organization, but when individuals have limited contacts across other teams, it is very difficult to build connections and practice teamwork. Collaborative learning enables individuals to become more productive by working in a team and find better ways to work with others, which in the long term helps organizations. By building this team spirit and departmental relationships, individuals develop strong connections with each other and, ultimately, become an asset for the organization (Stevanoviü et al. 2020).

12.5.3 Enhance Employee Engagement, Acquisition and Retention Rate

Collaborative learning leads to increased employee engagement and involvement in the organization, which improves organizational performance with high retention rate. Collaborative learning also allows employees to achieve better thinking and access useful information compared to what they might get in non-collaborative settings. It is also worth mentioning that collaborative learning enhances employee's skills by providing a better working environment where they can improve themselves and ultimately increase organizational performance. The performance of an organization directly and ultimately depends on employees and when the satisfaction level of employees is higher the organizational efficiency will be high as well (Stevanoviü et al. 2020).

12.6 Computer Aided Collaborative Learning (Figure 12.1)

Computer aided collaborative learning can be performed online or offline. Both methods can engage learners and are helpful throughout the learning process. (Sharples 2019).

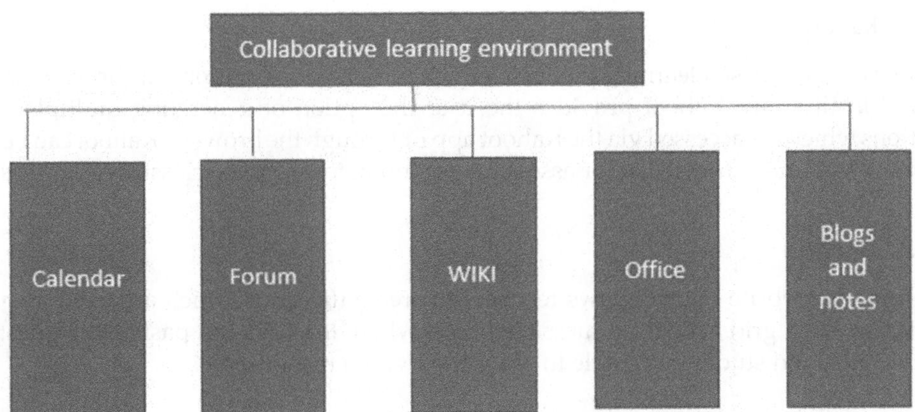

FIGURE 12.1
Collaborative Learning Environment.

The learning process which takes place in the regular classroom is always constructive, interactive and helps learners to incorporate their individual traits in their social relation with other learners. However, the capacity of computer-based learning should not be underestimated. The computer aided collaborative learning environment can be divided into: calendar, forum, Wiki, office, blogs and notes (Alur et al. 2020; Chen et al. 2018).

The mentioned tools are mostly interactive platforms which can be utilized online or offline. The type of environment has a great impact on the learner, which emphasizes the importance of collaborative learning here. The following platforms are all produced based on collaborative learning approaches.

12.6.1 BlackBoard Collaborate Ultra

Blackboard Collaborate is a real-time video conferencing tool that allows learners to use a virtual whiteboard, add files, and share applications and screens. The strength of this application is that there is no need to install any software to join a session and it easily opens in the browser.

12.6.2 WIZIQ

WIZIQ is a cloud-based education platform which is used to access training and teaching modules using desktops, laptops and smartphones. The platform allows the user to conduct the classes online with different packages being available as per the need of the customers (Al-Rahmi and Akram, 2017).

12.6.3 Google Apps for Education

Google for Education is a service that provides the customizable versions of different Google products using domain names provided by the customers. It features various web applications with similar functionalities aligned with traditional office suits including Gmail, Google Meet, Google Calendar, Google Drive, Google Docs, Google Sheets, Google Slides, Hangouts, Group, News, Play, Vault and Sites. Google for Education and Google apps are non-profits and are free, offering the same amount of storage as Google Apps for Work accounts.

12.6.4 Kahoot

Kahoot is a game-based learning platform which is used for educational technology in educational institutions. Kahoot provides the user the option of generating multiple choice questions which are accessed via the Kahoot app or through the browser. Kahoot can be used to review students' knowledge for assessments, and helps to create classroom activities.

12.6.5 FlipGrid

FlipGrid is a website which allows teachers to create the grids which are used for video discussion: each grid acts like a message board where teachers can paste their questions, called topics, and students are able to paste their video responses.

12.6.6 Skype in Education

Skype is also a free web-based communication tool which allows users to make calls, carry out video conferences and send instant messages. There are about 300 million active Skype users around the world. Skype provides students and teachers with the opportunity to participate in virtual tours of different places, communicate with authors and researchers, and also engage in conversations with classrooms around the world. In addition to that, Mystery Skype enables two classrooms to connect from different locations in a fun way and both classrooms can call each other on Skype and can ask questions.

12.7 Challenges and Opportunities for Designing Computer Aided Collaborative Learning

Computer aided collaborative learning is coming up with a lot of challenges and opportunities in the twenty-first century. The importance of computer-added collaborative learning significantly increased in the first quarter of 2020 due to the pandemic. The need for collaborative learning tools has increased significantly in the various sectors of education, whether those are universities, colleges or schools. Since March 2020, the whole world has been in a pandemic situation and learning has shifted to a new paradigm which is focusing on distance and e-learning. There are certain challenges and opportunities which are associated with computer aided collaborative learning, mentioned as follows.

The first and foremost challenge of collaborative learning is the availability of infrastructure, considering the fact that learning and educational tools are normally used in universities and in some cases in colleges, but are less used in schools. However, during the 2020 pandemic situation the need for online collaborative tools increased as students were not able to attend their regular classes and needed to study from home. Hence, there is a need to have collaborative learning tools which enable students to work in groups or pairs to perform their group tasks. There is a great need to enhance the existing infrastructure with respect to hardware requirements. The infrastructure requires high specification hardware with respect to processing power, RAM and storage capacity. There is also a great need for upgrading the internet infrastructure, because of the increase in multimedia traffic and to boost the learning management platforms.

Secondly, software and platforms which are running in the collaborative learning system should have the capacity to meet the requirements of the desired specification so that these tools and platforms can work properly.

The third and most important challenge associated with computer aided collaborative learning is education for children aged 3–11, in particular, as due to the pandemic situation the current available platforms are not suitable to help this age group in their learning. Educational institutions need to have a major shift in computer added collaborative learning tools which can address the issues faced by different levels of students, so that their learning will not be interrupted or stopped in any circumstances.

To conclude, computer aided collaborative learning tools are the ultimate solution to help students to gain knowledge from their homes in the pandemic situation without affecting their group studies by using these types of tools. To gain maximum benefit for twenty-first-century requirements, it is suggested that engineering tools such as Agile approach are applied to gather the necessary information and design the computer aided collaborative learning tools which are needed.

References

Ahmed, Amjed Sid, Mohamed Sid Ahmed, and Mazhar Hussain Malik. 2020. "Machine learning for strategic decision making during covid-19 at higher education institutes." In *2020 International Conference on Decision Aid Sciences and Application (DASA)*, pp. 663–668. IEEE.

Al-Rahmi, Waleed Mugahed, and Akram M. Zeki. 2017. "A model of using social media for collaborative learning to enhance learners' performance on learning." *Journal of King Saud University-Computer and Information Sciences* 29, no. 4: 526–535.

Allen, I. Elaine, and Jeff Seaman. 2007. *Online nation: Five years of growth in online learning*. Newburyport, MA: Sloan Consortium. 01950.

Alur, Rajeev, Richard Baraniuk, Rastislav Bodik, Ann Drobnis, Sumit Gulwani, Bjoern Hartmann, Yasmin Kafai et al. 2020. "Computer-Aided Personalized Education." *arXiv preprint arXiv:2007.03704*.

Bélanger, Paul. 2011. *Theories in adult learning and education*. Opladen: Verlag Barbara Budrich.

Bloom, Benjamin S., Max D. Engelhart, Edward J. Furst, Walquer H. Hill, and David R. Krathwohl. 1956. *Taxonomy of educational objectives: The classification of educational goals: Handbook I: Cognitive domain*. No. 373.19 C734t. New York: Mckay.

Chen, Juanjuan, Minhong Wang, Paul A. Kirschner, and Chin-Chung Tsai. 2018. "The role of collaboration, computer use, learning environments, and supporting strategies in CSCL: A meta-analysis." *Review of Educational Research* 88, no. 6: 799–843.

Federico, Pat-Anthony. 2000. "Learning styles and student attitudes toward various aspects of network-based instruction." *Computers in Human Behavior* 16, no. 4: 359–379.

Hadwin, A., Järvelä, S. and Miller, M., 2018. "Self-regulation, co-regulation, and shared regulation in collaborative learning environments." In D. H. Schunk & J. A. Greene (eds.), Handbook of Self-Regulation of Learning and Performance. London: Routledge/Taylor & Francis Group.

Huitt, W. 2011. "Bloom et al.'s taxonomy of the cognitive domain." Educational Psychology Interactive." 22.

Jeong, Heisawn, and Cindy E. Hmelo-Silver. 2016. "Seven affordances of computer-supported collaborative learning: How to support collaborative learning? How can technologies help?" *Educational Psychologist* 51, no. 2: 247–265.

Keegan, Desmond. 1998. "The two modes of distance education." *Open Learning: The Journal of Open, Distance and e-Learning* 13, no. 3: 43–47.

Kegan, Robert. 1982. *The evolving self*. Cambridge, MA: Harvard University Press.

Kegan, Robert. 1994. *In over our heads*. Cambridge, MA: Harvard University Press.

Khalifa, Mohamed, and Rinky Lam. 2002. "Web-based learning: Effects on learning process and outcome." *IEEE Transactions on education* 45, no. 4: 350–356.

Krathwohl, D.R., 1964. Bloom's Taxonomy of Educational Objectives: The Classification of Educational Goals. Hand book II: Affective domain. New York: David Mckay.

Nolan, Clare, Kim Ammann Howard, Kelley D. Gulley, and Elizabeth Gonzalez. 2019. "More than listening: Harnessing the power of feedback to drive collaborative learning." *The Foundation Review* 11, no. 2: 11–12.

Nyembe, Bangisisi Zamuxolo Mathews, and Grant Royd Howard. 2019 "The utilities of prominent learning theories for mobile collaborative learning (MCL) with reference to WhatsApp and m-learning." In *2019 International Conference on Advances in Big Data, Computing and Data Communication Systems (icABCD)*, pp. 1–6. IEEE.

Quitadamo, I.J., and Brown, A., 2001. Effective Teaching Styles and Instructional Design for Online Learning Environments. Washington, DC: Department of Education.

Rovai, A.P. 2002. "Building sense of community at a distance. the international review of research in open and distributed learning." [Sl], v. 3, n. 1. *Distances et médiations des savoirs. Distance and Mediation of Knowledge.*

Sharples, M. 2019. "Visions for the future of educational technology." In R. Ferguson *et al.* (eds.), Educational Visions: The Lessons from 40 Years of Innovation. London: Ubiquity Press.

Simpson, E. 1972. *The classification of learning objectives in the psychomotor domain*. Washington, DC: Gryphon House.

Stevanoviü, Jelena, Srdjan Atanasijeviü, Tatjana Atanasijeviü, and Monika Zahar. 2020. "Expanding the level of engineer knowledge for software modeling within corporate education by active and collaborative learning." In *2020 IEEE Global Engineering Education Conference (EDUCON)*, pp. 1807–1814. IEEE.

Tinto, Vincent. 1997. "Classrooms as communities: Exploring the educational character of student persistence." *The Journal of Higher Education* 68, no. 6: 599–623.

13

Estimating Attainment of Course Outcomes (COs) and Program Outcomes (POs) in the Digital Age

Nitin Tyagi

Department of Electronics and Communication Engineering, JIMS Engineering Management Technical Campus, Greater Noida, India

Manjula Jain

College of Management, Teerthankar Mahaveer University, Moradabad, India

Sandeep Gupta, Shekhar Singh, and Krishan Kumar Saraswat

Department of Computer Science and Engineering, JIMS Engineering Management Technical Campus, Greater Noida, India

13.1 Introduction

"Researchers examine what already is; Engineers make what has never been," is an axiom by Albert Einstein that conveys an effortlessness in engineering within the world. In the wake of finishing advanced education in the digital/online era, an undergraduate who picks an engineering qualification should have experienced various stages within the education framework. In the wake of picking a specific program for studying engineering, they need to gain entry to the institution. The institution will have a dream, which is the underlying driver for creating qualified specialists. It will set a mission, as indicated by authoritative guidelines. The vision and mission are overseen by a committee comprising individuals from the establishment. Partners are the board members from the organization. The partners are divided into inner and outer partners. The inner partners

DOI: 10.1201/9781003203070-15

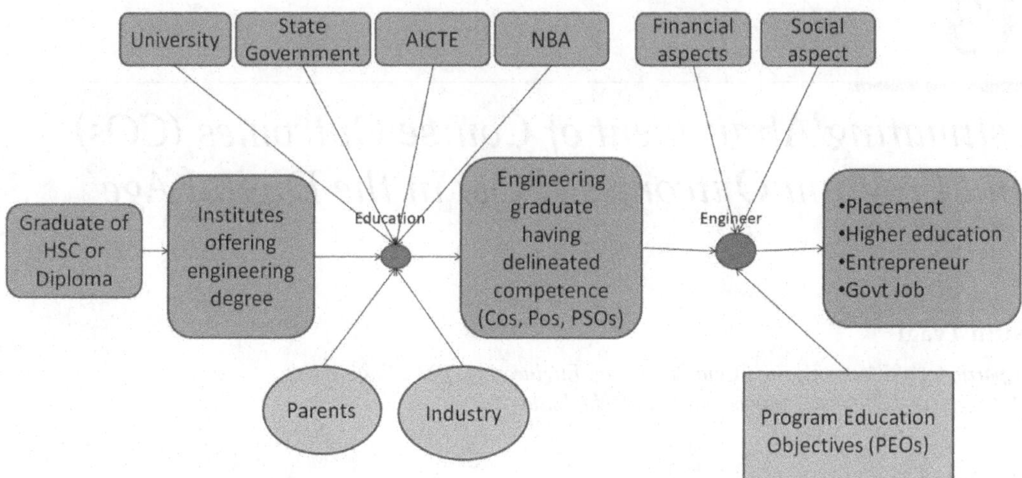

The layout shown in Figure 13.1 illustrates the structure of outcome based education. Different aspects of stakeholders are shown in figure, starting from admission of a undergraduate in engineering program to the placement of the undergraduate pass out.

FIGURE 13.1
Layout of OBE.

of an organization incorporate administration, administering board members, faculty individuals, non-teaching staff and undergraduates. The outer partners are guardians, management, industry specialists and alumni. The administration of self-financing engineering institutions offers fiscal stanchion to the administrative operation of the institution/college. The university offers alliance for the establishment subsequent to satisfying the standards. Later the organization will comply with the guidelines and educational program discharged by the affiliating university (Kavitha et al. 2018). Ordinarily the syllabus of the university is chosen by individuals from a leading body of study, which depends on crucial ideas, on-going patterns, and applications in innovation and industry demands. The employee of the foundation dealing with online education is to convey the educational program to undergraduates. The organization must have industry-institute collaboration.

The affiliating university operates within the regulations of the State Government to meet the standards of AICTE (AICTE 2018), which specifies all the required standards to the institutes, both for employees and undergraduates who work in technical areas. The National Board of Accreditation (NBA) awards the accreditation to the specific engineering program (branch), which needs to be satisfied to the standards of NBA (NBA 2015a and NBA 2015b). Undergraduates who finish an engineering degree should be given the chance to work in centre organizations, to seek a higher degree by going to GATE/GRE/IELTS/different exam(s), to land government positions through going to common administrations assessment, and, ultimately, to become technical entrepreneurs. Graduands can pick any of the above mentioned degrees, depending on their knowledge, ecomonic and social situation, and family circumstances. This decides the accomplishment of the Program Educational Objectives (PEOs) of the institute (Noureddine et al. 2013). This entire system provides the undergraduate with the best possible direction for e-learning.

The outcome, in addition to the object of teaching, is that scholars become skilled in the next step of a course. OBE focuses each slice of the didactic practice on goals or outcomes. So, the evaluation of outcome must include a total assessment of knowledge, skill and proficiency as well as attitude towards the fulfilment of the goal after completing four years of graduate study. To accomplish the advantage of the OBE, no single determined way is available for educating or appraisal techniques to be continued in the OBE framework (Askar 2009). It is achieved by delivering the content either by conventional, active or both learning methodologies that can be adopted based on the requirements. Some of the conventional methodologies that can be used are: assignments, Powerpoint presentations, case studies, seminars, guest lectures, Flip classes and workshops. Some of the active methodologies are: quizzes, role play, group discussions, brain storming sessions, implementing mini and major projects, industrial visits, industrial training and value added courses. An OBE framework deals with the competency requirement of students; further it organizes the assessment methods and curriculum to ensure sufficient learning methods.

13.2 Synopsis of Criteria

The manner of NBA accreditation has varied, starting with OBE practice near the role of Tier-I, then progressing toward Tier-II official approval processes (David et al. 2014). This OBE accreditation might be attained by effective use of autonomy through mission, vision, strategic planning and goals, of the college/institution. Success depends on the nine standards required by NBA to satisfy OBE to the sphere of Tier-II technical program:

i. Mission, Vision and PEOs
ii. Program Syllabus and Teaching-Learning Process
iii. COs and POs
iv. Undergraduates' Achievement
v. Faculty Knowledge and Contribution
vi. Teaching and Non-teaching staff
vii. Steady Enhancement
viii. Undergraduate Support System
ix. Governance, Financial Resources and Institutional Support

13.3 CO, PO and PSO Attainments

To handle the acquirement of COs and POs, moreover, Program Specific Outcomes (PSOs) one has to prepare proper COs for every course in the program starting from the first year to the final year engineering degree program. The COs are prepared by the relevant faculties of the department/course using knowledge levels as proposed by (Bloom 1956) and later by (Anderson and Krathwohl 2001). Now, a correlation is to be established among COs and POs within the scale of 1 to 3: 1 stands for low, 2 for medium, and 3 for high correlation. A matrix, which is called a mapping matrix, is then prepared in this regard for each and every course in the program, which also includes the elective subjects as

TABLE 13.1
Course Outcomes

COs	After taking this course students will be able to:
C106.1	Gain basic knowledge **(Remembering)** and discuss **(Understanding)** about semiconductor devices: diodes, BJT, FET and basic logic gates and its function.
C106.2	Analyse **(Analysing)** and distinguish **(Analysing)** the behaviour of semiconductor devices under bias and plot **(Draw)** their I-V Characteristics.
C106.3	Apply knowledge **(Remembering)** of semiconductor devices to design **(Creating)** basic analog and digital logic circuit using basic gates.
C106.4	Construct **(Creating)** the hybrid model of the semiconductor devices for further analysis.

TABLE 13.2
CO and PO Mapping

CO/PO Mapping
S/M/W indicates strength of correlation (3 = Strong, 2 = Moderate, 1 = Weak)

COs	Program Objectives (POs)											
	PO1	PO2	PO3	PO4	PO5	PO6	PO7	PO8	PO9	PO10	PO11	PO12
C106.1	3	2	1	2	-	-	-	-	-	1	-	2
C106.2	2	3	2	2	2	-	-	-		1	-	2
C106.3	3	3	3	2	2	-	-	-	2	2	-	3
C106.4	3	3	3	3	2	1	1					
C106	**2.75**	**2.75**	**2.25**	**2.25**	**2**	**1**	**1**	**-**	**2**	**1.33**	**-**	**2.33**

well. The curriculum outcomes in print as well as the mapping accompanied by POs are scrutinized recurrently, and then by a working group which includes superior teachers prior to finalization. Tables 13.1 to 13.3 program the COs then the COs-POs delineating matrix designed for a model subject (Kulkarni et al. 2017). Using the delineating grid of COs along with POs to every one of the programs, a 'Program Level Course-PO Lattice' to the considerable number of subjects incorporating first year subjects is readied. Table 13.3 shows a 'Course-PO' mapping network. For simplicity, just some of the courses appear, with hypothecated mapping esteems aside from C106 course.

13.4 CO Attainment

COs are smaller proclamations that depict what undergraduates are expected to know, and have the option to do toward the end of each course. These are aligned with the abilities, information and conduct that undergraduates gain in their registration through the course (NBA Tier II Manual 2013).

In a college partnered school, the CO achievement levels can be estimated dependent on the after-effects of the inner appraisal and outside assessment led by the college (Charles and Alberto 2003). It is known as direct estimation to fulfilment. Within the college which the creator's foundation is associated with, three inward appraisal (IA) exams are directed to every subject of that semester. For all exams, the number of undergraduates who accomplish a desired objective (normally, 60% to the most extreme imprints, that is 18 of 30) for the COs which are secured is processed. In the wake of all mid-term exams, the mean

TABLE 13.3
Program Level PO Outcomes Matrix

Course	PO1	PO2	PO3	PO4	PO5	PO6	PO7	PO8	PO9	PO10	PO11	PO12	Overall CO Attainment
C101	3	1.67	2.33	3	1.33	-	-	-	1.33	-	-	-	**1.5**
C102	2	-	-	-	3	1.33	2.33	1.67	-	-	-	-	**1.9**
-													
-													
-													
C106	2.75	2.75	2.25	2.25	2.00	1.00	1.00	-	2.00	1.33	-	2.33	**1.60**
-													
-													
C201	2	3	-	-	-	2.33	2	3	3	2.33	3	2.67	**2**
-													
-													
-													
-													
C305	3	1.67	1.33	3	-	-	1	2.33	-	-	2	3	**2.3**
-													
-													
-													
-													
C410	1.33	2	3	1.67	2.67	2.33	-	-	-	3	2.67	2.33	**2.33**

is figured for choosing the fulfilment level. The NBA has already provided, in its Self-Assessment Report (SAR) group, the accompanying model rules to achieve an accomplishment level:

- **Achievement Level 1**: If 60% of undergraduates score over 60% marks out of the maximum relevant marks.
- **Achievement Level 2**: If 70% of undergraduates score over 60% marks out of the maximum relevant marks.
- **Achievement Level 3**: If 80% of undergraduates score over 60% marks out of the maximum relevant marks.

In this manner, the normal level of undergraduates achieving every one of the COs chooses the COs fulfilment level. As an example, in the IA exams, the objective achievement level for every CO and for all undergraduates is aimed at 60% of the maximum marks for a question or a group of questions. The percentage of students achieving the target level of each and every CO is calculated and the mean of these percentages is examined to decide the *attainment level of the CO as discussed above in the example guidelines*. The way toward registering CO accomplishment in inside evaluation appears in Table 13.4.

Observing Table 13.4, it is discovered that the rates of undergraduates achieving CO1 to CO4 are 36%, 66.1%, 30.4%, and 29.1% separately. Consequently, the average level of undergraduates who achieved every one of the COs is 40.4%. This compares to Course Fulfilment Level 0.

Correspondingly, succeeding the statement to the college outcomes, the level of undergraduates who accomplished the COs is registered. Here, it is expected that the questions answered by the students cover all the COs designated for that course. As per Table 13.4 (kindly refer the last two columns), it is discovered that 55.4% of undergraduates

TABLE 13.4
Level of Undergraduates Achieving COs and Achievement Level

Sl No	Student Name	RollNo	Marks according to course outcomes								
			CO1 (5 Marks)			CO2 (4 Marks)					
			Q 3 (a)	%	Target Level (>=60%)	Q 1 (a)	Q 1 (e)	%	Target Level (>=60%)	Q 1 (b)	Q 1 (c)
1	Student 1	17225XX001	3	60	Y	2	2	100	Y	2	2
2	Student 2	17225XX002	4	80	Y	2	2	100	Y	2	2
3	Student 3	17225XX003	NA	NA	NA	2	2	100	Y	2	2
4	Student 4	17225XX004	2	40	N	2	2	100	Y	2	2
5	Student 5	17225XX005	3	60	Y	2	2	100	Y	2	2
6	Student 6	17225XX006	NA	NA	NA	2	2	100	Y	2	2
7	Student 7	17225XX007	NA	NA	NA	2	0	50	N	2	2
8	Student 8	17225XX008	0	0	N	2	2	100	Y	2	2
9	Student 9	17225XX009	NA	NA	NA	1	2	75	Y	2	2
10	Student 10	17225XX010	NA	NA	NA	2	NA	50	N	2	0
11	Student 11	17225XX011	0	0	N	NA	1	25	N	2	1
12	Student 12	17225XX012	NA	NA	NA	NA	1	25	N	2	NA
13	Student 13	17225XX013	2	40	N	0	2	50	N	2	2
14	Student 14	17225XX014	0	0	N	2	2	100	Y	2	NA
15	Student 15	17225XX015	3	60	Y	2	2	100	Y	2	1
16	Student 16	17225XX016	1	20	N	1	NA	25	N	NA	2
17	Student 17	17225XX017	NA	NA	NA	1	0	25	N	2	NA
18	Student 18	17225XX018	NA	NA	NA	2	2	100	Y	2	2
19	Student 19	17225XX019	1	20	N	2	2	100	Y	2	1
20	Student 20	17225XX020	NA	NA	NA	1	2	75	Y	2	1
21	Student 21	17225XX021	NA	NA	NA	1	2	75	Y	2	2
22	Student 22	17225XX022	3	60	Y	NA	0	0	N	1	2
23	Student 23	17225XX023	NA	NA	NA	2	1	75	Y	2	2
24	Student 24	17225XX024	NA	NA	NA	2	2	100	Y	2	2
25	Student 25	17225XX025	NA	NA	NA	2	1	75	Y	2	2
26	Student 26	17225XX026	NA	NA	NA	2	2	100	Y	2	2
27	Student 27	17225XX027	NA	NA	NA	NA	NA	NA	NA	NA	NA
28	Student 28	17225XX028	NA	NA	NA	1	NA	25	N	2	1
29	Student 29	17225XX029	NA	NA	NA	2	2	100	Y	2	2
30	Student 30	17225XX030	0	0	N	2	2	100	Y	2	2
31	Student 31	17225XX031	NA	NA	NA	2	2	100	Y	2	2
32	Student 32	17225XX032	NA	NA	NA	2	2	100	Y	2	NA
33	Student 33	17225XX033	NA	NA	NA	2	2	100	Y	2	2
34	Student 34	17225XX034	4	80	Y	2	2	100	Y	2	2
35	Student 35	17225XX035	NA	NA	NA	0	2	50	N	2	1
36	Student 36	17225XX036	5	100	Y	1	2	75	Y	2	0
37	Student 37	17225XX037	0	0	N	2	2	100	Y	2	1
38	Student 38	17225XX038	0	0	N	1	2	75	Y	2	1
39	Student 39	17225XX039	NA	NA	NA	2	2	100	Y	2	1
40	Student 40	17225XX040	NA	NA	NA	2	2	100	Y	2	2
41	Student 41	17225XX041	1	20	N	2	2	100	Y	2	2
42	Student 42	17225XX042	NA	NA	NA	2	NA	50	N	1	2
43	Student 43	17225XX043	3	60	Y	2	1	75	Y	2	2
44	Student 44	17225XX044	NA	NA	NA	2	2	100	Y	2	2
45	Student 45	17225XX045	NA	NA	Y	2	1	75	Y	2	1

Mapped with question number											
CO3 (21 Marks)						CO4 (10 Marks)				University Result	
Q 1 (d)	Q 2 (a)	Q 3 (b)	Q 4 (a)	%	Target Level (>=60%)	Q 2 (b)	Q 4 (b)	%	Target Level (>=60%)	100 marks	Target Level (>=60%)
2	NA	3	4	62	Y	NA	5	50	N	85	Y
2	NA	3	4	62	Y	NA	4	40	N	80	Y
2	5	NA	3	67	Y	3	4	70	Y	78	Y
1	4	3	NA	57	N	4	NA	40	N	79	Y
1	NA	4	5	67	Y	NA	4	40	N	57	N
1	4	NA	4	62	Y	4	5	90	Y	85	Y
NA	3	NA	4	52	N	2	4	60	Y	47	N
2	NA	2	3	52	N	NA	3	30	N	75	Y
0	5	NA	2	52	N	3	1	40	N	40	N
1	NA	3	3	43	N	NA	4	40	N	55	N
2	3	3	NA	52	N	3	NA	30	N	49	N
2	3	NA	4	52	N	3	4	70	Y	40	N
1	NA	2	3	48	N	NA	4	40	N	72	Y
NA	NA	3	NA	24	N	NA	NA	NA	NA	70	Y
2	5	3	NA	62	Y	3	NA	30	N	56	N
NA	3	NA	NA	24	N	2	NA	20	N	30	N
1	2	NA	5	48	N	3	5	80	Y	48	N
2	4	NA	5	71	Y	5	4	90	Y	41	N
NA	NA	3	4	48	N	NA	4	40	N	41	N
NA	3	NA	2	38	N	NA	1	10	N	40	N
2	5	NA	5	76	Y	4	4	80	Y	63	Y
NA	3	2	NA	38	N	3	NA	30	N	64	Y
2	2	NA	4	57	N	3	4	70	Y	73	Y
2	2	NA	4	57	N	2	4	60	Y	70	Y
2	4	3	NA	62	Y	3	NA	30	N	79	Y
2	NA	NA	1	33	N	NA	1	10	N	34	N
NA	NA	NA	NA	NA	NA	NA	NA	NA	NA	A	NA
2	3	NA	5	62	Y	NA	4	40	N	76	Y
1	2	NA	2	43	N	2	1	30	N	30	N
2	NA	4	3	62	Y	NA	4	40	N	62	Y
2	5	NA	5	76	Y	3	4	70	Y	61	Y
1	0	NA	4	33	N	1	4	50	N	74	Y
2	4	NA	4	67	Y	4	4	80	Y	87	Y
2	NA	4	5	71	Y	NA	5	50	N	69	Y
1	3	NA	3	48	N	NA	3	30	N	54	N
2	NA	NA	4	38	N	NA	5	50	N	79	Y
NA	NA	4	3	48	N	NA	3	30	N	46	N
1	NA	4	4	57	N	NA	4	40	N	79	Y
1	2	NA	4	48	N	NA	4	40	N	73	Y
2	3	NA	4	62	Y	2	4	60	Y	62	Y
2	NA	4	5	71	Y	NA	4	40	N	70	Y
NA	1	NA	2	29	N	2	1	30	N	46	N
1	NA	1	4	48	N	NA	3	30	N	82	Y
1	1	NA	4	48	N	2	5	70	Y	63	Y
1	1	NA	NA	24	N	1	NA	10	N	49	N

(continued)

TABLE 13.4 (CONT.)
Level of Undergraduates Achieving COs and Achievement Level

Sl No	Student Name	RollNo	Marks according to course outcomes								
			CO1 (5 Marks)			CO2 (4 Marks)					
			Q 3 (a)	%	Target Level (>=60%)	Q 1 (a)	Q 1 (e)	%	Target Level (>=60%)	Q 1 (b)	Q 1 (c)
46	Student 46	17225XX046	NA	NA	NA	NA	NA	NA	NA	NA	NA
47	Student 47	17225XX047	2	40	N	1	2	75	Y	2	2
48	Student 48	17225XX048	0	0	N	2	NA	50	N	2	2
49	Student 49	17225XX049	NA	NA	NA	2	1	75	Y	2	2
50	Student 50	17225XX050	NA	NA	NA	2	1	75	Y	2	1
51	Student 51	17225XX051	0	0	N	1	0	25	N	0	0
52	Student 52	17225XX052	NA	NA	NA	1	NA	25	N	2	NA
53	Student 53	17225XX053	0	0	N	2	2	100	Y	2	1
54	Student 54	17225XX054	NA	NA	NA	2	NA	50	N	2	2
55	Student 55	17225XX055	1	20	N	2	NA	50	N	2	1
56	Student 56	17225XX056	NA	NA	NA	NA	2	50	N	2	1
57	Student 57	17225XX057	NA	NA	NA	1	0	25	N	0	0
58	Student 58	17225XX058	NA	NA	NA	1	NA	25	N	2	0

have scored over 60% of the most extreme stamps in the course. Henceforth, the fulfilment level for this situation is 0 according to the model rules proposed within the SAR of the NBA.

- **Achievement Level 1**: If 60% of undergraduates scores over 60% checks out of the most extreme pertinent imprints.
- **Achievement Level 2**: If 70% of undergraduates scores over 60% checks out of the most extreme applicable imprints.
- **Achievement Level 3**: If 80% of undergraduates scores over 60% checks out of the most extreme applicable imprints.

In a gathering of senior employees in the creator's establishment, numerous talks were held on setting the objective achievement level (per cent of imprints scored by an undergraduate in a subject) to choose the subject fulfilment level. The creator contended that this objective ought to be put together not just with respect to the college's outcomes for the last 3–4 years but additionally on the sort (subject) and the nature of undergraduates conceded. In designing projects, there are hardly any courses which undergraduates feel are more troublesome in contrast with different courses. Some model courses to refer to in the Electronics and Communication Engineering program are 'Analog Electronics', 'Digital Electronics', 'Analog and Digital Communication System', 'Electromagnetic Field Theory and Antennas', and so forth, where college results fluctuate.

For the situation model contemplated within this chapter, the objective per cent of imprints achieved by undergraduates is aimed by the subject employee dependent on the college consequences to the subjects in the foundation in the previous 3 years. The normal qualifying rate in a particular subject was about 40%, of which only around 55% of undergraduates achieved 60 imprints or more out of 100 (maximum) marks. Henceforth, the objective is diminished to 50% (that means an undergraduate must achieve 50 imprints or higher for achieving the COs). Then the rules for choosing the fulfilment levels were altered as:

Mapped with question number											
CO3 (21 Marks)						**CO4 (10 Marks)**				**University Result**	
Q 1 (d)	**Q 2 (a)**	**Q 3 (b)**	**Q 4 (a)**	**%**	**Target Level (>=60%)**	**Q 2 (b)**	**Q 4 (b)**	**%**	**Target Level (>=60%)**	**100 marks**	**Target Level (>=60%)**
NA	NA	NA	NA	NA	NA	NA	NA	NA	NA	32	N
1	3	3	NA	52	N	5	NA	50	N	74	Y
1	NA	0	2	33	N	NA	2	20	N	53	N
1	3	NA	4	57	N	3	4	70	Y	48	N
1	4	NA	4	57	N	0	5	50	N	68	Y
0	0	0	NA	0	N	0	NA	0	N	Not Allowed	NA
NA	4	NA	3	43	N	3	2	50	N	63	Y
1	NA	3	5	57	N	NA	4	40	N	59	N
1	2	NA	3	48	N	3	3	60	Y	61	Y
1	NA	3	3	48	N	NA	4	40	N	59	N
2	4	NA	3	57	N	5	3	80	Y	74	Y
0	2	NA	0	10	N	NA	1	10	N	50	N
2	5	NA	4	62	Y	NA	4	40	N	51	N

- **Achievement Level 1**: If 60% of undergraduates scores over 50% checks out of the most extreme pertinent imprints.
- **Achievement Level 2**: If 70% of undergraduates scores over 50% checks out of the most extreme applicable imprints.
- **Achievement Level 3**: If 80% of undergraduates scores over 50% checks out of the most extreme applicable imprints.

Table 13.4 shows that 71.4% of undergraduates have scored over 50% of imprints. Thus, the CO achievement level in the university exam is TWO.

13.5 By and Large Co Fulfillment

The general COs accomplishment level in the subject contemplated is figured as:

$$\begin{aligned}\text{Comprehensive COs Fulfilment Level} &= 20\% \text{ of COs fulfilment in IA} \\ &\quad \text{test} + 80\% \text{ of COs fulfilment in} \\ &\quad \text{University Exam} \\ &= 0.2 \times 0 + 0.8 \times 2 \\ &= 1.6\end{aligned}$$

It is accepted here that every one of the COs characterized for the course are canvassed in the university exam. Be that as it may, this is troublesome for the inclusion of COs, question wise, because the paper is adjusted and settled by various employees. The model rules as per the SAR recommend for utilizing an extent of 80% priority for university exam and 20% priority for IA for processing by and large CO fulfilment for a course.

13.6 POs Attainment

POs are more extensive articulations as compared to COs, which portray what undergraduates are expected to know and what they have the option to do after graduation. These identify with the abilities, information and conduct that undergraduates procure in their registration throughout the course (NBA Tier-II Manual 2013). Prior to the June 2015 organization of SAR, the projects used to characterize the POs were dependent on alumni properties. The June 2015 organization of SAR incorporates POs prepared commonly for all the programs. In any case, NBA proposes projects to characterize 2–4 POs explicit to a designing system which are known as Program Specific Outcomes (PSOs) (NBA 2015). This is compulsory to register the achievement levels to PSOs notwithstanding processing accomplishment of POs.

POs and PSOs are accomplished by the fulfilment of COs. It is known as the direct fulfilment to POs as well as PSOs. The general COs fulfilment, as discussed within section 13.4, and the COs-POs delineating esteems, as processed by Table 13.2, are utilized for figuring out the achievement to the POs. So also, the general COs achievement, as registered in section 13.4, and COs-PSOs mapping values (not included in this chapter) are utilized for figuring out the accomplishment of the PSOs.

According to the rules of the SAR, the general accomplishment of POs is registered by including direct achievement and backhanded fulfilment esteems in the extent of 80:20 (NBA 2015). That is, 80% of direct achievement and 20% of aberrant accomplishment are considered.

For deciding circuitous achievement of POs and PSOs, SAR proposes undergraduate leave reviews, business studies, co-curricular exercises, extracurricular exercises, and so forth. The students exit survey may be considered in this regard. A poll is structured (not included in this chapter) for such reason and the normal reactions by the active undergraduates for every PO are registered and recorded in the comparison line of Table 13.5 (Akash et al. 2019). Finally, in general, POs accomplishment esteems are figured by including immediate and backhanded PO fulfilment esteems in the extent of 80:20 separately (NBA Tier-II Manual 2013) and (Surendar and Shruti 2015). The processed qualities are contrasted and the set objective estimations to POs. The objective qualities are set in conference within the individuals from a 'Departmental Advisory Board' alongside the employees of the course/program. This is contended that the objective POs accomplishment esteem for every PO might be distinctive as the commitment of subjects for POs fulfilment is unique. In like manner, all POs were set within various objective incentives, which appear in the final column of Table 13.5. The table shows that every one of the POs is accomplished. An activity plan for the POs which don't arrive at the objective fulfilment esteem might be actualized in the ensuing scholastic year. Paradigm 7 as per SAR manages target estimations of the POs, and activity ideas required for accomplishing POs whose fulfilment esteems are not exactly the targeted objective qualities.

TABLE 13.5
Attainment of POs

Course	PO1	PO2	PO3	PO4	PO5	PO6	PO7	PO8	PO9	PO10	PO11	PO12	Overall CO Attainment
C101	3	1.67	2.33	3	1.33	-	-	-	1.33	-	-	-	**1.5**
C102	2	-	-	-	3	1.33	2.33	1.67	-	-	-	-	**1.9**
-													
-													
-													
C106	2.75	2.75	2.25	2.25	2.00	1.00	1.00	-	2.00	1.33	-	2.33	**1.60**
-													
-													
C201	2	3	-	-	-	2.33	2	3	3	2.33	3	2.67	**2**
-													
-													
-													
-													
C305	3	1.67	1.33	3	-	-	1	2.33	-	-	2	3	**2.3**
-													
-													
-													
-													
C410	1.33	2	3	1.67	2.67	2.33	-	-	-	3	2.67	2.33	**2.33**
Direct PO Attainment	2.35	2.22	2.23	2.48	2.25	1.75	1.58	2.33	2.11	2.22	2.56	2.58	
Indirect Attainment	2.55	2.67	2.66	1.90	1.00	1.33	1.66	2.66	2.00	2.50	2.13	2.67	
Overall PO Attainment	**2.39**	**2.31**	**2.31**	**2.36**	**2.00**	**1.66**	**1.60**	**2.40**	**2.09**	**2.28**	**2.47**	**2.60**	
Set Target	**2.00**	**2.00**	**2.00**	**2.00**	**2.00**	**1.50**	**1.50**	**2.00**	**2.00**	**2.00**	**2.00**	**2.00**	

13.7 Conclusion

Standard 3 of SAR of NBA is a significant rule and is a contribution for basis 7. The measure indicates how a program is performing as far as fulfilment estimation results and course/program results. The chapter has suggested a disentangled strategy for estimating or processing the fulfilment results and consequently program results and PSOs. The attainment of PSOs and POs computed here might be compared with the target attainment values and an action plan can be laid for the specific PSOs and POs whose attainment value is less than the initial set target value. The philosophy may likewise be utilized for the estimation of PSOs and POs as well as COs in a self-sufficient, non-subsidiary foundation.

13.8 Discussion

The OBE usage of COs and POs fulfilment has been investigated for Course Design and Development which were proposed to all students of the first year engineering program of JIMS Engineering Management Technical Campus, Greater Noida, India. Two techniques have been combined, that is, indirect assessment and direct assessment. The indirect assessment suggests that the CO accomplishment straightforwardly mirrors the PO fulfilment. Then again, the direct assessment suggests every individual segment in the evaluation is planned to its separate COs and POs and will be surveyed in an isolated way. CO and PO achievement joining direct estimation and indirect estimation display a differing result. The indirect assessment technique is more sensitive towards distinguishing the issues that influence accomplishment of COs as well as POs. Issues identified with non-satisfaction of one or the other COs or POs may be attributed to the awareness with regards to the problem synthesizing, product sustainability, and student's attitude towards citing genuine literature information throughout the development of their product. Consistent improvement might be actualized by zeroing in on the current issues. In any case, managing the extensive data utilizing segregated method might be time-consuming and deters the commitment of academicians with regards to effective OBE implementation. Subject facilitators have a major duty of planning the subject/course curricula, which may facilitate the achievement examination measure. All appraisals to be actualized in the course (as an example task, exam, project, and final assessment) could be set up prior to the start of the semester. This is feasible if the subject coordinator has been involved in the same subject for at least one semester so they have sufficient insight on preparing the teaching plan and the CO as per the predetermined PSOs and POs.

Likewise, the establishment ought to build up a framework that gives normalized CO-PO accomplishment examination. The framework should consider the requirements among scholastic individuals which are straightforwardly associated with information assortment and inform the board action. The framework interface could be effortlessly explored as it assumes a huge function towards empowering the responsibility of scholastic individuals. Information move action might be created as reasonable as one can be to evade excess cycle.

Finally, the viability of OBE usage returns to the act of the connected scholarly individuals. They must be proactive in dealing with information on schedule so that their workload does not become overwhelming toward the end of the semester. Appropriate arrangements will prompt productive outcomes, with fewer problems in dealing with the additional prerequisite of the accreditation body.

References

AICTE, 2018. CII Survey of Industry Linked Technical Institutes 2018 available at www.aicte-india.org/sites/default/files/AICTE-CII-Survey-Report-2018_1.pdf.

Ali Askar, S. M. 2009. "Implementation of OBE in engineering education: Are we there yet?" in International Conference on Engineering Education (ICEED), pp. 164–166.

Anderson, L. W., and Krathwohl, D. R. 2001. A taxonomy for learning, teaching, and assessing, Abridged Edition. Boston, MA: Allyn and Bacon.

Asch, David, Sean Nicholson, Sindhu Srinivas, Jeph Herrin, and Andrew Epstein, 2014, "How Do You Deliver a Good Obstetrician? Outcome-Based Evaluation of Medical Education", in Academic Medicine, 89, 1, pp. 24–26.

Bloom, B. S. 1956. Taxonomy of Educational Objectives, Handbook I: The Cognitive Domain. New York: David McKay Co Inc.

Charles Desforges and Alberto Abouchaar, 2003. "The Impact of Parental Involvement, Parental Support and Family Education on Pupil Achievement and Adjustment: A Literature

Review", Research Report RR433, Produced by the Department for Education and Skills, Nottingham: DfES Publications.

Kavitha, A., K. Immanuvel Arokia James, K. A. Harish and V. Rajamani, 2018. "An Empirical Study on Co-Po Assessment & Attainment for NBA Tier-II Engineering Accreditation Towards Empowering the Students Through Outcome Based Education", International Journal of Pure and Applied Mathematics, 118, 20, pp. 2615–2624.

Kulkarni, V.A., B. B. Ahuja, and MR Dhanvijay, 2017. "CO-PO Mapping and Attainment Booklet for Tier-II students with Rubrics Assessment", Journal of Engineering Education Transformations, 30, 3, pp. 28–34.

NBA, 2015a. National Board of Accreditation Self-Assessment Report (SAR) For Engineering Programs of Tier-II Institutions – First Time Accreditation, June 2015, available at www.nbaind.org/En/1079-self-assessment-report-tier-ii.aspx.

NBA, 2015b. Evaluation guidelines by NBA, available at www.nbaind.org/files/evaluation-guidelines-tier-ii-0.pdf.

NBA Manual for UG Engineering Programmes (Tier-II), 2013. Available at www.nbaind.org/Files/NBA%20-%20Tier%20II%20Manual.pdf.

Rajak, Akash, Ajay Kumar Shrivastava, Shashank Bhardwaj, and Arun Kumar Tripathi, 2019. "Assessment and Attainment of Program Educational Objectives for Post Graduate Courses", I.J. Modern Education and Computer Science, 2, pp. 26–32.

Rawat, Surendar and Shruti Karkare, 2015. "An Empirical Study on Assessment of PO Attainment for a Diploma Program", International Journal of Advanced Research in Engineering and Technology, 6, 11, pp. 50–58.

14

Influence of Digital Issues on Cloud-Based Higher Education Quality

N. Viswanadham

Sr. Assistant Professor, Department of Accounting and Finance, Faculty of Business Administration, St. Augustine University of Tanzania, Mwanza, Tanzania

Aarti Singh

Assistant Professor, Strategy Management, FORE School of Management, New Delhi

DOI: 10.1201/9781003203070-16

14.1 Introduction

Higher education is a key area for economic development. Capacity development is possible by improving the overall quality of higher education. The higher education authorities or institutions have considerably expanded and diversified (Henard & Roseveare 2012). Following globalization and privatization in India, many structural reforms were introduced in the higher education sector. The economic and societal development of the country is directly determined by the quality of higher education, which depends upon the effective use of technical skills of human resources with their subjective knowledge, thus generating creative thinking and moral values in society (Abbas 2020). The university education system needs to focus on offering more than just degree programs, so that it also provides graduates with a better understanding of right and wrong. The quality provision of the developed education system must satisfy different stakeholders, such as employers, government and academicians. The improvised education system also tries to capture the student's ideas about the quality of higher education in both public and private higher education institutions (Szczepankiewicz et al. 2019). The updated education system impacts the usage of various digital issues and technology and thus is highly dependent upon information technology. The information technology-based curriculum of a developed education system always helps to access the latest information about the learning environment through inquiry-based activities (Stephenson 2001).

The use of digitalization in the education system shows that information technology plays a key role in higher education learning, thus affecting higher education institutions. The use of information technology in terms of digitalized classrooms and effective virtual learning platforms like Google Classroom, for instance, shows that information technology and digital technology have become the backbone of the modern education system (Hamidi & Chavoshi 2018). Before COVID-19, every higher education institution had its own internal quality assessment cell to maintain the desired quality to meet standards in the education sector. These internal quality assessment cells focus on various vital issues of higher education, like teaching requirements, performance assessment, class strategies to make education more effective, and through quality to enhance student's performance (Ali 2020). Students' quality education helps to enhance their performance, as well as the institute but the sudden change that occurred due to COVID-19 distracted and changed the education system of almost all institutions. Thus the pandemic has become the cause of revolutionary change in the education system, changing ways of learning and affecting both educational institutes and students. The changed education system can be understood from two perspectives: the first considers the effect of change in students' learning; the second considers the role of the higher education system which adopts the change generated by the COVID-19 pandemic to survive and enhance learning.

14.1.1 Role of Cloud Computing in Higher Education

In the current competitive situation, all higher education institutions must provide high-quality education; otherwise, they won't survive in the sector. Institutions have to adopt new technologies and establish updated information technology-based infrastructure. This is expensive to maintain in crises as well as at the outset and in times of expansion. This type of technology transformation requires huge funding and investment. To address this situation most higher education institutions aim to adopt cost-effective measurements (Oke & Fernandes 2020). The cloud computing concept has emerged as an assured solution to the challenges associated with information technology budgets. Cloud computing is a convenient enabling model with demand network access. Students of higher education institutions are highly networked and globally connected. There are three cloud technology models: infrastructure as a service; platform as a service; and software as a service. World-renowned universities use cloud technology to manage thousands of students from worldwide branches. Cloud computing software in the education sector leads to cost effectiveness. Instead of arranging data centers, a cloud mitigation ecosystem can simply be established, then the management can easily predict the operating costs. The cloud management system creates the largest collaborative platforms between educators, students, parents and other stakeholders in the education system. It creates the latest learning ambiance and new digital experience for all stakeholders. Security of data is the greatest benefit of cloud computing in education because much of the latest research data should maintain confidentiality (Qasem et al. 2020). This study considered factor analysis to capture both perspectives on the changed education system by identifying vital factors and their related variables.

14.1.2 The Objective of the Study

To measure the influence of digital issues on the quality of higher education.

14.2 Theoretical Construction

To measure the effect of overall quality on the education system various theories have been studied which were used in the past to understand the role of higher education institutions in delivering education. These theories built the foundation of understanding flows of learning to build strong pillars in terms of good students. Understanding these theories helps in identifying how the educational system adapts to change and what may be the vital factors that should be considered while understanding the change. The theories used in this study, which develop the theoretical background, offer an explanation to help higher education institutions on basic ideas about the implementation of cloud-based technologies.

14.2.1 The Organismic Integration Theory

Intrinsically, people need to be skilled (e.g. to be knowledgeable, creative, innovative or skillful) in order to achieve the outcome they desire. For individuals to improve their competencies, they need to acquire knowledge, skills, relatedness and ability through digital learning. Unfortunately, the digital learning process is often difficult or frustrated by external factors such as leadership, regulations and culture. This shows how individuals learn from the outer environment and understand the change which helps in generating responses toward change. Thus, if a change is to be sustainable outside of a controlled environment individuals must fully internalize perceived values from behavior to be learned. Currently, this theory plays a vital role, because individual competency development is in the hands of learning institutions by providing quality training.

14.2.2 Technology Acceptance Theories

According to Fred Davis, technology plays a vital role in enhancing performance. This shows that technology affects performance but the outcome depends upon the apparent acceptance and understanding of technology. This view tries to portray the picture of performance after the integration of the technology acceptance model and information system technology. This theory offers an overview of how people accept and use technology for growth through enhanced performance. Hence technology acceptance theories show that by accepting technology, performance can be improved. Thus higher education institutions can consider the change and adopt it by using technology to defiantly improve their performance. Due to the COVID-19 pandemic, educational institutions depend on technology to provide new ways of learning. Because cloud technology implementation leads to cost effectiveness for institutions, nowadays students utilize technology for all sorts of aspects. Cloud technology changes the scenario of technology adoption with low cost. Particularly from a professional course point of view, cloud-based learning is essential.

14.2.2.1 Adoption of New Technology

The application of digitalization improves our abilities and efficiency to change the global scenario quickly. Information and computer technology (ICT) is often embedded within hardware and software, so that we can operate them even without knowing their operating instructions. Technical innovation is an advanced digitalization concept based on updated knowledge that provides solutions to various problems (Akbar 2013; Savage & Sterry 1990).

14.2.3 Theory of Planned Behaviour Approach

Bansal & Taylor (2002) identified that when planned behavior is lower, and the tasks are difficult, intentions often do not translate into required actions. Joynathsing & Ramkissoon (2010) identified that both individual attitude and subjective norm help to determine behavioral intent, but planned behavioral control was not significantly influencing behavioral intention or any issues. Lin and Cheng (2012) found that the intention of graduate business school students was to get involved in innovative and technical activities by adding development-based strength in the TPB. Their modified TPB is a good indicator of students' intention and ability to participate in innovative activities.

14.2.4 Technology Acceptance Model (TAM)

According to the technology acceptance model (TAM), a person always has the option to either make complete utilization of an innovation or to partially accept it for improving their performance (Spanos 2009). Davis (1989) established a TAM based on an expectancy value model. This technology acceptance model discussed that adoption of new technology and systems completely depends upon the individual intention towards adopting the technology, and the acceptance theory explains this by considering two views:

The first view depends upon the ease of use of the existing technology and system, and the second view depends upon the usefulness of the newly developed technology and system. Both views are interrelated as with perceived ease of using the existing technology and system one can understand the usefulness of an innovative new technology and system. Davis (1989) identified that both views – perceived ease of use of the existing technology and system, and perceived usefulness of the new innovative technology and system – will affect the acceptance of new innovative technology. Davis (1989) also explains the perceived usefulness as the degree of control of personal beliefs which have been used in adopting the new innovative technology and system to enhance their performance; while perceived ease of use has been explained as the degree of control to an individual belief which helps in understanding the existing system and technologies. Davis (1989) identified that personal use is the strongest predictor of a person's intention in their TAM. TAM has been discussed in various studies and contexts with supportive empirical research studies. Park (2009) used structural equational modeling to analyze and explain the technology acceptance model to understand university students' behavioral intention to use the e-learning and digitalization concept. The TAM model has also been used to describe the digital classroom, usage of e-learning platforms, and other technological and subjective issues in system accessibility by considering perceived usefulness and perceived ease of use. This TAM concept also develops the acceptance attitude towards technology and other digital learning systems. Studies proved TAM (combination of perceived usefulness and perceived ease of use) as a good theoretical tool to understand the acceptance behavior of users toward digitalization.

14.3. Review of Literature

Higher education institutions in India have adopted the change as per requirement and need. India's education system can be assessed on the trust of students and their guardians with supportive data. Improvement in the education system can be made by academic quality standards in terms of students and welfare issues, which should be equated with quality in higher education institutions. This view was explained by Kenneth Clark when he was Secretary of State for Education and Science (Evans & Morrison 2011; Eisenhardt and Graebner 2007).

Funding Council sector institutions focused on increasing the number of students with both firsts and upper seconds. Harvey (1995) stated that change should always be rapid and continuous; he also explained the role of new adaptive behavior towards improvement in the education system. This study also generates the requirement of measuring change and addictiveness towards change and requirements. Other studies have identified that the approach lies in the responsibility aspect of continuous quality assurance and assessment (Harvey & Green 1993). The need for improvement has been witnessed for decades. It has been identified that change is occurring in the requirement of education and ways to deliver it but failures occur when it comes to delivery of the conceptual framework to students. These issues were treated with common tolerance when the students were part of a gifted elite (Naisbitt & Aburdene 1989).

To avoid misunderstanding on quality valuation there must be a treaty internationally on the meaning of terms such as 'level', 'standards', 'effectiveness' (De Weert 1990).

A. Level: Doctoral programmer is at a higher level than one leading to a baccalaureate. This does not mean that those programs are of higher quality than baccalaureate programs.
B. Standards: Specific criteria for each student and program must be conveyed before programs can be presented to the students.

C. Effectiveness: It is always possible to achieve 'easy' low customary goals. In other words, excellence in higher education cannot only be a question of directed attainments but must also include assessments about the goal of the program.

The higher ranked universities are working with a professional working system; they have trained staff, qualified professors and a well-developed education system to meet all required standards. These developed universities are known to students and other professionals because of their output in terms of highly qualified and well-trained students. They not only developed a professional attitude in students but also teach them working ethics to meet the university objectives (Chickering & Reisser 1993). In higher education institutions the regular improvement in education quality has been made through regular assessment and improving accordingly. This regular assessment helps to understand and adapt the change according to the environment; it also helps in meeting the essential standards and objectives that are known to all related stakeholders (Chickering & Reisser 1993).

Papert (1980) studied the role of technology in terms of gadgets and tools to empower the learning system. With the enhancement of technology, educational quality can be improved and assessed regularly. This study also considers the relationship between technology and constructivism: this can be understood in terms of critical thinking. Critical thinking is a unique approach which helps to understand the change and take decisive actions accordingly. Critical thinking also helps in developing problem-solving attitudes in students. This approach is beneficial to students in developing their skills within society as well as the institute.

Bates (1997) reported the nonexistence of adequate training and compulsory skills as a hindrance to the information technology used in higher education institutions in Tanzania. The study shows that training is also a vital part of accepting the change. During the COVID-19 pandemic, the sudden change required proper training and understanding to adopt the new learning environment. Krysa (1998) identified the requirements for digital preparation. This study tries to explain the role of technology in terms of digital preparation. Hence preparation helps in enhancing the performance of faculties working in institutions. In the COVID-19 pandemic, proper training and understanding of digital technology not only enhance the performance but also create a new learning environment for students. Hence digital teaching mechanisms require ICT training for students and faculty to increase the education limits.

Digital technology usage enables learners to explore, share and develop team skills. Learners can improve their knowledge by sharing diversified and different experiences in the group to direct and reflect knowledge and skillsets. Digital technology in higher education institutes helps students to emphasize high order subjective concepts rather than just thinking and not implementing tasks (Levin and Wadmany 2006).

McMahon's study (2009) identified the statistical correlations between learning with information technology, like a digital classroom and digital delivery of concepts, and important analytical thinking skills. The study identified that higher exposure to digital technology for learning would lead to higher critical thinking and analytical skills in students. Thus, learning institutes require a strong focus to assimilate information technology among all of the subjective and learning areas at each class level. This change, if implemented properly, enables students to apply technical aids to accomplish higher levels of cognitive thinking in each domain of learning contexts.

Serhan (2009) demonstrated that information technology increases independence by allowing learners to create their study inputs and materials; it is possible then to get more exposure than in the traditional learning system provided in classrooms. This can be discussed concerning capability, once higher education students are more assured in technical skills and their operations, they can develop their skill and knowledge to apply their learning and transfer skills in their area while using new technology with efficiency and effectiveness. Information technology in terms of digital learning is always considered in different ways rather than objective support to traditional learning systems (Tezci 2011). Tezci (2011) identified that academic staff must learn the usage of technology in all possible ways to enhance traditional teaching to escalate productivity and performance. The technology should also be learning from a student-focused perspective to understand the role of digitalization as a part of classroom accomplishments, which helps to enhance students' learning ability. This shows that in higher education institutions academic professionals must use technology in creative and industrious ways which enhance the engagement of students by using productive activities during class sessions (Birch and Irvine 2009). In support of this view, they pointed out that academic staff always use a creative approach for information technology amalgamation in the classroom. This integration helps faculty to learn more about the digital classroom or virtual teaching strategies and leads to adapting innovative learning instruments while using digital gadgets during classroom sessions. Grossman et al. (2009) found that cloud computing infrastructure helps to access various updated domain information for higher education institutions. Higgins et al. (2012) notice that digital learning in the education system has a huge impact on the writing skills of learners.

14.3.1 Research Gap

Many studies focused on only specific quality issues in the higher education sector, but very little information is available on overall quality in the higher education sector. This study tries to fill the gap (Nasim et al. 2020).

14.3.2 Conceptual Framework (Figure 14.1)

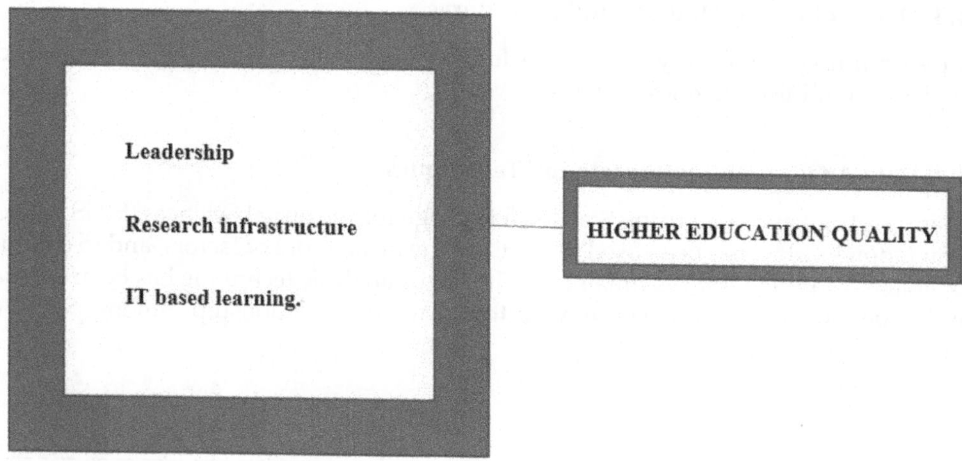

FIGURE 14.1
Conceptual Framework.
Source: Researcher's data (2021).

14.4 Methodology

The research methodology used for this study is explained below.

14.4.1 The Study Area

Our research study focused on higher education institutions like colleges as well as universities. In this study, the institutions have been chosen randomly based on the availability of network and reputation of the institutions, and so on.

14.4.2 Research Design

This research study used the descriptive methodology to utilize the survey design, aimed at studying the digitalization determinants that influence the quality of learning in higher institutions which occur because of the change due to the COVID-19 pandemic. Many institutions were in lockdown, so communication has been over the phone and by email. The study used both quantitative and qualitative approaches to assess the factors.

14.4.2.1 Population and Sample

The study population comprises all stakeholders of higher education institutions. The sample size of the study is 200. The convenience sampling method is used to get accurate results (Hollensen 2003).

14.4.2.2 Sampling Technique

A cross-sectional design was adopted, as it is appropriate for descriptive studies. This design was suitable for this study due to constraints in time and other resources, particularly financial issues and virtual data collection.

14.4.3 Data Collection Methods and Procedures

This research used the survey method. Data have been collected for the research study through self-administered questionnaires.

14.4.4 Data Analysis and Interpretation Techniques

The data has been analyzed using Statistical Package for the Social Sciences (SPSS version 16 for windows). SPSS has been used to calculate the mean score of factors, and to conduct factor analysis through the Friedman test. The factor analysis technique has been used as a data reduction technique by simplifying the correlation relationships among points of continuous variables.

14.5 Data Analysis

The data have been analyzed in Tables 14.1 and 14.2.

TABLE 14.1
Statistical Calculation of Study Variables

	Mean	Std. Deviation[a]
Academics	3.05	.932
Courses	3.21	1.008
Research and development	3.17	1.038
Infrastructure	3.82	1.029
Core issues	3.00	.853
Leadership of the institute	2.92	.725
Challenges	2.97	.816
ICT based learning	3.02	.788
Cyber security	3.06	.920
Misc.	3.29	1.084
Soft skills	3.56	1,143
Faculty external contacts	3.29	.901

[a] Standard Deviation – Standard deviations of the variables used in the study.

Source: Data analysis (2021).

Tables 14.1 and 14.2 indicate that there are many academic challenges in higher education institutions; quality staff retention, in particular, is a big issue. Many of the respondents noted that it is a big academic challenge. So the management has to think about it and make a clear policy on employee retention.

Another issue is the ICT based course curriculum: because of COVID-19, all higher education institutes started online teaching as per the government of India instructions. But many academic staff have been confused as to how to create online modules successfully and present as per the requirement. Moreover, some courses have equations and lengthy explanations needed, so it becomes a big challenge. Research and development is another issue with higher education institutions. Because many of them only focus on academic results and placements, so it is an issue for quality research and development. It is recommended that all higher education institutions invest and focus on research activities; otherwise, without research, it is not to be considered as a standard institution. Though this generation has the advantage of digitalization, a big threat from technology is cyberattacks. So it is very important to maintain good internal control systems to face cybercrime and prevent the stealing of information from the various online platforms.

Sampling Adequacy – This test measures variance between 0 and 1, and values closer to 1 have been considered (see Table 14.3).

All these tests are considered together to satisfy a minimum standard and accuracy to perform factor analysis.

Communalities – It is a proportion of each variable's variance from the components, which can be described by the factors (see Table 14.4). Communalities can also be defined as the total of square factor loadings for the variables. The outcome should sum to 4.86 i.e., 4.86/ 12 = 46% of the variance is common variance and 60% is unique.

Factor – In this study the number of variables are the same as the number of factors used in the factor analysis (see Table 14.5). However, out of 12 factors only the first 4 factors have been retained during the analysis.

From the scree plot graphs (Figure 14.2) it is observed that after the third factor the line is almost flat, which means each successive factor is accounting for little aggregates of the total variance.

TABLE 14.2
Correlation Matrix[a]

		Academics	Courses	Research and development	Infrastructure
Correlation	Academics	1.000	.005	.070	.329
	Courses	.005	1.000	.531	.169
	Research and development	.070	.531	1.000	.000
	Infrastructure	.329	.169	.000	1.000
	Core issues	.381	.229	.325	.190
	Leadership of the institute	–.039	.043	.057	.004
	Challenges	.316	.026	–.119	–.097
	ICT based learning	.350	–.157	.015	–.034
	Cyber security	.209	–.046	.132	–.083
	Misc.	.481	–.028	–.096	.007
	Soft skills	.230	.370	.330	.139
	Faculty external contacts	.326	.217	.062	.253
		Core issues	**Leadership of the institute**	**Challenges**	**ICT based learning**
Correlation	Academics	.381	–.039	.316	.350
	Courses	.229	.043	.026	–.157
	Research and development	.325	.057	-.119	.015
	Infrastructure	.190	.004	-.097	–.034
	Core issues	1.000	-.024	.044	.158
	Leadership of the institute	–.024	1.000	.098	.055
	Challenges	.044	.098	1.000	.307
	ICT based learning	.158	.055	.307	1.000
	Cyber security	.174	.282	.244	.458
	Misc.	.180	.221	.113	.084
	Soft skills	.233	.162	.018	.125
	Faculty external contacts	.079	–.198	–.050	–.049
		Cyber security	**Misc.**	**Soft skills**	**Faculty external contacts**
Correlation	Academics	.209	.481	.230	.326
	Courses	–.046	–.028	.370	.217
	Research and development	.132	–.096	.330	.062
	Infrastructure	–.083	.007	.139	.253
	Core issues	.174	.180	.233	.079
	Leadership of the institute	.282	.221	.162	–.198
	Challenges	.244	.113	.018	–.050
	ICT based learning	.458	.084	.125	–.049
	Cyber security	1.000	.393	.343	.089
	Misc.	.393	1.000	.371	.396
	Soft skills	.343	.371	1.000	.256
	Faculty external contacts	.089	.396	.256	1.000

[a] Determinant = .038

Source: Data analysis (2021).

TABLE 14.3
Sampling Adequacy and Chi-Square Analysis

KMO and Bartlett's Test[a]	
Sampling adequacy	.522
Approx. chi-square	1710.417
Df.	66
Sig.	.000

a Bartlett's Test of Sphericity tests the null hypothesis developed in the study

Source: Data analysis (2021).

TABLE 14.4
Communalities

	Initial	Extraction
Academics	.595	.976
Courses	.464	.541
Research and development	.469	.591
Infrastructure	.322	.193
Core issues	.279	.268
Leadership of the institute	.254	.161
Challenges	.304	.185
ICT based learning	.387	.493
Cyber security	.457	.624
Misc.	.583	.871
Soft skills	.375	.451
Faculty external contacts	.375	.352

Extraction method: Principal axis factoring.
Source: Data analysis (2021).

This can be understood from the result that factor 1 correlates 0.782 with component 1, and the outcome shows that 10 factors have been correlated to the first item. Hence it is understood from the result that there are some miscellaneous issues in academics, like admission criteria as per the statutory bodies like the Universities Grants Commission (UGC) and All India Council for Technical Education being followed, but many of the institutions adopt cheap marketing techniques to attract lower profile or low graded students to get admission into different courses. So it will impact the class discipline and lesson plan implementation and also faculty recruitment. As per the criteria higher education institutions must appoint good academic profile from the quality process, but as they are following their policies to control the cost, many institutions in India are unable to implement UGC scales, and simply recruit under the probationary period of two years. The major condition is if the incumbent demonstrates good performance during probation, then they confirm the appointment scale will be given, but unfortunately those new will not be able to continue, because of indiscipline and the unprofessional environment with colleagues, so they resign from the service. But UGC or All India Council for Technical Education never raises queries on these issues. These bodies also never suggest digitalization; if they made it mandatory for the higher education system, it would give positive results on the digitalization of institutions and all staff would need to acquire new digital skills according to the market requirement. The majority of private colleges recruit old

TABLE 14.5
Total Variance Explained

	Initial Eigenvalues[a]			Extraction sums of squared loadings[e]		
Factor	Total[b]	% of Variance	Cumulative %	Total	% of Variance	Cumulative %
1	2.833	23.606	23.606	2.458	20.483	20.483
2	1.928	16.068	39.674	1.440	11.997	32.479
3	1.512	12.599	52.273	1.013	8.439	40.919
4	1.217	10.145	62.418	.798	6.647	47.566
5	.959	7.996	70.414			
6	.882	7.348	77.762			
7	.758	6.314	84.076			
8	.535	4.462	88.539			
9	.486	4.048	92.587			
10	.393	3.273	95.860			
11	.311	2.594	98.454			
12	.186	1.546	100.000			

Extraction Method: Principal Axis Factoring.

a **Initial Eigenvalues** – The correlation matrix has been used to conduct the factor analysis, and during factor analysis all the variables are standardized, so that variance of each variable should be 1. The total variance is equal to the number of variables used in the analysis, in this study total variables are twelve.

b **Total** – So it is understood that each successive factor will account for less and less variance.

c **% of Variance** – The percentage of variance is the percentage of total variance accounted by each factor in this study.

d **Cumulative %** – This shows the variance percentage and cumulated values of all factors as shown in the fourth row where the value is 62.418, it means that the first three factors together account for 62.418% of the total variance.

e **Extraction sums of squared loadings** – This shows that the total number of rows is linked to the total number of factors retained in this study.

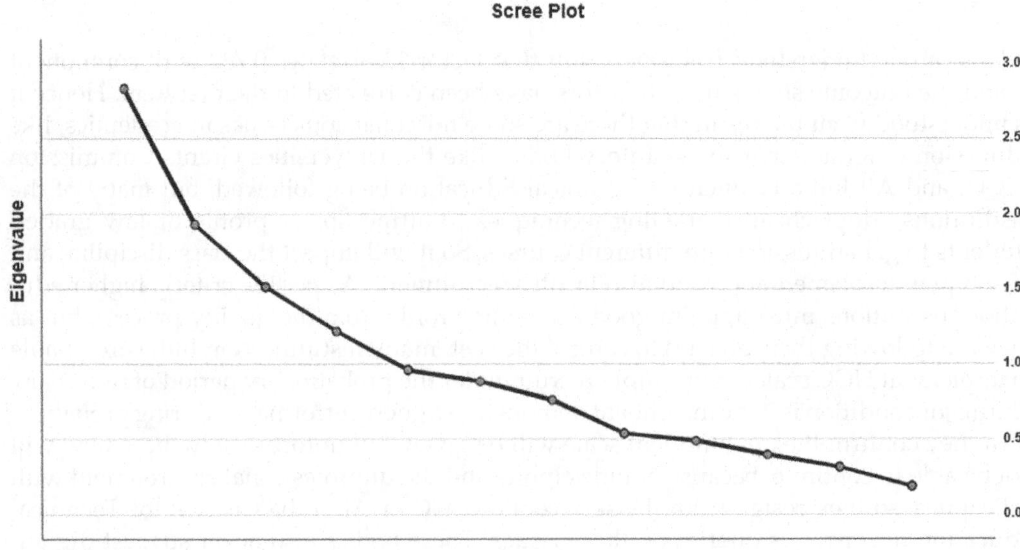

FIGURE 14.2
Scree plot of eigenvalue.

TABLE 14.6
Factor Matrix

	Factor			
	1	2	3	4
Academics	.782	–.195	–.413	.395
Courses	.255	.686	.079	–.006
Research and development	.284	.627	.310	.141
Infrastructure	.212	.185	–.316	.121
Core issues	.428	.204	.008	.209
Leadership of the institute	.154	–.077	.307	–.192
Challenges	.244	–.275	.133	.181
ICT based learning	.379	–.366	.310	.346
Cyber security	.556	–.267	.482	–.107
Misc.	.688	–.263	–.182	–.543
Soft skills	.558	.281	.154	–.192
Faculty external contacts	.389	.163	–.378	–.176

Extraction Method: Principal Axis Factoring.

Source: Data analysis (2021).

retired professionals from various industries to maintain good replacement assistance for their outgoing batch students, but it won't constructively help those institutions, because those professionals from different industries are new to the digital educational environment. It is another big challenge and the top management of the universities must develop a concrete solution for this issue.

Factor Matrix – Table 14.6 has the unrelated factor loadings. The factor matrix shows the correlations between the variables and factors used in this study as the correlation is possible among range –1 to +1.

From Table 14.7, we understood that faculty external contacts is also an important issue, because faculty has to interact with the students, and different stakeholders to provide maximum output. This study noted earlier that many of the faculty in different colleges and universities are frequently leaving. Management of those higher education institutions never try to conduct any exit interviews and simply calculate the final salary and settle the account. Because of the high supply of deemed universities doctorate degrees, many doctorates are available for lower salaries (Flores 2019). It is one of the cheapest and most common practices in higher education institutions: official bodies from the government pass comment on it but they do not take any serious action or punishment, and never question these issues so they become common practice.

Many colleges have a shortage of faculty on specialized degrees, and experience in the domain area is another problem. They simply put the tag as a multi-discipline and recruit academicians from unrelated areas. It is very common, particularly in management schools or business schools, and must be reviewed by the government (Coppage 2019).

14.6 Conclusion

The education sector is dynamic and changes its strategies according to the market scenario, but at the same time, those changes must be acceptable to various stakeholders. As in

TABLE 14.7
Factor Score Coefficient Matrix

	Factor			
	1	2	3	4
Academics	.470	–.147	–.622	.826
Courses	.143	.484	.016	–.033
Research and development	.209	.454	.271	.087
Infrastructure	–.008	.108	–.113	–.022
Core issues	.062	.109	.073	.034
Leadership of the institute	.055	–.039	.132	–.009
Challenges	.022	–.107	.133	.058
ICT based learning	.080	–.246	.410	.187
Cyber security	.240	–.229	.626	.054
Misc.	.349	–.182	–.232	–1.009
Soft skills	.157	.200	.135	–.074
Faculty external contacts	.015	.154	–.189	–.128

Extraction Method: Principal Axis Factoring.

Source: Data analysis (2021).

Table 14.7, particularly on education programs offered, courses must be industry-linked and able to provide updated knowledge on core issues. Organizational culture is very important for discipline issues, and any higher education institutions must maintain proper discipline: only then shall they be able to make a lot of curriculum amendments and facilitate industry-based programs. We found that the majority of institutions' management focus highly on students admission by adopting different marketing techniques, rather than the quality of teaching. A teamwork culture should be adopted for more effective learning and quality delivery in the digital age, and the right technology tools should be chosen to support an information technology-based curriculum. Higher education institutions must encourage original research by adopting the latest technology and encouraging digitalization at all administrative and research levels, and in consultancy issues. Universities should aim to be at least in the top 500 in world rankings. Digitalization of institutions is highly encouraged, but before that, all higher education institutions must adopt discipline, academic integrity, quality teaching, and work life balance for management staff. Higher educational institution students expect digitalized systems with industry-based linked courses and top placements. Hence this study identifies that information technology and highly professional standards play a major role in all academic activities.

Digital-based learning is breaking down cultural and geographical boundaries. Digitalization helps to create different learning modules in a faster way. Academicians can join online professional development programs to improve their domain knowledge. Digitalization of universities solves many of the above challenges, so new ICT and innovative practices find solutions for many problems. Cloud computing is the main provider for effective learning resources to students because of lower budgets and faster access. Cloud technology helps to access all stakeholders at once. When we think about it critically from a stakeholder's perspective, higher education institutions still have to develop quality teaching, technology-based learning, updated syllabuses, global level accreditations and world ranking institutions. Many educational institutions, mostly private, failed to implement proper salary scales and basic facilities even though the role of inspection authorities is normal, particularly in some states in India. Higher education institutions failed to provide updated technology infrastructure – it is a big challenge for them (Deep et al. 2019).

14.7 Implications

Quality is the only area by which to judge the competency and standard of higher education institutions. Their objective is to develop competency among citizens and find solutions for current economic, technical and societal problems through quality and high-level research, but the reality is different. Deemed universities, in particular, are awarding doctorates to diplomas in a liberal manner. There is a lot of lobbying with different agencies, which creates an unhealthy environment in higher education and leads to cut-throat competition, not only in awarding degrees but admissions procedures following different practices and offering promises to gain admission. Due to this criteria, those who are admitted through this channel, behave without due studiousness during college hours, having no discipline at all, and this type of culture is encouraged by many private universalities and colleges. It is a very bad sign for future higher education. It is an indication of the leadership failure of some private higher education institutions. The government and respective bodies should consider these issues seriously to ensure quality. Only quality research helps to find real solutions to all kinds of economical, societal and technical problems. But what type of research is carried out with educational institutions? It is a million dollar question. There is very poor quality research, institutions only conduct international conferences, many papers are prepared in a hurried manner with information copy-and-pasted and phrases just changed to avoid plagiarism, because faculties are busy with overloaded teaching hours and administration work (NBA and NAAC preparation). It is one of the key issues to change age criteria to ensure quality research and publishing papers with reputed journals. Eligibility for academic staff is another big challenge, particularly in management education where those who join are not aware of the fundamentals of management but are teaching with business departments. So it is good to have a governmental policy for those teaching management courses to study a one-year specialized course on the fundamentals of management; otherwise they may not be able to prepare good managers through their teaching. It is very important for all management disciplines in universities and colleges. Particularly with a science and engineering background, staff should be limited to only operations research, quantitative, business mathematics, and systems areas; otherwise it will impact on the learning and delivering lectures, and finally leads to a degree without a conceptual background. It is very important to recruit qualified staff along with the latest techno-based learning like cloud computing infrastructure. Information technology plays a key role in higher education; anyone, from top-level to lower-level management, can help to avoid delays in communication and make quick decisions to run the institutions smoothly. But it is seen that many of the senior faculties from different colleges are unable to transform and are unwilling to learn new digital skills, simply depending on younger staff members. It is one of the biggest hurdles to strict implementation of the digital environment within the respective universities. So the government of India higher education statutory bodies must take this issue seriously and made it a mandatory requirement for all academic staff to be computer literate, and able to operate virtual classes without further assistance.

The curriculum should be based on industry-related topics and market demanded skills should be the learning objectives for all professional courses. Topics of each course must be updated and students should have the opportunity to visit specific industry and learn from there. Even here there are difficulties from some academic staff members being unable to reach up to the mark, and still working with old theoretical knowledge. Many colleges and universities recruit old retired professionals from the industry to fill this gap, but their outdated attitudes and perceptions create a hurdle for the younger generation. So, our main suggestion is not to consider retired people for key positions at universities, as it is a waste of economic resources. If the management of colleges do consider retired professors they should come from reputed and dynamic institutions.

Management of higher education institutions should try to collaborate with the top 500 universities in the world: collaboration helps to initiate student exchange programs, learn a new skill through virtual modes, and adopt new technological innovative policies to reach global standards. Finally, all universities must adopt new technologies and try to upgrade to the latest versions, adhere to rigorous admissions policies, maintain strict discipline, and recruit experienced academicians from a variety of multicultural backgrounds. The curriculum must be industry-focused, with specific budget allocation for research and development activities. Consultancy with local business firms must be initiated. All this is only possible if the universities and colleges accept digitalization and acquire new information technology skills.

14.8 Limitations

Due to the COVID-19 outbreak, this study collected data online only; if data were collected through meeting with respondents personally there could be some more important information that may provide more insight to this study. This study tries to capture experts' views by considering primary data; secondary analysis can be done to further validate the study.

14.9 Future Research

The following areas are to be further studied.

1. Role of cloud computing infrastructure on quality administration of universities.
2. Impact of cloud computing on the ranking of higher education institutions.
3. Impact on education quality before and after implementation of cloud-based technology learning.

References

Abbas, Jawad. 2020 "Impact of total quality management on corporate sustainability through the mediating effect of knowledge management." *Journal of Cleaner Production* 244: 118806.

Akbar, F. 2013. "What affects students' acceptance and use of technology? Test of UTAUT in the context of a high-education institution in Qatar." Senior Honors Thesis, Information Systems, Dietrich College, *Carnegie Mellon University* (4): 1–30.

Ali, Wahab. 2020. "Online and remote learning in higher education institutes: A necessity in light of COVID-19 pandemic." *Higher Education Studies* 10 (3): 16–25.

Bansal, H. S., and S. F. Taylor. 2002. "Investigating interactive effects in the theory of planned behavior in a service-provider switching context." *Psychology & Marketing* (19): 407–425.

Bates, Anthony W. 1997. "The impact of technological change on open and distance learning." *Distance education* 18 (1): 93–109.

Berger, P. L. 1967. *The sacred canopy: Elements of a sociological theory of religion*, New York: Anchor Books.

Birch, Anthony, and Valerie Irvine. 2009. "Preservice teachers' acceptance of ICT integration in the classroom: Applying the UTAUT model." *Educational media international* 46 (4): 295–315.

Chickering, Arthur W., and Linda Reisser. 1993. *Education and identity. The Jossey-Bass higher and adult education series*. San Francisco, CA: Jossey-Bass Inc., Publishers.

Coppage, Cynthia Ann. 2019. "African American registered nurses in post-secondary faculty positions: A qualitative phenomenological study." PhD diss., University of Phoenix.

Davis, F. D. 1989. "Perceived usefulness, perceived ease of use, and user acceptance of information technologies." *MIS Quarterly*, 13 (3): 319–340.

Deep, Sadia, Berhannudin Mohd Salleh, and Hussain Othman. 2019. "Study on problem-based learning towards improving soft skills of students in effective communication class." *International Journal of Innovation and Learning* 25 (1): 17–34.

De Weert, Egbert. 1990. "A macro-analysis of quality assessment in higher education." *Higher Education* 19 (1): 57–72.

Eisenhardt, K. M. and M. E. Graebner. 2007. "Theory building from cases: Opportunities and challenges." *Academy of Management Journal* 50 (1): 25–32.

Evans, Stephen, and Bruce Morrison. 2011. "Meeting the challenges of English-medium higher education: The first-year experience in Hong Kong." *English for Specific Purposes* 30 (3): 198–208.

Flores, Maria Assunção. 2019. "Unpacking teacher quality: Key issues for early career teachers." In *Attracting and keeping the best teachers*, eds Anna Sullivan, Bruce Johnson, and Michele Simons, pp. 15–38. Singapore: Springer.

Grossman, Robert L., Yunhong Gu, Michael Sabala, and Wanzhi Zhang. 2009. "Compute and storage clouds using wide area high performance networks." *Future Generation Computer Systems* 25 (2): 179–183.

Hamidi, Hodjat, and Amir Chavoshi. 2018. "Analysis of the essential factors for the adoption of mobile learning in higher education: A case study of students of the University of Technology." *Telematics and Informatics* 35 (4): 1053–1070.

Harvey, Lee. 1995. "Beyond TQM." *Quality in Higher Education* 1 (2): 123–146.

Harvey, Lee, and Diana Green. 1993. "Defining quality." *Assessment & Evaluation in Higher Education* 18 (1): 9–34.

Henard, Fabrice, and Deborah Roseveare. 2012. "Fostering quality teaching in higher education: Policies and practices." *An IMHE Guide for Higher Education Institutions*: 7–11.

Higgins, Steven, Z. Xiao, and Maria Katsipataki. 2012. "The impact of digital technology on learning: A summary for the education endowment foundation." *Durham, UK: Education Endowment Foundation and Durham University*.

Hollensen, Svend. 2003. *Marketing management: A relationship approach*. Harlow: Financial Times Prentice Hall.

Joynathsing, C. and H. Ramkissoon. 2010. *Understanding the behavioral intention of European tourists*, International Research Symposium in Service Management.

Kraft, P., J. Rise, S. Sutton, and E. Roysamb. 2005. "Perceived difficulty in the theory of planned behaviour: Perceived behavioural control or affective attitude?" *British Journal of Social Psychology* (44): 479–496

Krysa, R. 1998. "Factors Affecting the Adoption and Use of Computer Technology in Schools." University of Saskatchewan. Retrieved from: www.usask.ca/education/coursework/802papers/krysa/krysa.PDF Accessed 23/03/12.

Levin, Tamar, and Rivka Wadmany. 2006. "Teachers' beliefs and practices in technology-based classrooms: A developmental view." *Journal of Research on Technology in Education* 39 (2): 157–181.

Lin, M. L., and P. Cheng. 2012. "The willingness of business students on innovative behavior within the theory of planned behavior." *World Academy of Science, Engineering and Technology* 6 (2012): 384–388.

McMahon, Graham. 2009. "Critical thinking and ICT integration in a Western Australian secondary school." *Journal of Educational Technology & Society* 12 (4): 269–281.

Naisbitt, John, and Patricia Aburdene. 1989. *Reinventing the corporation.* William Morrow and Company.

Nasim, Kanwal, Arif Sikander, and Xiaowen Tian. 2020. "Twenty years of research on total quality management in higher education: A systematic literature review." *Higher Education Quarterly* 74 (1): 75–97.

Oke, Adekunle, and Fatima Araujo Pereira Fernandes. 2020. "Innovations in teaching and learning: Exploring the perceptions of the education sector on the 4th industrial revolution (4IR)." *Journal of Open Innovation: Technology, Market, and Complexity* 6 (2): 31.

Papert, Seymour. 1980. *Mindstorms: children, computers* and powerful ideas. London: Harvester Press.

Park, S. Y. 2009. "An analysis of the technology acceptance model in understanding university students' behavioral intention to use e-learning." *Educational Technology & Society,* 12 (3): 150–162.

Qasem, Yousef A. M., Shahla Asadi, Rusli Abdullah, Yusmadi Yah, Rodziah Atan, Mohammed A. Al-Sharafi, and Amr Abdullatif Yassin. 2020. "A multi-analytical approach to predict the determinants of cloud computing adoption in higher education institutions." *Applied Sciences* 10 (14): 4905.

Savage, E., and Sterry, L. 1990. "A conceptual framework for technology education." *The Technology Teacher* 50 (1): 6–11.

Serhan, Derar. 2009. "Preparing pre-service teachers for computer technology integration." *International Journal of Instructional Media* 36 (4): 439–448.

Spanos, Y. E. 2009. "Innovation adoption: an integrative model." *SPOUDAI Journal of Economic Business* 95 (1–2), 100–124.

Stephenson, J. 2001. "Learner-managed learning: An emerging pedagogy for online learning and teaching." New Era in Education, 83 (3), 81–82.

Szczepankiewicz, Elżbieta, Jan Fazlagić, and Windham Loopesko. 2019. "A conceptual model for developing climate education in sustainability management education system." *Sustainability* 13 (3): 1241.

Tezci, Erdogan. 2011. "Factors that influence pre-service teachers' ICT usage in education." *European Journal of Teacher Education* 34 (4): 483–499.

15

Dimensions of Cloud Computing-Based Brand Equity Measurement in the Education Sector of Oman and India

Marshal Fith

Research Scholar, Waljat College of Applied Sciences, Muscat, Sultanate of Oman

Dr. S. L. Gupta

Dean & Professor, Birla Institute of Technology, Mesra, Ranchi, India

Dr. Niraj Mishra

Assistant Professor, Department of Management
Birla Institute of Technology, Mesra, Ranchi, India

Mohammad Yawar

Waljat College of Applied Sciences, Muscat, Sultanate of Oman

DOI: 10.1201/9781003203070-17

15.1 Introduction

Cloud computing and artificial intelligence (AI) are the new mediums in many fields, for example, advertising, education, marketing, business decision, buying decision, and so on ... the full extent of AI possibilities are yet to be discovered. AI is a systematic approach of a computational device, allowing the user to use it to their best advantage. For example, when a user is streaming through Netflix, they get a lot of suggestions; the same goes for YouTube, Spotify, Vimeo, Gaana, and other video streaming or audio streaming websites or applications. Other examples are Amazon, eBay, Alibaba, Indiamart, and other shopping websites: on browsing these sites the user finds that the suggestions being displayed are based on their supposed needs.

The way these websites and applications suggest products and services as per our needs is based on the fact that all these companies are storing our data and using it to make predictions. This is a very basic level of understanding of AI. A more detailed understanding involves a lot of computer know-how and other technical understanding.

This chapter is focused on the measurement of brand equity of educational institutions in Oman and India, through the use of cloud computing to measure brand equity in the education sector. Typically, the brand equity of a brand depends on various factors such as brand loyalty, reach, and awareness. The same goes for the education sector, but since it is a service sector it is difficult to increase these factors in the prospective students before they avail the services because unlike a product, a service is not tangible and does not have any physical properties. So, in the case of educational institutions, they cannot increase these factors in the students beforehand and then admit them into the institution.

The only way to increase these factors in prospective students is by increasing them in current students. The institution will not be able to do it effectively through typical branding processes, so AI must be used to enhance the process. By introducing AI into the process, the institution is capable of increasing the effectiveness of the branding as well as simulating what prospective students are going to experience in this institution.

The chapter revolves around the fact that cloud computing is the new normal in branding and that brand equity will increase if cloud computing is introduced into the branding process. This will help to not only increase the brand equity among the current students but also simulate this equity among prospective students.

15.2 Literature Review

15.2.1 Cloud Computing

Cloud computing resources include data storage, servers, databases, networking, and software, among other tools and applications. Students, instructors, and administrators all profit from cloud computing in education. Students can access homework from wherever they have internet access, tutors can immediately upload learning resources, and administrators can conveniently communicate with each other and cut costs on data storage.

Despite the fact that cloud computing is an existing technology, there is no general or common description for it. Recent advancements in hardware, virtualization technologies, distributed storage, and internet-based service delivery have spawned cloud computing. The term "cloud" refers to the universal availability and access to computing resources made possible by internet technologies. Cloud-based applications provide enterprises and consumers with low-cost access to vast computing resources. Organizations will lower their total IT costs by transferring IT functions like storage, business applications, and services to the cloud (Oliveira et al. 2014).

Cloud computing is quickly becoming a strategic option for educational institutions, businesses and individuals, providing significant cost savings as well as versatile and convenient scalability for startups (Abu-Shanab and Qasem 2014). However, the use of cloud computing in brand equity measurement in the education sector has proved to be a lot more beneficial to students all over the world. Cloud computing-based techniques allow teachers to use different tools and pedagogies to interact with the students and increase the brand equity measurement in the education sector.

15.2.2 Brand Awareness

When consumers face a vast commodity brand, the higher the brand awareness, the easier it is to attract consumers (Zhang 2020). The same goes for educational institutes: the prospective student face the dilemma of which school to join, because of the increasing number of schools and education programmes. The placement of brand recognition plays an important role in shaping customer buying intentions (Gerber et al. 2016). So, which institute to pick is entirely in the hands of the institutions, whether they are able to create a brand awareness about their education institutions and whether they are able to engrave the brand into the minds of prospective students. According to Rup et al. (2020) and Chaney et al. (2018), brand recognition is described as consumers' ability to recognize products under a variety of circumstances, as evidenced by brand restoration and recalling of past results. Starting at the lowest level, not remembering the brand, and progressing to brand identification, the top-of-mind recalling point, there are many stages of brand awareness. Brand identity may indicate a company's life, dedication, and core values, all of which are critical to its success. (Ilyas et al. 2020). Several reasons contribute to a company's strong brand awareness: advertising on a regular basis, and being linked to the presence and sale of brands that target different demographics (Foroudi et al. 2014; Mashur et al. 2019).

Brand awareness, according to Dabbous and Barakat (2020), has become a significant variable that affects customer expectations of a brand. Certain brands will attempt to control consumers' minds in order to sway their preferences, making the brand a viable competitor among other brands (Curina et al. 2020). Most academics agree that brand recognition and memory are essential factors for customers when making purchasing decisions (Emma and Sharp 2000; Thoma and Williams 2013).

15.2.3 Brand Loyalty

The behavioral viewpoint of brand loyalty, such as buying habits or the likelihood of repurchasing, is emphasized in early views of brand loyalty (Srinivasan, Anderson and Ponnavolu 2002). However, this viewpoint alone is insufficient to assess loyalty, as buying behavior is a deceptive indicator of loyalty. The 9 psychological predispositions, which include behaviors, desires, and devotion to a company, are other components of loyalty (Ebrahim, 2019). As a result, attitudinal loyalty identifies the conditions that influence repeat buying behavior (Tatar and Eren-Erdogmus 2016). The term "attitudinal loyalty" refers to a consumer's favorable attitude toward a company (Cossío-Silva et al. 2015).

Customers with a high level of loyalty have a close bond with the company and are more likely to make frequent purchases than customers with a low level of loyalty (Kandampully, Zhang, and Bilgihan, 2015; Šerić and Praničević, 2018).

Applied to the abundance of real-time data (Big Data), AI is marketed as a means to transform education in ways that deliver more customized, versatile, inclusive, and stimulating learning.

15.2.4 AI Brand Awareness

Companies may use social media to raise brand awareness by introducing their products to a large number of people (Kumar, Choi, and Greene 2017). For businesses, social media has been essential for effectively communicating with clients, establishing long-term partnerships, sharing content, and promoting brands (Ismail 2017). Joining social media gives businesses a rare chance to strengthen their identities by increasing market equity and brand recognition, credibility, and loyalty (Alberghini, Cricelli, and Grimaldi 2014). Customers' views on the impact of social media on brand interaction have been the subject of several surveys (Hollebeek, Glynn, and Brodie 2014; Laroche, Habibi, and Richard 2013), and on brand communities (Heydari and Laroche 2018), brand trust (Habibi, Laroche, and Richard 2014) and brand equity (Hsu and Lawrence 2016). Corporations are constantly using social media to communicate, exchange ideas, develop long-term relationships with committed clients, gain new customers who could otherwise be out of reach (Gallaugher and Ransbotham 2010; Tsimonis and Dimitriadis 2014), and create brand loyalty (de Vries, Gensler, and Leeflang 2017; Swani et al. 2017; Yoshida et al. 2018).

Firms will further connect with their loyal clients in a variety of ways through the social media world (Krishen, Berezan, Agarwal, and Kachroo 2016), by building strong and intimate partnerships and providing exclusive and seamless customer interactions (Rapp et al. 2013). Companies that use online networking in an immersive, personalized, diligent, and receptive manner, as outlined by Raab et al. (2016), are more prepared to gain customers and enhance brand loyalty.

AI refers to the theoretical structure and architecture of computers that are capable of performing repetitive activities that require human intelligence. Integration of AI into the education sector creates a revolution through its result-driven approach. The applications for solving issues such as language processing, reasoning, planning, and cognitive modelling increase the demand for AI in the education sector. AI can also help organize and synthesize content to support content delivery.

AI-enabled solutions and services perform various functions in the AI education sector, such as information distribution, performance grading and grouping of students, and intelligent teaching systems to enhance the learning experience of students and teaching faculty. To boost performance and the learning experience in education and learning apps, AI technologies such as deep learning, machine learning, and neuro-linguistic programming are used. To create instructional systems, AI technologies are used in conjunction with teaching strategies such as the learner model, pedagogical model, and domain model to optimize knowledge delivery and assessment. The global market AI learning is anticipated to register USD 3.68 billion by 2023, growing at a compound annual growth rate of 47% from 2018 to 2023.

15.2.5 Predictive Analytics to Enhance Brand Equity in Education

Institutions in higher education are using predictive analytics as a way to respond to the many businesses and operational changes happening in the education industry. The three key motives universities use this instrument are as follows.

15.2.5.1 Targeted Student Advising

Few colleges have an adequate number of advisors on staff, and as a result, students often cannot receive the individualized attention they need.

However, systems based on predictive analytics like early-alert and program recommender can help identify students who require support and allow staff and faculty to assist.

15.2.5.2 Adaptive Learning

Predictive analytics is now being used by colleges to create self-learning courseware; designed to modify the learning route of a student based on their interactions with the technology. Using predictive analytics in adaptive learning platforms can help instructors pinpoint learning gaps in the student's learning process and then customize the educational journey so that it better aligns with how students learn.

The AI-based tool can help students accelerate their learning by allowing them to quickly go through content they already know while providing additional support in areas where they struggle.

15.2.5.3 Manage Enrolment

Colleges are also using predictive analytics to better predict enrolment and the consequent management plans. This data aids schools in predicting the scale of new and returning classes. It assists the school in narrowing the scope of their recruiting and promotion activities such that only the most qualified candidates apply, graduate, and excel. Predictive analytics aids colleges in predicting the financial needs of new and returning classes, as well as determining whether or not a recipient will need a financial aid grant.

Brand equity is an integral component of a business's identity. Every day, we witness the influence of brand value. Consider that more consumers pay almost twice the price for well-established brands than for generic store brands. In general, the more optimistic the brand equity, the higher the price of goods and services.

Education is a substantial expense in a lifetime. The brand image an institution holds is the effort of years of persistence, yet it can deteriorate in a few days. Branding of education is not the same as branding of any other products. All the typical branding techniques employed by the marketer to create a superior brand image for a product cannot be utilized in education branding.

15.3 Research Questions

1. To what degree is the student attracted when using AI branding for educational institutions?
2. What are the governing problems that the students face while creating an image of the institution based on digitally marketed institutions?

15.4 Research Hypothesis

There is no association with the variables/constructs given and brand equity when branding higher education institutes using AI.

15.5 Research Objectives

The objectives of the research are:

- To study the perceptual or psychological response of students to measure brand equity dimension of AI.
- To determine the various factors that affect the brand image of the institution.
- To study how AI branding will enhance the brand image of the institution.
- To evaluate the demographic variable impact on the student-based brand equity of institutions in India and Oman.
- Future scope of use and impact of cognitive modelling through AI.

15.6 Research Problems

Many educational institutions are not able to keep up with the expectations of students. Hence there is a dynamic shift in the selection and loyalty of students to institutions. The changes in branding practices have taken a toll in the reduced brand equity; the introduction of AI in all walks of life has penetrated education and cannot be avoided. The study will be discussing the effects of AI in branding to increase the brand equity of an educational institution among students.

15.7 Research Methods

The chapter aims to showcase different models based on the research methods. The results found from the study can be studied in later sections.

The theoretical architecture of current and proposed models of cloud computing-based brand equity assessment in the education industry is presented in the following section.

15.7.1 Theoretical Background

15.7.1.1 Existing Model (Figure 15.1)

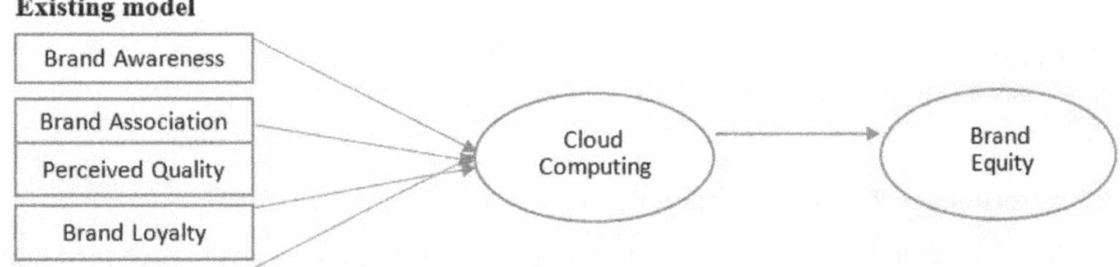

FIGURE 15.1
Existing models.

15.7.1.2 Proposed Model (Figure 15.2)

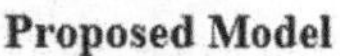

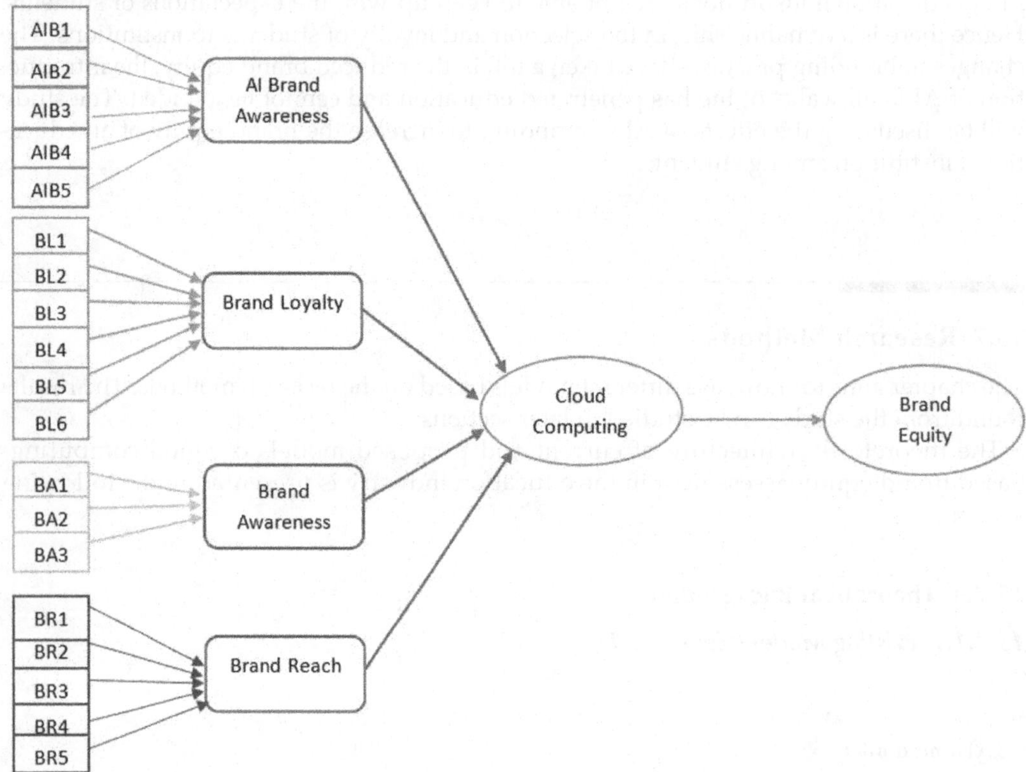

FIGURE 15.2
Proposed model to attain brand equity through cloud computing.

15.7.2 Secondary Research Method

The research method employed is exploratory research design. This gives scope to identify all the dimensions related to branding in an educational institution and the factors influencing brand equity while using AI as tools for teaching and learning.

15.7.3 Scale Development

For scale growth, Nunnaly's (1978) guidelines were followed. This included creating initial scale variables, variable screening and refining by panel evaluations, a systematic pretest of variable purification and revision, additional monitoring for variable filtration, and finally a field survey for confirmation. Related approaches for scale production have been used in a number of other tests.

15.7.4 Sampling Method

The sampling was done in two stages, initially random sampling then, in the later stage, we used convenience sampling.

15.7.5 Data Collection

The study revolved around primary data through a structured questionnaire. The sample size was 390 students from 20 institutes (10 from Oman and 10 from India). To supplement details in the study and to justify our variables, secondary data were collected from various reliable sources.

15.7.6 Data Analysis

The study was analyzed using structural equation modeling, and we used exploratory factor analysis to verify the variables' correlations and Cronbach's alpha to determine the variables' reliability.

15.8 Results and Discussion

Figure 15.3 depicts the overall measurement model comprising five constructs. Some of the values of the model fit indices were not within the prescribed limits in the initial measurement model. Therefore, after co-varying some of the error terms, a final measurement model was constructed (see Figure 15.4). All the model fit indices of the final measurement model were within the prescribed limits.

15.8.1 Regression Weights

The sign of a regression coefficient indicates whether each independent variable and the dependent variable have a positive or negative relationship. A positive coefficient indicates that the mean of the dependent variable continues to rise as the value of the independent variable rises. (See Tables 15.1-15.3.)

15.8.2 Model Fit

The fit indices in structural equation modeling decide if the formula is correct overall. If the model is right, it can then be determined if those paths are relevant. Acceptable fit indexes do not always mean close relationships. The fit indices can be categorized into a few different groups. Discrepancy functions, such as the chi square test and relative chi square, and RMS tests that equate the target model to the null model, such as the CFI, NFI, TFI, and IFI, fall into this category.

All the fit indices obtained met the defined criteria. Bentler (1990) recommended the following cut off values for these indices: (i) CMIN/*df* (normed chi square) < 3, (ii) AGFI (adjusted goodness of fit index) > 0.80, (iii) CFI (confirmatory fit index) > 0.90, (iv) RMSEA (root mean square error of approximation) < 0.05, (v) p-value (model) > 0.05, and (vi) GFI (goodness of fit index) > 0.90.

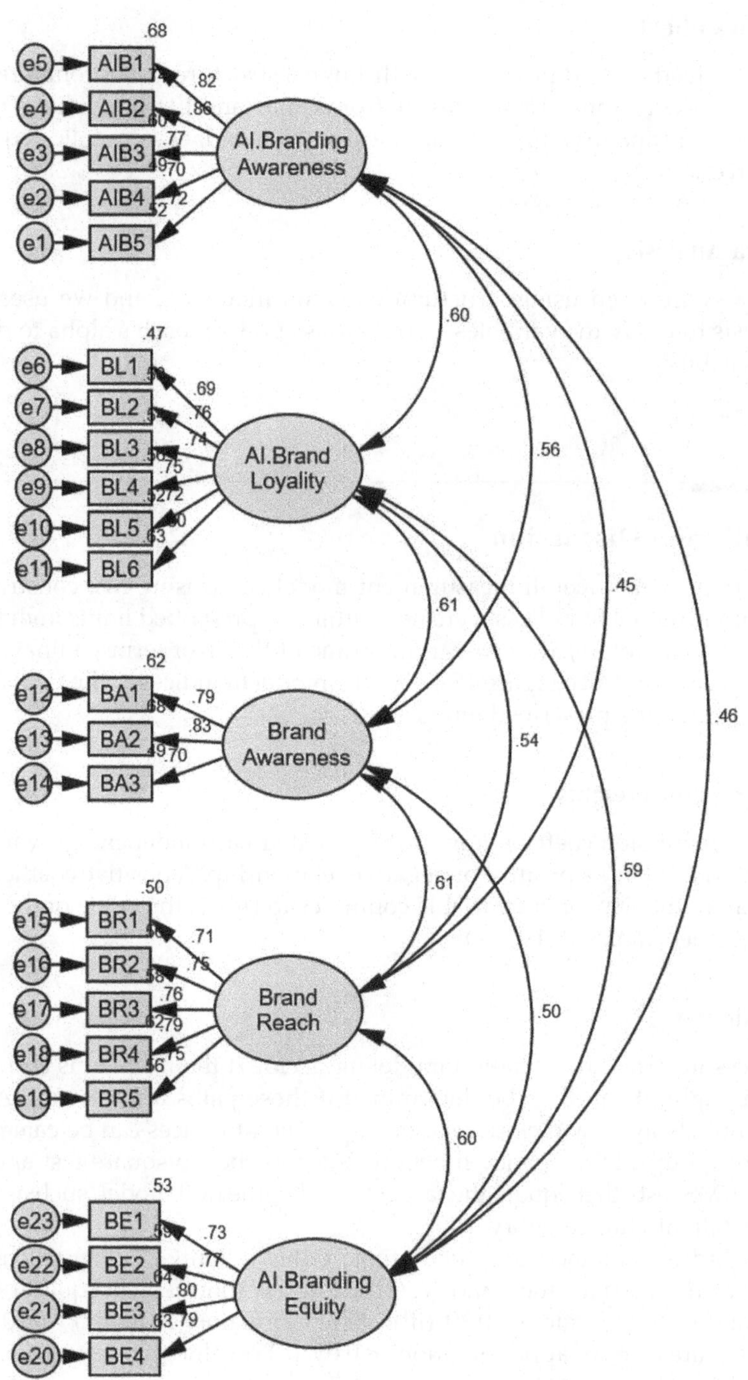

FIGURE 15.3
Initial measurement model.

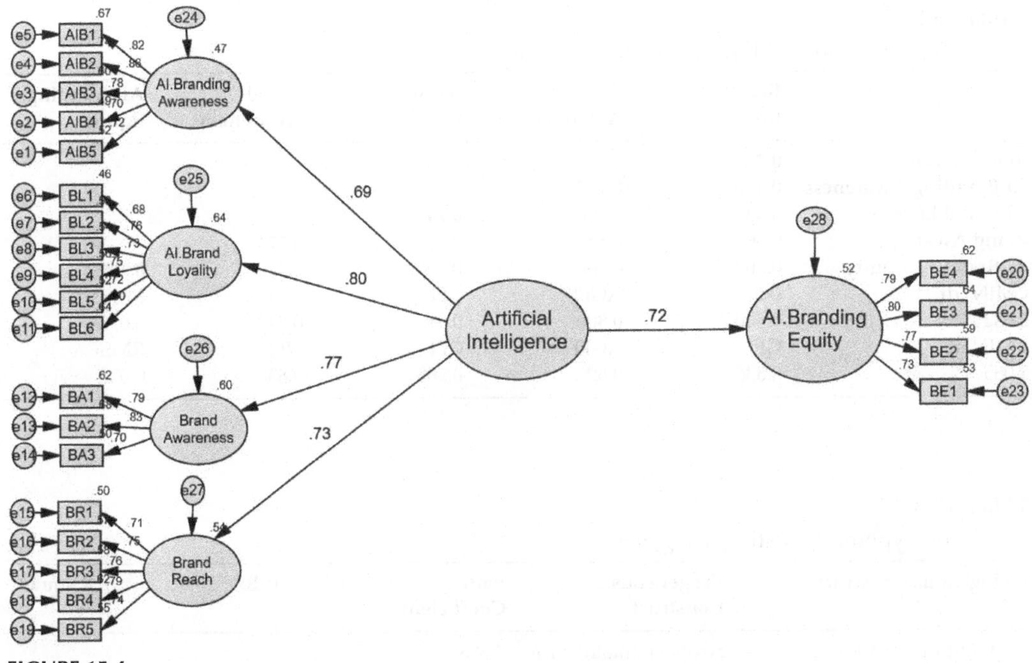

FIGURE 15.4
Final measurement model.

TABLE 15.1
Regression Weights and Factors

			Construct Loadings	S.E.	Composite Reliability	Average Variance Extracted	Maximum Shared Variance	Cronbach Alpha
AIB5	<---	AI Branding	0.720		0.883	0.604	0.355	
AIB4	<---	Awareness	0.699	0.097				
AIB3	<---		0.773	0.096				
AIB2	<---		0.859	0.099				
AIB1	<---		0.822	0.101				
BL5	<---	AI Brand Loyalty	0.719		0.880	0.550	0.375	
BL4	<---		0.746	0.106				
BL3	<---		0.736	0.105				
BL2	<---		0.762	0.112				
BL1	<---		0.685	0.111				
BL6	<---		0.796	0.117				
BA3	<---	Brand Awareness	0.702		0.817	0.599	0.375	
BA2	<---		0.827	0.119				
BA1	<---		0.787	0.117				
BR5	<---	Brand Reach	0.745		0.866	0.563	0.370	
BR4	<---		0.789	0.102				
BR3	<---		0.759	0.096				
BR2	<---		0.751	0.102				
BR1	<---		0.707	0.096				
BE4	<---	AI. Branding	0.791	0.107	0.855	0.596	0.362	
BE3	<---	Equity	0.798	0.100				
BE2	<---		0.769	0.096				
BE1	<---		0.728					

TABLE 15.2
Values of Different Brand Equity Measurement Factors

	Brand Reach	AI Branding Awareness	AI Brand Loyalty	Brand Awareness	AI Branding Equity
Brand Reach	**0.751**				
AI Branding Awareness	0.450	**0.777**			
AI Brand Loyalty	0.539	0.596	**0.741**		
Brand Awareness	0.608	0.555	0.612	**0.774**	
AI Branding Equity	0.602	0.460	0.590	0.499	**0.772**
CMIN/df	GFI	AGFI	CFI	NFI	RMSEA
2.082	0.840	0.800	0.910	0.842	0.072
CMIN/df	GFI	AGFI	CFI	NFI	RMSEA
2.085	0.836	0.800	0.908	0.838	0.072

TABLE 15.3
Results of Hypothesis Testing using SEM

Endogenous Construct		Exogeneous Construct	Path Coefficient	S.E.	C.R.	P	R square
AI Branding Awareness	<---	Artificial Intelligence	0.688				
AI Brand Loyalty	<---		0.800	0.133	6.616	***	
Brand Awareness	<---		0.774	0.147	6.347	***	
Brand Reach	<---		0.734	0.140	6.427	***	
AI Branding Equity	<---	Artificial Intelligence	0.720	0.134	6.289	***	52%

15.9 Conclusion, Implication, and Future Scope

The response yielded by the study adequately states that the introduction of AI in all aspects of education is inevitable. The application of AI in branding and increasing brand equity is vast, and the institutions that have leveraged this opportunity have seen exceptional results in terms of new admissions of students, retention of students, increased levels of loyalty by students by recommending the institution to prospective students, and high levels of satisfaction among students.

15.9.1 Administrative Implications

Concurrent school activities aim to provide a pleasurable learning environment in order to provide ostensibly high-quality schooling. The best use of AI in the instruction and value addition of the university will help academic administrators to benefit greatly, because it would enable them to assess students' general understanding and feelings about the educational institution. It will provide immediate input on branding activities in terms of operation, education system accountability, organization culture, and quality of education and learning environment. Understanding students' experience-based responses can aid managers in better managing schools and universities and coordinating their initiatives to maintain an improved educational experience.

15.9.2 Scope for Future Research

In this research the AI branding has been considered for educational institutions. In the future, this topic can be extrapolated to other service sectors like hospitals, the hospitality industry, banking, insurance, and public utility services.

References

Abu-Shanab, Emad, and Qasem, Huda. 2014. Cloud Computing Adoption: Brand Equity Impact On.

Alberghini, E., Cricelli, L., and Grimaldi, M. 2014. A methodology to manage and monitor social media inside a company: a case study. Journal of Knowledge Management, 18(2), 255–277. doi.org/10.1108/JKM-10-2013-0392

Bentler, P. M. 1990. Fit indexes, Lagrange multipliers, constraint changes and incomplete data in structural models. Multivariate Behavioral Research, 25(2), 163–172

Chaney, I., Hosany, S., Wu, M.-S. S., Chen, C.-H. S., and Nguyen, B. 2018. Size does matter: Effects of in-game advertising stimuli on brand recall and brand recognition. Computers in Human Behavior, 86 (September), 311–318. doi.org/10.1016/j. chb.2018.05.007

Cossío-Silva, F. J., Revilla-Camacho, M.Á., Vega-Vázquez, M., and Palacios-Florencio, B. 2015. Value co-creation and customer loyalty. Journal of Business Research, 69(5), 1621–1625. doi.org/10.1016/j.jbusres.2015.10.028

Curina, I., Francioni, B., Hegner, S. M., and Cioppi, M. 2020. Brand hate and non-repurchase intention: A service context perspective in a cross-channel setting. Journal of Retailing and Consumer Services, 54 (May), 102031. doi.org/10.1016/j.jretconser.2019.102031

Dabbous, A., and Barakat, K. A. 2020. Bridging the online offline gap: Assessing the impact of brands' social network content quality on brand awareness and purchase intention. Journal of Retailing and Consumer Services, 53 (March), 101966. doi.org/10.1016/j.jretconser.2019.101966

De Vries, L., Gensler, S., and Leeflang, P. S. H. 2017. Effects of traditional advertising and social messages on brand-building metrics and customer acquisition. Journal of Marketing, 81(5), 1–15. doi.org/10.1509/jm.15.0178

Ebrahim, R. 2019. The role of trust in understanding the impact of social media marketing on brand equity and brand loyalty. *Journal of Relationship Marketing*, 19(4), 287–308. doi.org/10.1080/15332667.2019.1705742

Emma, K. M., and Sharp, B. M. 2000. Brand awareness effects on consumer decision making for a common, repeat purchase product: A replication. *J. Bus. Res.*, 48, 5–15. doi.org/10.1016/s0148-2963(98)00070-8

Foroudi, P., Melewar, T. C., and Gupta, S. 2014. Linking corporate logo, corporate image, and reputation: An examination of consumer perceptions in the financial setting. Journal of Business Research, 67(11), 2269–2281. doi.org/10.1016/j.jbusres.2014.06.015

Gallaugher, J., and Ransbotham, S. 2010. Social media and customer dialog management at Starbucks. MIS Quarterly Executive, 9(4).

Gerber, C., Ward, S., and Goedhals-Gerber, L. 2016. The impact of perceived risk on on-line purchase behavior: Risk governance and control. Financial Markets and Institutions, 4(4), 13–18. doi.org/10.22495/rgcv4i4c1art4

Habibi, M. R., Laroche, M., and Richard, M. O. 2014. The roles of brand community and community engagement in building brand trust on social media. Computers in Human Behavior, 37, 152–161. doi.org/10.1016/j.chb.2014.04.016

Heydari, A., and Laroche, M. 2018. Cross-cultural study of social media-based brand communities: An abstract. In Krey, N., Rossi, P. (Eds.), Back to the Future: Using Marketing Basics to Provide Customer Value. AMSAC 2017. Developments in Marketing Science: Proceedings of the Academy of Marketing Science. Cham: Springer (pp. 331–332). doi.org/10.1007/978-3-319-66023-3_115

Hollebeek, L. D., Glynn, M. S., and Brodie, R. J. 2014. Consumer brand engagement in social media: Conceptualization, scale development and validation. Journal of Interactive Marketing, 28(2), 149–165. doi.org/10.1016/j.intmar.2013.12.002

Hsu, L., and Lawrence, B. 2016. The role of social media and brand equity during a product recall crisis: A shareholder value perspective. International Journal of Research in Marketing, 33(1), 59–77. doi.org/10.1016/j.ijresmar.2015.04.004

Ilyas, G., Rahmi, S., Tamsah, H., Munir, A., and Putra, A. 2020. Reflective model of brand awareness on repurchase intention and customer satisfaction. *The Journal of Asian Finance, Economics and Business*, 7(9), 427–438. doi.org/10.13106/jafeb.2020.vol7.no9.427

Ismail, A. R. 2017. The influence of perceived social media marketing activities on brand loyalty. Asia Pacific Journal of Marketing and Logistics, 29(1), 129–144. doi.org/10.1108/APJML-10-2015-0154

Kandampully, J., Zhang, T., and Bilgihan, A. 2015. Customer loyalty: A review and future directions with a special focus on the hospitality industry. International Journal of Contemporary Hospitality Management, 27(3), 379–414. doi.org/10.1108/ IJCHM-03-2014-0151

Krishen, A. S., Berezan, O., Agarwal, S., & Kachroo, P. 2016. The generation of virtual needs: Recipes for satisfaction in social media networking. Journal of Business Research, 69(11), 5248–5254.

Kumar, V., Choi, J. B., and Greene, M. 2017. Synergistic effects of social media and traditional marketing on brand sales: Capturing the time-varying effects. Journal of the Academy of Marketing Science, 45(2), 268–288. doi.org/10.1007/s11747-016-0484-7

Laroche, M., Habibi, M. R., and Richard, M. O. 2013. To be or not to be in social media: How brand loyalty is affected by social media? International Journal of Information Management, 33(1), 76–82

Mashur, R., Gunawan, B. I., Fitriany, Ashoer, M., Hidayat, M., and Aditya, H. P. K. P. 2019. Moving from traditional to society 5.0: Case study by online transportation business. Journal of Distribution Science, 17(9), 93–102. doi.org/10.15722/ jds.17.09.201909.93

Nunnally, J. C. 1978. Psychometric theory. New York, NY: McGraw-Hill

Oliveira, Tiago, Thomas, Manoj, and Espadanal, Mariana. 2014. Assessing the determinants of cloud computing adoption: An analysis of the manufacturing and services sectors. Information and Management 51(5): 497–510

Raab, C., Berezan, O., Krishen, A. S., and Tanford, S. 2016. What's in a word? Building program loyalty through social media communication. Cornell Hospitality Quarterly, 57(2), 138–149. doi.org/10.1177/1938965515619488

Rapp, A., Beitelspacher, L. S., Grewal, D., and Hughes, D. E. 2013. Understanding social media effects across seller, retailer, and consumer interactions. Journal of the Academy of Marketing Science, 41(5), 547–566. doi.org/10.1007/s11747-013-0326-9

Rup, J., Goodman, S., and Hammond, D. 2020. Cannabis advertising, promotion and branding: Differences in consumer exposure between "legal" and "illegal" markets in Canada and the US. Preventive Medicine, 133 (January), 106013. doi.org/10.1016/j.ypmed.2020.106013

Šerić, M., and Praničević, D. G. 2018. Consumer-generated reviews on social media and brand relationship outcomes in the fast-food chain industry. Journal of Hospitality Marketing and Management, 27(2), 218–238. doi.org/10.1080/19368623.2017.1340219

Srinivasan, S. S., Anderson, R., and Ponnavolu, K. 2002. Customer loyalty in e-commerce: An exploration of its antecedents and consequences. Journal of Retailing, 78(1), 41–50. doi.org/10.1016/S0022-4359(01)00065-3

Swani, K., Milne, G. R., Brown, B. P., Assaf, A. G., and Donthu, N. 2017. What messages to post? Evaluating the popularity of social media communications in business versus consumer markets. Industrial Marketing Management, 62, 77–87. doi.org/10.1016/j.indmarman.2016.07.006

Tatar, S. B., and Eren-Erdogmus, I. 2016. The effect of social media marketing on brand trust and brand loyalty for hotels. Information Technology and Tourism, 16(3), 249–263. doi.org/10.1007/s40558-015-0048-6

Thoma, V., and Williams, A. 2013. The devil you know: The effect of brand recognition and product ratings on consumer choice. *Judgm. Decis. Mak.*, 8, 34–44

Tsimonis, G., and Dimitriadis, S. 2014. Brand strategies in social media. Marketing Intelligence and Planning, 32(3), 328–344. doi.org/10.1108/MIP-04-2013-0056

Yoshida, M., Gordon, B. S., Nakazawa, M., Shibuya, S., and Fujiwara, N. 2018. Bridging the gap between social media and behavioral brand loyalty. Electronic Commerce Research and Applications, 28, 208–218. doi.org/10.1016/j.elerap.2018.02.005

Zhang, Xuefeng. 2020. The influences of brand awareness on consumers' cognitive process: An event-related potentials study. Frontiers in Neuroscience, 14, 549. www.frontiersin.org/article/10.3389/fnins.2020.00549. doi.org/10.3389/fnins.2020.00549

Index